CW00687735

The Anatomy of
Major Projects

The Anatomy of
Major Projects

A Study of the Reality of Project Management

PETER W. G. MORRIS

and

GEORGE H. HOUGH

Major Projects Association
Templeton College, Oxford

JOHN WILEY & SONS
Chichester · New York · Brisbane · Toronto · Singapore

Copyright © 1987 by Major Projects Association

Reprinted June 1990

All rights reserved

No part of this book may be reproduced by any means,
or transmitted, or translated into a machine language
without the written permission of the publisher.

Library of Congress Cataloging-in-Publication Data:

Morris, Peter W. G.
  The anatomy of major projects.

  Bibliography: p.
  Includes index.
  1. Industrial project management.   I. Hough,
George H. I. Hough, George H.   II. Title.
HD69.P75M674   1987   658.4'04   87–8176

ISBN 0 471 91551 3

British Library Cataloguing in Publication Data:

Morris, Peter W. G.
  The anatomy of major projects: a study
  of the reality of project management.
  1. Industrial project management—
  Case studies
  I. Title   II. Hough, George H.
  658.4'04'0722   HD69.P75

ISBN 0 471 91551 3

Typeset by Input Typesetting Ltd, London SW19 8DR
Printed by Antony Rowe Ltd, Chippenham, Wiltshire

Contents

Foreword

I believe this book is important for at least two reasons. First, it broadens considerably the existing literature on project management. Second, it focuses our attention on large, complex projects—those undertakings which are essential to the development of society but which are poorly understood and too often inadequately managed.

Those of us who have worked in project managment, particularly at a senior level, have long been conscious that the textbooks on project management have singularly failed to treat effectively, or in many cases at all, those issues which most have a bearing on the final success or otherwise of projects—issues such as contract strategy, design management, politics, community action, client changes and industrial relations. Instead, textbooks have dwelt on planning and control techniques and methods of organization, many of which are too complex to find ready application in the real world of projects.

Further, projects are generally fun, yet too few books on project management—indeed perhaps on management generally—reflect the drama and interest of real life.

This book, it seems to me, by describing eight case studies 'in the round' admirably captures the challenges and satisfaction to be found in initiating and managing projects. And in taking this case study approach, it succeeds in at least indicating some of the crucial areas of project managment not covered in other texts. Chapter 11, the major 'theory' chapter in the book, is almost exclusively about such issues.

The book is valuable too in the way it brings together a very broad collection of information from around the world on the several different technologies that project management these days serves.

It further provides a useful service in showing how project 'success' can be viewed from several different perspectives, some of them quite independent of each other.

As a project management text, then, it is to be welcomed as a major milestone, perhaps even as the beginning of a new era of writing about projects from a broader, more senior perspective. But the book is more than just a project management text. It is a detailed study of major industrial undertakings.

As the authors point out, academic research and teaching of company management is relatively new. Yet many of society's most important endeavours span several companies. Such ventures are becoming increasingly common in industry, particularly as costs and risks increase and as regulatory pressures and marketing become more complex. They demand leadership of the highest calibre in welding together diverse interests, dealing with government, raising finance, recruiting excellent staff and negotiating contracts. Yet our ability to understand and articulate what this involves, let alone to begin teaching it, is still rudimentary. Formal writing and teaching of such multi-organizational undertakings is almost non-existent. *The Anatomy of Major Projects* provides much basic information upon which such an understanding might be based.

This book springs from the interests and research of the Major Projects Association. The MPA is a unique association of governmental and business institutions concerned with such large, complex undertakings. It has been meeting since 1981 to explore the issues involved in effectively initiating, assessing, securing and accomplishing such projects. It is the Association's intent that this work be only the first of several such studies aimed at improving our understanding of, and ability to implement more effectively, these very important endeavours. This book certainly helps the reader towards these goals.

SIR ALISTAIR FRAME
Chairman, Major Projects Association
Chairman, Rio Tinto-Zinc Corporation plc

Preface

The Major Projects Association comprises over 60 member institutions representing owners, bankers, consultants, contractors, manufacturers, insurers, lawyers and government. The MPA defines major projects as those which require knowledge, skills or resources that exceed what is readily or conventionally available to the key participants. Major projects are commonly found in construction, information technology and aerospace as well as in biotechnology, agriculture, the social services and other industries.

The aim of the MPA is to enhance the ability of its members to initiate, assess, secure and accomplish major projects successfully. To these ends members actively share their knowledge and experience to yield a better, multi-disciplined understanding of the subject and to draw conclusions and develop improved methods.

The MPA' activities include Oxford seminars, lectures and symposia in London and an annual conference. The MPA also sponsors a research programme at Templeton College, the Oxford Centre for Management Studies.

The work reported here is the first large-scale research specifically undertaken as part of this research programme. The work was conducted by Dr Peter Morris, Director of the Major Projects Association and an Associate Fellow of Templeton College, and Dr George Hough, a consultant to the MPA.

While there is inevitably much in this report which reflects the opinions of others, the accounts of the cases studied, their analyses and the conclusions drawn from them are solely those of the authors. They are not necessarily those of the companies or individuals involved in the projects nor of the Major Projects Association.

Acknowledgements

We would like to acknowledge the help of a great many people without the assistance of whom this research would not have been possible. We would particularly like to recognize the efforts of the many people who helped us with the case studies. We would also like to mention the Research Steering Committee: Patrick Hodgson (Chairman), Robert Cochran, Terry Lewis, Janine Nahapiet and Allen Sykes. Our thanks go to them all.

We also wish to thank Jane Thompson for her tireless efforts in preparing the many drafts of the initial research report and Victoria Meek for her assistance with preparing the drafts of this book.

PART ONE

Major Projects and Project Management

Chapter One

The Study of Major Projects

Project management is by now a relatively well developed management discipline. Projects, on the other hand, have been but barely studied. Major projects, those representing substantial opportunities but posing above average risk, are especially poorly understood. The purpose of this book is to explore the anatomy of major projects so that these large, complex endeavours may be undertaken more efficiently, to the benefit of everyone. In doing so, our understanding of managing other kinds of projects may also be improved.

Project management, which had its origins in the chemical industry just prior to World War II, was developed in the 1950s, essentially in the defence and petrochemical industries. It has since been developing steadily as an important management discipline. Project management is clearly identified as a separate discipline in the Atlas missile programme of 1954 and in the Polaris Programme, particularly the Special Projects Office created by Admiral Raborn for the management of Polaris in 1955 [1]. By 1970 several professional societies had been established in Europe, the USA, Australia and Japan. Degree courses are now offered at several universities throughout the world [2]. More and more companies in many different industries are perceiving that their business has important project dimensions.

A project is an undertaking to achieve a specified objective, defined usually in terms of technical performance, budget and schedule. There are basically two kinds of projects: those which are complete in themselves, like an oil platform or a tunnel, and those which represent a series, or programme, of products or projects, like an aircraft or an aid programme.

Projects are accomplished according to a common life-cycle. Every project, no matter of what kind or for what duration, essentially follows the activity sequence of prefeasibility/feasibility, design and contract negotiation, implementation, handover and in-service support. While this life-cycle of projects is relatively straightforward—a single sequence from prefeasibility to handover—a programme can be of two kinds: either a series of individual projects (as, for example, a series of telephone exchanges) or a programme with an R & D 'project' phase followed by the manufacture of that product (Figure 1.1). The skill of the project manager rests, in many fundamental respects, on an innate appreciation of the requirements of progressing the project through this life-cycle. In doing so, many issues arise which are common to all kinds of projects, e.g. those of leadership and organization, financing, planning and control, and the contracting of third parties.

Like Molière's Bourgeois Gentilhomme, we are surrounded by projects without necessarily realizing it. Many projects are commonplace. Going on holiday is a project: it has an end objective, it follows a life-cycle, it requires financial analysis and funding, it needs planning (during which trade-offs are made between objectives), it even requires organization, control and leadership. Such familiar 'projects' can be accomplished without resort to complex, formal management tools. Project management becomes important when the project itself becomes sufficiently difficult that it warrants the application of specific project management concepts, skills, tools and techniques.

Project management is in essence simple. Project management pulls together the functional disciplines needed to achieve the project's budgetary, schedule and technical objectives. As Olsen defined it,

> Project management is the application of a collection of tools and techniques (such as CPM and matrix organization) to direct the use of diverse resources towards the accomplishment of a unique, complex, one-time task within time, cost and quality constraints. Each task requires a particular mix of these tools and techniques structured to fit the task environment and life-cycle (from conception to completion) of the task [4].

In pulling together these functional disciplines a number of special techniques are used as the project develops through its life-cycle. Typical of these are design management, scheduling, work breakdown analysis, task-responsibility matrices, performance measurement, project organization, cost control, contract administration, quality management and team selection and building [5] (Figure 1.2).

Through the sustained outpouring of the many thousands of articles, books and seminar proceedings on project management which have been written over the last 20 to 30 years, our understanding of project management is now relatively mature. It remains, however, essentially an understanding of how the implementation of a project can be managed. It still fails to take a strategic interest in how projects can better achieve the objectives of those promoting, undertaking or being affected by them.

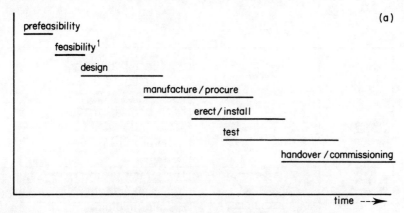

Figure 1.1 Project/programme life cycles (a) One-time projects

[1] Hammond and Fox distinguish a pre-investment stage between feasibility and design in which financial sponsorship is secured [3].

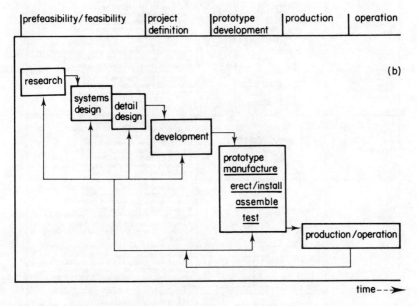

(b) Product development programmes

It is true that there are other disciplines which take a more strategic view of projects. Project analysis[1], for example, in many ways a sister art to project management and generally taught as a separate discipline

[1] Project analysis is also called project appraisal and project evaluation, though some organizations tend to use one of these terms as ex-ante and the other as ex-poste, e.g. the World Bank appraises projects, implements them and then evaluates them [6].

Specifications		A traditional engineering tool, specifications play a fundamental part in establishing the project baseline. Specifications can be very detailed or 'merely' performance
Work breakdown structures		Developed in the US defence industry, a WBS is officially defined as: 'A product-oriented family tree division of hardware, software, services and other work tasks which organizes, defines and graphically displays the product to be produced, as well as the work to be accomplished to achieve the specified product.' The top 2-4 hierarchic levels define the functional basis of the project, the bottom 1-2 define the project's activities
Configuration management		The technique of defining and monitoring the project's engineering configuration and, when used with change control, of ensuring all parties are using the same appropriate, up-to-date configuration information
Bar charts		Developed by Gantt in the early 1900 bar charts show activities as horizontal bars displayed against a horizontal time scale. Bar charts do not show activity interrelationships
Network scheduling		Network schedules are of two types: activity-on-node (precedence) and activity-on-arrow (i-j). Developed in the late 1950s, networks show activity interrelationships. Essentially, no activity can leave a node until all those entering it are completed. (Activities usually proceed from left to right.) Precedence is considered by novices to be more difficult to use but probably is not, does have greater communicative power, and avoids dummies (dotted arrows) which are often necessary for purely logic reasons on i-j. The critical path is the longest path through the network (zero slack)
Task-responsibility matrices		T-R matrices range organizational unit against WBS elements so that responsibilities are clear (e.g. S = Supervision, C = Control, E = Execution). This is particularly valuable on large, complex projects
Performance measurement		Project control requires knowing accurately the actual progress achieved. This necessitates that progress be measured physically. Measurement based on invoices is too imprecise. Combining physical and financial reporting is difficult. Measured Bills of Quantities is one method; Earned Value (illustrated opposite) is another
Matrix organization		There are essentially three kinds of organization found on projects: functional, project and matrix. In functional organizations, responsibility and authority lie with functional managers (e.g. engineering, procurement); in projects, with the project manager. In a matrix, they are shared. A team member thus has two 'bosses'. The three forms are not mutually exclusive
Cost control		As with performance measurement, cost control necessitates knowing actual costs. There are four basic classes of cost data: budgeted (approved and appropriated); committed; incurred (earned and invoiced) and forecast
Contract administration		At the contract management level, project management often becomes the skill of negotiating and administering the contract, its risks, contingencies and clauses – particularly when variations are introduced
Quality assurance		Quality control is the checking that quality is satisfactory. Quality assurance is 'all activities and functions concerned with the attainment of quality', it is a whole philosophy of management geared to this end. In the USA, a key aspect of QA is documentation
Team building		Selecting the group of people who will work on the project, and welding them into a team by providing leadership and motivation and by properly handling conflict, is a prerequisite of effective project management. Specific tools exist to facilitate this task

Figure 1.2 Project management techniques

[7], in principle looks at those issues of project economics and viability which are broader than the implementation skills of accomplishing the project on schedule, in budget, to scope. In practice, however, project analysis has often tended to give too little attention to the management and implementation aspects of projects [8] and has dwelt too exclusively on the economic and financial aspects. What is needed is the bringing together of the disciplines of project analysis and project management, particularly at the senior management level. We might then talk, perhaps, not so much of project management as of the management of projects, the focus being not the tools and techniques of bringing the project in on schedule, in budget, to technical performance but the phenomenon of projects and how they can be managed successfully.

Why, though, is this so important, especially given that there has already been so much written about project management and project analysis?

Curiously, despite the enormous attention project management and analysis have received over the years, the track record of projects is fundamentally poor, particularly for the larger and more difficult ones. Overruns are common. Many projects appear as failures, particularly in the public view [9]. Projects are often completed late or over budget, do not perform in the way expected, involve severe strain on participating institutions or are cancelled prior to their completion after the expenditure of considerable sums of money.

Table 1.1 summarizes all the reports publicly available on the record of project overruns. There is no selectivity whatsoever in the data contained in the table. While there is undoubtedly additional information held in company files, we believe this to be as full a representation of the information that is currently publicly available as is possible.

There are hardly any reports showing underruns (the reports of Hufschmidt and Gerin [10] and Merewitz [11] of almost 400 US, mostly relatively small projects show many instances of underruns but also a greater proportion of overruns). In all the other cases, representing some 3,500 projects drawn from all over the world in several different industries, overruns are the norm, being typically between 40 and 200 per cent, although greater percentage overruns are found in a number of groupings, particularly certain defence projects and in the US nuclear industry. As examples, consider the following.

—For several years, studies by the General Accounting Office (GAO)—the auditing arm of the US Congress—have consistently shown that federally funded projects typically overrun their initial (or baseline) budgets. A 1975 GAO report, for example, showed that major federally funded projects were overrunning on average 75

Table 1.1 *Project Overrun Record* (detailed references are given in the bibliography)

Study Title	Projects studied	Overrun	Principal reasons
General Accounting Office, 1979	940 US civil and military projects	75% cost increase ($346 billion to $607 billion)	Inflation, quantity increases, engineering changes, schedule changes, underestimating
General Accounting Office, 1982	444 US civil and military projects	140% cost increase ($460 billion to $842 billion)	Quantity changes, inflation, underestimation, support costs, engineering changes, schedule changes
Harman, 1970	25 US weapon systems projects	50–700% cost increase	Project size, complexity, technological advance and development strategy
Large, 1974	8 US weapon systems projects	200–400% cost increase	Underestimate difficulty and cost
Marshall and Meckling, 1959	22 US weapons projects	200–300% cost increase, 30–50% schedule increase	Differences in technological advance
Merrow et al, 1979	10 US energy prototype projects	100–200% cost increase	Technology advance/uncertainty
Myers and Devey, 1984	55 US process plants (33 having pioneer technology)	140–210% cost increase 0–30 months schedule increase	Cost: technological innovation and poor project definition. Schedule: concurrency and solid feedstock
Perry et al, 1969	19US weapon system projects	0–460% cost increase	Government-induced scope changes

Source	Projects	Overrun	Causes
Peck and Scherer, 1962	12 US weapon systems	0–600% cost increase 0–130% schedule increase	Unforeseen technical difficulties or opportunities to improve technical performace
Perry et al: 1971	36 US weapon systems projects	0–220% overrun	Technical uncertainty (30%), scope changes (50%), underestimating (20%)
Summers, 1965	22 US weapon systems projects	15–150% cost overrun	Technological uncertainty and programme length
Blake et al: 1976	Various US power plants	58–258% cost overrun	
Canaday, 1980	35 US nuclear power plants	58–408% cost overrun	Inflation; increased safety requirements; interest charges
Cochran, 1978	BART, TAPS, SRAM	36–200% cost overrun	Concurrency and resource shortages
General Accounting Office, 1981	2 large US coal liquefaction plants	43% cost overrun	Poorly defined and administered contracts
General Accounting Office, 1984	3 US nuclear power plants	362–548% cost overrun	
Hufschmidt and Gerin, 1970	61TVA projects 68 Corps of Engineers projects 79 Bureau of Reclamation projects	−18% to +16% cost overrun −35% to +55% cost overrun −34% to +80% cost overrun	Design changes, relocation, land acquisition, schedule changes, mis-estimation, scope changes inflation, scope changes, quantity changes
Mason et al: 1977	199 US nuclear power plants	26% cost growth 88% schedule growth	Inflation and interest charges

Table 1.1 Continued

Study Title	Projects studied	Overrun	Principal reasons
Merewitz, 1973	49 US highway projects 49 US water projects 59 US building projects 15 US other projects	−40% to +80% cost overrun −30% to +110% cost overrun −20% to +145% cost overrun −20% to +250% cost overrun	
Utility Data Institute, 1985	42 US nuclear plants	190–3,900% cost overrun	
Baum and Tolbert, 1985	World Bank Projects, 1945–85	30–40% cost overrun	
World Bank, 1985	1,014 World Bank projects	30–40% cost overrun	Inflation, especially 1979–80; delays due to increased innovation and complexity; an institutional capability in host countries which did not keep pace with this; and changes
Arditi et al: 1985a, 1985b	384 Turkish projects	40–110% cost overrun 34–44% schedule overrun	Inflation; shortage of materials; delays; payment problems, contractors' financial problems
Healey, 1964	13 Indian irrigation and power projects	12–230% cost increase	Design changes; escalation; increase in scope; mis-estimation
Ministry of Programme Implementation	187 Indian public sector projects	19 to +45% cost increase 0–19% schedule overrun	Late approvals; site acquisition and clearing; equipment supply; slow performance; scope and design changes; estimating uncertainties; increased interest charges; funding availability

Source	Projects	Result	Causes
Department of Energy, 1976	Various North Sea projects	100–44% cost overrun	Inflation; underestimation
Institute of Industrial Economics, 1979	20 oil projects	10–780% cost overrun	
National Economic Development Office, 1970	13 UK power projects, 16 UK oil and chemical plants, 7 UK oil gasification projects	0–50% cost increases 0–27 month (35%) schedule increase	Inappropriate contract policies; late design information and too many changes; insufficient training; poor industrial relations management
National Economic Development Office, 1976	3 ethylene units, 3 distillation units, 3 refineries, 3 methanol plants, 6 power stations	0–68% schedule overrun	Site management represents heart of problem, particularly industrial relations
Wilson, 1969	36 CEGB power plants	43% of units have 12 months schedule overrun	Adverse site conditions; manufacturing difficulties; design faults; labour problems
Allen and Norris, 1970	84 UK laboratory research projects	45% cost overrun, 206% schedule overrun	No obvious reasons
Segelod, 1986	35 Swedish large-scale private projects	10% average overrun, −30% +40% variance	Estimating uncertainty; escalation; technical innovation; generally difficult to isolate causes
Pugh, 1985	71 UK aerospace projects	Cost overruns normal	Insufficient work in project definition, concurrency, high risk (particularly new materials)

per cent while the overrun on projects of $1 billion or over was 140 per cent [12]; by 1982 the figures were 140 per cent and 189 per cent respectively [13].

—Studies by the Rand Corporation show a consistent pattern of overrun for technically complex projects,whether in aerospace or construction projects [14].

—Studies of US nuclear power plant, tunnelling, highway, water, building and other projects show overruns to be extremely common [15].

—World Bank projects in general have consistently overrun [16].

—Studies of irrigation, power and construction projects in India and Turkey have shown delays to be common and serious [17].

—North Sea projects had a history of significant overruns, at least until recently [18].

—Large scale UK power and civil projects had a record of substantial overruns, at least until recently [19].

—Research in Sweden on local government and industrial projects shows overruns to be common [20].

—Defence projects have a record of frequent overruns [21].

Why does the record so consistently show project overruns to be the norm? Is this the indictment of project management that it seems? After all, if the stated task of project management is to accomplish a project to technical specification, in budget, on schedule, then despite all the thousands of papers, hundreds of books and years of discussion, project management is patently not performing adequately.

Though incompetence must sometimes be to blame for this record of overruns, it is almost certainly less significant than might at first be imagined. The very frequency of overruns across so many different industries suggests that there must be other reasons. In fact, analysis of the reasons quoted in the reports for the overruns suggests that the causes of this poor performance are generally to be found in areas which have traditionally not been the concern of project management. It would thus seem that if we are to manage our projects better we must learn to manage these other factors more effectively. Such factors include escalation, government or client induced changes, increased order quantities, increased safety requirements, interest charges, land acquisition charges and so on. Indeed, many projects overrun because of circumstances 'external' to the project—whether price escalation, government action, strikes, corporate decisions, or acts of God (a fact which, curiously, most of the writing and teaching of project management seems to ignore [22]).

It is this seemingly appalling record of missed targets which undoubtedly has led to the scepticism the public typically feels towards large projects. Yet in fact, the presence of a numerical overrun is only indicative of the possibility of project failure. It is not in itself a proof of incompetence, imprudence or even necessarily of problems [23]. For example, certain of the GAO overruns are due to increased order quantities—the GAO studies show an overrun since the final programme cost is greater than the initial budget—but an increased order quantity is surely a sign of success. Much of the cost growth in early US defence programmes was due to government requested changes [24]. Similarly, regulatory changes in the US nuclear industry are responsible for a substantial proportion of the cost growth in this industry [25].

There are other potential distortions in the figures. The treatment of contingencies is one example. The Apollo programme, for example, came in at $21 billion, only $1 billion over its initial estimate. Few know that the initial estimate included $8 billion of contingencies, a thing rare in itself. Very few public projects have even semiformal contingency budgets, for several reasons—politicians are less likely to approve expensive projects and in competitive bid situations it is extremely difficult for government to admit that its estimate has that extra bit of 'fat' in it [26]). Contingencies are not even always common practice on civil projects: the Trans-Alaskan Pipeline (TAPS), which began with $900 million as the ballpark estimate for a simple pipeline laid over 800 miles of frozen tundra and ended at $8.5 billion after enormous engineering and regulatory changes, had no contingency in its initial budget.

Other distortions include price escalation—most private sector projects include a line item for inflation (though TAPS did not) whereas most government projects are calculated in current prices with no budget item for escalation[2]; accounting practices, e.g. on depreciation, which affect the way items are charged; and exchange rate fluctuations, which can play havoc on multi-currency projects.

Indeed for the project sponsor—its owner or his financial backers—overruns are not necessarily even the best measure of project success. The project may still be profitable even though it exceeds its original budget or is late. Market conditions might have changed, for example. Such was the case in the early North Sea oil projects. Similarly, the reverse might be true. This happened on numerous commodity and primary metals projects, such as copper, bauxite and steel, in the late 1970s and early 1980s. Instead, internal rate of return may well be a more appropriate measure of success for the project sponsor.

---

[2] Thus the Central Electricity Generating Board (CEGB) discounts all costs back to the project's budget base dates. This makes comparison of overruns on UK nuclear power projects with those experienced by the US nuclear plants, for example, almost impossible to make accurately—US plant costs include not only inflation but generally the finance charges for funds used during construction (AFUDC: Amortized Funds Used During Construction) [27].

A contractor may achieve his project management targets but in doing so suffer severe financial loss, e.g. because of an inadequate bid or unforeseen circumstances arising which are unrecoverable under contract conditions. Meeting original targets would in this case be a poor measure of business success. Alternatively, there are many situations where contractors explicitly wish to have initial targets exceeded, normally because their initial bid was low and their only chance of profit is through changes to the contract conditions.

Even given the above caveats, however, overruns are at minimum at least indicative of problems. As such they provide support for the contention that many projects come out worse than the parties involved budgeted, especially the larger and more complex ones. Indeed, there is a significant feeling among many in the project world that major projects in particular have an unhealthily high rate of failure. This feeling is shared by the public at large which often resents the enormous dislocation caused by such projects and the way they absorb huge quantities of money when so many others in society suffer from lack of needed funds.

But what are major projects and how are they different from other projects? Is it really worth studying their management as an exercise in its own right?

Some projects are so large or complex or difficult that they require an exceptional level of management [28]. Such major projects are generally of great importance to those undertaking them. Indeed one would be foolish to undertake them were they not so, for invariably the risk they pose is extraordinary. Major projects are those which are particularly demanding either because of their size, complexity, schedule urgency or demand on existing resources or know-how [29]. Importantly, the term 'major' is relative. There may be complex, difficult projects which while not large in monetary terms are nevertheless clearly major to those undertaking them, e.g. major R & D projects or a refit at a process plant. Again therefore, we are all surrounded by major projects without necessarily realizing it. Both as individuals and as companies we invariably find ourselves at some time in our lives embarking upon a project which exceeds our experience, or which poses special problems of size or urgency, or which represents some other form of major difficulty.

In fact, some of the most important undertakings that our society embarks upon are in effect major projects [30]. Society does not always grow in small increments. Often the most important developments occur through step-like progressions. The development of the railways; the building of major road systems; the construction of the electricity system; the development of airports and harbours; the installation of telecommunications networks; the development of major new products, such as computers, motor cars, aeroplanes and drugs; the gradual exploration and development of space; the implementation of major health, education and welfare programmes: all are examples of major projects which have been and continue to be central to the development of our society [31]. Yet too often we seem to manage such important developments poorly.

The study of major projects ought, therefore, to be of immense importance and interest to society. Until now, however, it has been neglected almost totally. The very great majority of our educational efforts have been focused on individual topics, such as languages, economics and science. Latterly, education has moved to a second phase, being focused more on the specific needs of individual companies. The development of business school education over the last few decades has responded to and created an awareness of the value of education directed towards individual institutions' needs. A third phase is the focusing of knowledge and education at the major projects which institutions undertake. Just as the challenge of orientating education to the needs of specific companies was difficult and required great conceptual effort, so the focusing of knowledge at the major project level will require similar conceptual and organizational ability. For like the effort to generalize usefully across companies, at the project level we need to be able to recognize common features in projects in different industries, utilizing the lessons and tools of the many disciplines which come together to work on a project: finance, insurance, law, politics, economics, management, engineering and so on.

There is, further, a particular difficulty in developing knowledge on major projects. For while companies represent obvious sponsors of such work, projects, being aggregations of the efforts of many different organizations, often lack such an obvious sponsor. It is largely for this reason that several societies have been formed since the late 1970s with the specific intent of developing a multi-industry understanding of major projects. Such societies include The American Society for Macro-Engineering [32] and the Large Scale Programs Institute in the United States; Le Centre International de Recherche et Formation en Gestion des Grands Projets and the Canadian Major Projects Association in Canada; the Mitsubishi Research Institute, the Japan Institute of Macro-Engineering and the Japan Project Industrial Council in Japan; the Spanish Society for Macro-Engineering; and the Major Projects Association in the United Kingdom.

These societies are different from the professional project management societies such as the European International Association of Project Managers (INTERNET), the US's Project Management Institute (PMI), the Australian Project Management Forum (PMF) or the Japanese Engineering Advancement Association (ENAA) [33]. They are groupings of senior people concerned with large and complex projects who want to understand better the broader issues involved in the successful initiation, assessment, securing and accomplishment of major projects. The project management societies, on the other hand, being typically associations for projects managers, tend to be concerned with the specific concepts, tools and techniques of project management rather than these broader, more strategic issues.

Given the frequently poor record of major projects and our generally imprecise understanding of their management, is it imprudent to embark upon a major project? Certainly the large risk these projects pose ought to make participants exceptionally cautious. But advocating caution is not the same as advocating that major projects should necessarily be avoided. To go unnecessarily for large, complex undertakings is clearly foolish, but there are many instances in both industry and government where such projects simply cannot be avoided. The very great majority of today's defence projects are inescapably expensive and complex, for example. The aircraft industry is perforce a major projects one. The petroleum, gas and petrochemical industries are predominantly major too. There are, further, occasions where major undertakings may so obviously make a major contribution to society— be it a second Panama Canal, a space station, a telecommunications link, a refoliation programme for the deserts, or a major infrastructure development such as a tunnel, a bridge, or a waste-water scheme in a Third World city [34]—that it would be almost criminal to ignore the opportunity such a major project would offer. In all cases, however, participants must be wary of the very great challenges to management— the hazards to success— that come with such major projects.

Big is not necessarily beautiful. But neither is it necessarily ugly. Where major efforts are called for, management must respond appropriately, using all the skills and experience at its disposal. The problem is that we have very little formal understanding of how to manage such major projects effectively.

One of the purposes of this book is to explore what is involved in managing such major undertakings. The book does so by describing, in Part Two, eight major projects undertaken during the last 20 or so years in the United Kingdom and Europe. In Part Three it analyses the management challenges posed by these and similar projects and the lessons which can be drawn from their study. The lessons which are derived from the analysis tell us much that is new about the management of major projects.

The analysis of the case studies also extends greatly our understanding of the management of projects in general. For in exploring the strategic issues which emerge as important in these case studies—

issues such as technology management, the role of government, contract administration—our formal understanding of the management of projects is extended quite considerably. This book is thus also as much a text on the new peceptions of project management as a study of major projects.

REFERENCES

1. Beard, E., 1976; Putman, W. D., 1972; Sapolsky, H., 1972.
2. *Project Management Journal*, 1984.
3. Hammond, R. and Fox, D., 1985.
4. Olsen, R. P., 1971.
5. Archibald, R. D., 1976; Cleland, D. I. and King, W. R., 1983; Delp, P. *et al*, 1977; Dinsmore, P. C., 1984; Dunne, E., 1983; Harrison, F. L., 1985; Johnston, K. F. A., 1971; Kerzner, H. D., 1979; Lock, D., 1984, 1987; Maciariello, J. A., 1978; Marsh, P. D. V., 1969; Martin, C. C., 1976; Meredith, J. R. and Mantel, S. J., 1985; *Project Management Journal*, 1986; Roman, D. D., 1986; Ruskin, A. M. and Estes, W. E., 1982; Scott, P., 1974; Wearne, S. H., 1984; Webster, F. M., 1981.
6. Baum, W. C., and Tolbert, S. M., 1985.
7. Fremgem, J. M., 1973; Gittinger, J. P., 1972; Little, I. M. D. and Mirless, J. M., 1968; Merrett, A. J. and Sykes, A., 1963; Rowley, C. S., 1973; Squire, L. and van der Tak, H. G., 1975.
8. Baum, W. C. and Tolbert, S. M., 1985; Carter, E. E., 1972; Hertz, D. B. and Thomas, H., 1983; Hellings, J., 1985; Hodder, J. E., and Riggs, H. E., 1985; Mao J. C. T., 1970.
9. Ellis, W., 1985.
10. Hufschmidt, N. M. and Gerin, J., 1970.
11. Merewitz, L., 1973.
12. General Accounting Office, 1980.
13. General Acounting Office, 1983.
14. Harman, A. J., 1970; Large, J. P., 1974; Marshall, A. W. and Meckling, W. H., 1959; Merrow, E., Chapel, S. W. and Worthing, C. A., 1979; Myers, C. W. and Devey, M. R., 1984; Perry, R. L. *et al.*, 1969; Summers, R., 1965.
15. Blake, C., Cox, D. and Fraize, W., 1976; Cochran, E. G., Patz, A. L. and Rowe, A. J., 1978; Hufschmidt, N. M. and Gerin, J., 1970; General Accounting Office, 1981, 1984; Mason, G. E. *et al.*, 1977; Merewitz, L., 1973; National Committee on Tunnelling Technology, 1974; Utility Data Institute, 1985.
16. Baum, W. C. and Tolbert, S. M., 1985; World Bank, 1985.
17. Arditi, D., Akan, G. T. and Gurdamar, S., 1985a, 1985b; Healey, J. M. 1964; Ministry of Programme Implementation, 1986.
18. Department of Energy, 1976; Frankhouser, H. S., 1981; Institute of Industrial Economics, 1979; Stinchcombe, A. L., 1979b; Vicklund, C. A. and Craft, W. S., 1981.

19. National Economic Development Office, 1970; Wilson, A., 1969.
20. Segelod, E., 1986
21. Connell, J., 1986; Fox, J. R., 1984; General Accounting Office, 1985; Large, P., 1974; Peck, M. J. and Sherer, F. M., 1962; Pugh, P. G., 1985.
22. Morris, P. W. G. and Hodgson, P. J., 1985.
23. Fox, J. R., 1984.
24. Large, J. P., 1974; Perry, R. L. *et al.*, 1969.
25. Canaday, H. T., 1980; Kutner, S., 1979.
26. Large, J. P., 1984.
27. Canaday, H. T., 1980.
28. Fraser, D. C., 1984; Morris, P. W. G., 1985a, 1985b; Morris, P. W. G. and Hough, G. H., 1986.
29. Fraser, D. C., 1984.
30. Davidson, F. P., 1986.
31. Davidson, F. P., Giacoletto, L. J. and Salkeld, R., 1978; Davidson, F. P., Meador, C. L. and Salkeld, R., 1980; Davidson, F. P. and Meador, C. L., 1982; Salkeld, R., Davidson, F. P. and Meador, C. L., 1981.
32. Horwitch, M., 1987.
33. *Project Management Journal*, 1985.
34. Davidson, F. P., 1986.

PART TWO

The Case Studies

Chapter Two

The Channel Tunnel, 1960–75

The idea of a fixed link across the English Channel goes back at least to Napoleonic times. In 1802 a French mining engineer, Albert Mathieu, proposed a detailed tunnelling scheme. This was commended by Napoleon to Charles Fox during the signing of the Treaty of Amiens. In 1803 a British engineer named Mottray proposed a large diameter iron pipe laid on the sea bottom—an immersed tube. Since then a myriad of schemes of all kinds have been proposed. People have talked of canals with double jetties, of viaducts, of dams with locks, of tidal engineering and power generation, but most studies throughout history have concentrated on a tunnel. During the period from about 1833 to 1869 many serious studies were carried out, and many proposals made. The British Channel Tunnel Company was formed in 1872. The French company was formed three years later.

The French Geological Commission ordered a major study in 1876. A geological map of the route was produced which has been the basis for all subsequent tunnel studies. It confirmed that there is a single stratum of chalk marl which is ideal tunnelling material. To demonstrate the validity of the plan, each of the Channel Tunnel companies sank a shaft on its own coast and bored out for over a mile. These tunnels can be seen to this day. They were remarkably free of trouble and proved that the stratum was impermeable to water. The work was stopped because of British fear that the tunnel posed a threat to national security. This argument prevailed for another 70 years.

After World War I, Prime Minister Ramsay MacDonald called four ex-prime ministers to discuss the project. They devoted the whole of 40 minutes to the proposed project and then rejected it. Churchill commented, 'There is not doubt of the promptitude. The question is: was their decision right or wrong? I do not hesitate to say that it was wrong.'

In 1930 a British Government commission approved the tunnel: it went to the House of Commons and was lost by a few votes. In the late 1930s a road tunnel was proposed and this again failed to attract a sufficient vote.

After World War II it became obvious that the traffic across the Straits of Dover was building up to a level which caused uncomfortable congestion in peak periods. It was felt by many people that a brake would be put on our economic expansion if something was not done about it. In 1955 a parliamentary question was put to the Minister of Defence, Harold Macmillan. Macmillan's reply finally ended the long and rather dismal history of British objection to the tunnel on military grounds: 'Of the military objections to this tunnel,' he said, 'scarcely any remain.'

Two years later, in 1957, the Channel Tunnel Study Group was formed. This group comprised four parties: the British Channel Tunnel Company, the French equivalent, the French Suez Company and an American company. The group excluded vested interests and looked with an open mind at possible options. They concluded that economically and technically a bored tunnel offered the best solution at the time. They proposed a rail tunnel since a road tunnel of that length could not be ventilated without coming up in mid Channel, which they saw as posing maritime hazards. The rail tunnel would be sufficiently large to take rolling stock on which large lorries, caravans, cars and so forth could be carried. Most of the traffic, of course, would arrive at each side of the Channel by road. The tunnel was therefore planned to cater for both road and rail traffic. This design concept, 'the rolling motorway', was the key technical concept in the tunnel. Because most of the traffic arrived by road, the British Channel Tunnel Company thought it necessary that whoever carried out the project should not be dominated by the railways.

At the end of 1960 the French formed an entirely French Channel Bridge Study Group made up of banks and tourist and motor car organizations. They carried out studies for a bridge. This gave the two governments the problem of deciding between the tunnel and bridge proposals. A civil service working group was set up to review the two schemes and reported in September 1963 [1]. It came down firmly in favour of a tunnel on grounds of cost, practicability, profitability and general acceptability. Six months later, in February 1964, the two governments issued a joint policy declaration that they had agreed on a bored rail tunnel. As an earnest of their intentions, the governments financed a major geological survey with something like 500 sea-bed bore holes across the Channel. This was carried out by the Channel Tunnel Study Group with government money and with government supervision.

In February 1967 the two governments invited private interests to submit proposals for the financing and construction of the tunnel. Three international groups were formed, one being the Channel Tunnel Study Group, another being an Anglo-French banking consortium led by Hill-Samuel, and a third being led by Warburgs. The Channel Tunnel Study Group was joined by most of the leading British merchant banks, and Morgan Stanley, First Boston and White Weld from the United States. All three groups submitted proposals during 1967 and 1968, but none of them was wholly acceptable. The UK and French governments therefore asked the three groups to get together. The final British group comprised the British Channel Tunnel Company, seven of the leading merchant banks (headed by Morgan Grenfell) and British Rail. The three major American investment banks retained a small stake. The French company comprised nine banks and merchant banks, and SNCF.

The 1963 White Paper had assumed that the project would be in the private sector but subject to government regulation to prevent excessive profits. This changed fundamentally with the British Labour Government in 1966. Barbara Castle, the new Minister of Transport, seemed to want the project carried out by the public sector. The French remained keen on the private sector. The tunnel was thus to be built and financed privately with loans guaranteed by both governments for between 70 and 90 per cent of the cost.[1] The project was to be handed over to a nationalized Anglo-French operating authority, to be created at some future date, which would be government owned. The project was to be organized, financed and built, however, by the two private-sector consortia, each building half of the facility. The 10 to 30 per cent of private capital would be supported by 90 to 70 per cent of government guaranteed loan capital. Although it was conceded that there had to be risk capital, there was a clear ceiling on the reward for that risk capital. That ceiling tended to take much of the interest out of that project. It was not, strictly speaking, equity capital under the scheme; it was more like participating preference capital with the preference aspect more dominant.

From the outset, the organization of the Channel Tunnel took on its characteristic feature of duplication. The organization structure of the project was consequently complex (Figure 2.1). The project was being

---

[1] Companies were required to raise not less than 10 per cent of the estimated out-turn costs as at the start of construction as equity. The balance of the actual costs—whatever they turned out to be—was to be raised by loans guaranteed by the British and French governments. If the actual costs exceeded the original estimated out-turn costs, the companies were to use their best endeavours to raise not less than 10 per cent of the additional costs as equity. Thus the two governments were in the position of being the lenders of last resort who would provide the cash required to complete the project; by virtue of their guarantees they were also the providers of any deficiency finance that might be required if the tunnel cash flows were insufficient to service the loans.

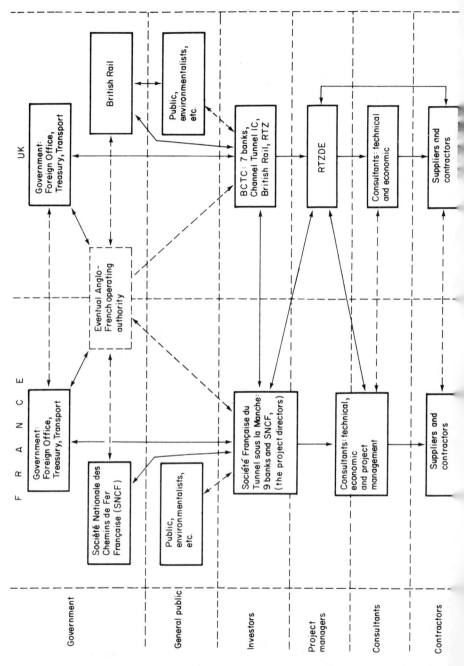

Figure 2.1 Channel Tunnel organization

Source: *Major Projects Association*

undertaken on the initiative of two countries, France and the United Kingdom, of very different temperament and character. Both the public and private sectors of each country were substantially involved. Further, the project was without a client: there were the two governments and various banks, but looking at the project from an operations point of view, there was no single decision-taking body, no single overall head. The French side was dominated by banking interests and was to be managed by individual consultants. On the British side there were seven merchant banks, British Rail, Rio Tinto-Zinc (RTZ) and the old Channel Tunnel Company. Sir Val Duncan, Chairman of RTZ, had been approached by Prime Minister Edward Heath to see whether RTZ would be interested in taking a lead management role in the project.[2] RTZ were appointed in the summer of 1970 as project managers of the British organization.

A fundamental principle of the Channel Tunnel, in spirit if not in letter, was *moitié-moitié* (half and half): the work was to be divided equally, half the costs being borne by each side. The theoretical reasons for this were obvious; in practice they were far from clear. For example, the excavation on the French side was much tougher, and hence more expensive, than that on the British; the cost of the rail improvements on the British side were known to cost more than those on the French side. Figure 2.2 shows the bore holes and the line of the tunnel; Figure 2.3 shows the tunnel in section.

Economic analyses of the tunnel's viability had been carried out in 1957–9 for the Channel Tunnel Study Group. These were too dated to be of use in the 1970s, however. A study by British and French government officials which was produced in 1963 was similarly dated. SETEC, a French firm of consultants who had worked on the 1959 study, worked on a number of updates between 1966 and 1969. These studies still showed a tunnel to be economically preferable to a bridge, that the rate of return would be very high and that therefore it should be possible to finance the project with private capital.

In March 1971 an agreement was signed between the two governments which committed them to studies costing £1 million, to be completed by April 1972. These would be followed by a final decision on the tunnel. The general belief about this time (the summer of 1970) was that the project would be in existence and operational within six or seven years.

RTZ felt that a first task of theirs had to be a review of the existing studies. Their conclusion following this review was that the traffic fore-

---

[2] This to a large extent followed RTZ's outstanding achievement on Churchill Falls [2].

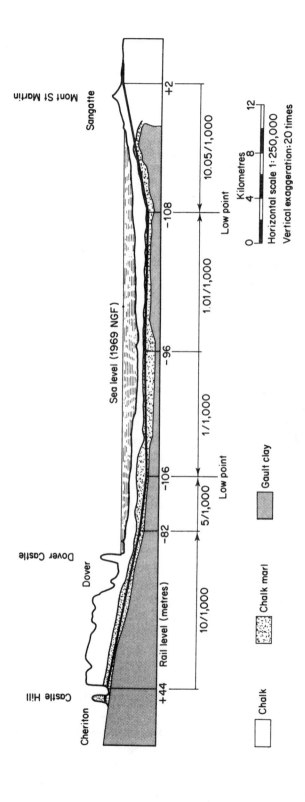

Figure 2.2 Vertical alignment of the 1970 route

Source: *Major Projects Association*

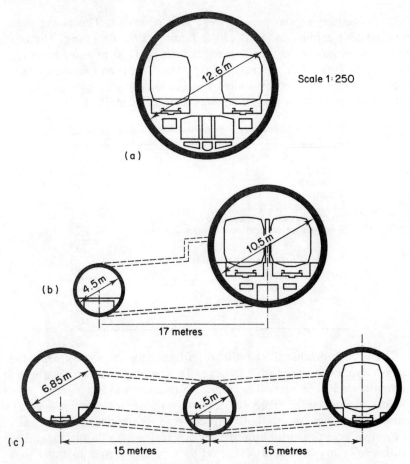

Scale 1:250

(a)

(b)

17 metres

(c)

15 metres   15 metres

Figure 2.3 Cross-sections of possible tunnels (a) Single tunnel with integral service gallery (b) Single tunnel with separate service tunnel (c) Twin tunnels with separate service tunnel
Source: *Major Projects Association*

casts were crude and outdated, that further study was necessary and that £500,000 should be allocated for such a study. On the *moitié-moitié* principle, this meant that the French would have to undertake a similar study, at a cost, that is, also of £500,000. Despite French misgivings that this was a British trick to stall the project, the studies were duly undertaken (not without some argument). The studies were begun in April 1971 and completed in May 1972. New traffic forecasts were produced. There was a fresh look at the technical design of the tunnels and terminals (although the British Government would not allow any options to be studied other than a bored tunnel). The budget, financing and profitability of the project were also reviewed. The new budget totalled £366 million in terms of the January 1972 £ sterling. The out-turn cost in money value was expected to be £630 million, however, because of escalation, interest during construction and financing fees. The estimate, obtained by adding French costs to sterling costs, at the rate of exchange then prevailing, was built up as in Table 2.1.

Table 2.1   Estimates for constructing Channel Tunnel

	£m
Tunnels	202
Terminals	58
Rolling stock	33
Project development	7
Land purchase & insurance	5
Engineering supervision & management	28
	333
Provision for contingencies (10%)	33
Total (January 1972 value)	366
Provision for escalation	168
Interest during construction	96
	630

The French produced an estimate in francs for their work while the British produced theirs in £ sterling. To combine the two required a common exchange rate. The logical approach was to forecast how exchange rates were likely to move over the construction period. However, discussions by both project management teams with their respective governments showed that this was not to be the case. The British Treasury informed RTZ that they could assume anything they liked provided they did not show the pound falling against the franc! At the same time, the French consultants were told that they could assume anything they liked except that they must not show the franc falling against the pound! So a date was chosen—the end of the study— and the exchange rate at that time was taken. There was strong disagreement between the French and the British as to the financial returns resulting from different traffic forecasts and different tolls. The British figures were less bullish than the French.

In September 1971 the two sides signed heads of agreement on the method of financing the project. The document was later called 'Agreements Number 1', the plural being used because the versions in English and French were not quite the same (even after allowing for translation difficulties). The agreement required the two companies to raise at least 10 per cent of the capital required in the form of equity, and to use their best efforts to raise 30 per cent in this way. The capital required was defined as the out-turn cost, including escalation and interest during construction. The balance of the funds was to be raised under guarantees provided by the British and French governments.

The governments took the view that since they would be the main risk bearers, in so far as they would be providing guarantees for up to 90 per cent of the capital, they should be the main beneficiaries of any equity surplus. This meant that the equity capital as defined would not be normal equity but would have a negotiated return. The return was to be such that would just allow the money to be raised, consistent with market conditions at the time of issue and based on the then current estimates of capital and operating costs. There were some first attempts to define a formula which included two factors, called X and Y. X was to be a percentage of the gross revenue of the tunnel and Y was to be a percentage of the net receipts of the tunnel. Net receipts were defined in a way which bore little resemblance to anything that an accountant would recognize. They were effectively the net cash flow of the tunnel, after servicing loan repayments.

The project teams were working well by this stage, although better on the engineering side than the economic. Significantly, however, British Rail was in effect absent from the British team. The relationship between the French Channel Tunnel Company and SNCF was very much better. One of the main reasons was that the person who was in charge of the French economic studies was seconded from SNCF. There was no such person from British Rail, even though much of the revenues of the tunnel would be generated by through rail traffic and British Rail was a significant shareholder within the British Channel Tunnel Company. British Rail would obviously have a large part to play in the operating authority yet within the Rail Board the tunnel was viewed as unnecessary and unrealistic: it was not going to happen and did not warrant the investment of senior management time. The part of British Rail responsible was Southern Region. Rail investment funds were in short supply and Southern Region's business revolved around London which was in need of further rail investment.

Throughout the Preliminary Phase, the project team was actively working with the government on the various documents that had to be passed, signed, ratified and put into place before the project could proceed. There was a large list of them. There were the Agreements Numbers 1, 2 and 3, and there was to be an Anglo-French Treaty. There were to be several parliamentary debates and select committees for which material had to be prepared. There would have to be enabling legislation to allow various changes to take place. The parliamentary legislative programme was going to be immense. A target was set that it should be completed before the end of 1974. The Heath Government was in power; it had been elected in June 1970 and was expected to stand for re-election during the first half of 1975. It was hoped that this complicated body of legislation would not be interfered with by any election run-up or a change of government. (In fact, in 1974 there was a change of government in the United Kingdom and two general elections.) For the French, the procedure was much easier. All their planning requirements could be handled through a Declaration de l'Uti-litée Publique which led to a straightforward planning inquiry which, it seemed, was unlikely to encounter serious public opposition.

The report on the Preliminary Phase was not published because of the different forecasts developed by the British and French using different methods. After completion of the Preliminary Phase, great pressures were applied that the next phase should not produce anything as embarrassing.

Agreements Number 1 were signed on 20 October 1972. The esti-mated cost of Phase I was £5.5 million; £2.5 million of this was to be contributed by the companies as equity and the balance was provided as government-guaranteed loans. Phase I of the project now began and was to last until June 1973.

One of the first tasks in the new phase was the refinement of the traffic and market studies. Much time was devoted to the way in which certain variables likely to have an important effect on the level of traffic were likely to move in the future. The basic problem was that the two governments were unwilling to produce forecasts on gross domestic products, inflation, exchange rates and such like, since they felt that these might be made available to a wide audience. The consultants were therefore obliged to produce a number of alternative sets of such variables which they showed to the governments, who then indicated whether or not they would be embarrassed by their eventual publi-cation. Traffic patterns were agreed and optimum toll charges outlined. The competition offered by the ferries was particularly studied. Tech-nical studies now concentrated on developing the design of rolling stock, on tunnel linings and on modifications to the site of the place where the tunnel crossed the British shore. Additional geological work was carried out on the French side. Planning consents were sought, e.g. from the Kent County Council; local inhabitants were consulted. Profitability forecasts were reviewed in further detail. This time the differences in traffic forecasts between the French and the British were much narrower. Problems were still experienced in obtaining politically embarrassing national economic forecasts. The result was that two sets of traffic forecasts were produced: those accepted by the governments based on higher economic growth and those accepted by the companies based on lower economic growth. These were respectively called the

Central Growth Forecasts and the Low Growth Forecasts. The capital costs had also been re-estimated during Phase I. Much was made in the press of the 'dramatic increase of costs' but the increases were mainly due to non-engineering matters such as exchange rate movements and inflation. The new estimated cost was £468 million in January 1973 terms compared with £366 million using January 1972 costs. Comparing like with like, the estimated cost increased by £25 million (or about 7 per cent), most of which was due to scope changes. The estimated out-turn cost of the tunnel in money values was £846 million made up as in Table 2.2:

Table 2.2   Estimated out-turn cost of Channel Tunnel

	£m
Estimate in January 1973 values	468
Escalation of costs during construction	186
Interest during construction	192
Total	846

The main criterion used to measure the overall profitability of the tunnel was the internal discounted cash flow rate of return in real terms on the total capital employed. Since some £7.5 million of risk money (25 per cent of the total) was to be raised towards the cost of Phase II, a remuneration formula had to be agreed based on the forecasts existing at the end of Phase I. This proved to be the single most difficult aspect of Phase I. Agreement was never reached on which of the two sets of traffic forecasts was to be used and, in the end, the remuneration formula was based on the arithmetical average of the Low Growth and Central Growth forecasts.

Organizationally, the project was working well at this time. Most organizational problems stemmed from the number of different organizations involved and the lack of an overall supremo. The ultimate internal authority was the Quadripartite Committee consisting of representatives of the two governments and the two companies. This met regularly and was, in the main, a useful and successful forum. There were specialized committees such as:

Project Management Executive Committee
Finance Committee
Traffic Forecasts Committee
Engineering Committees
   Tunnel Design
   Terminals
   Rolling Stock

They met regularly and liaised with respective experts in the governments.

Two problems became apparent. One was that there was insufficient liaison with British Rail management, especially on the design of the London-to-Dover high-speed rail link—British Rail's team was very small (half a dozen or so), and this for a project which represented the first major rail project this century—so that RTZ ended by making several rail decisions on their own, e.g. on the train configuration. The other was that there had been a complete change in the British officials working with the project management team and in the economic studies areas.

Public interest in the project grew substantially in 1973. Partly this was the fascination for a tunnel which at last would have given Britain a fixed connection to the Continent. Another important reason was that the project followed three other large public-sector transport projects—the Motorway Box, Maplin and Concorde—which had been strongly endorsed by government and become the subject of intense public debate over a prolonged time period [3]. Two of these projects were eventually cancelled. To some extent, the Channel Tunnel was the victim of its predecessors.

There was also suspicion that although the two Channel Tunnel Companies were claiming that this was a private-sector project, they might not be risking their own money. Most of the finance was guaranteed by public funds, and hence there was a feeling that the private sector was getting an easy ride on the back of the public sector. The shipping lobby began to make itself felt. Keith Wickenden began to emerge as an effective lobbyist and champion against the tunnel. There was worry about the danger of overdevelopment in Kent and about the environmental impact of the proposed terminal at Cheriton. Lively debate developed on where the London terminal should be: British Rail wished to use the White City, while the Greater London Council preferred the Surrey Docks and most passengers preferred Central London. The politicians in particular appeared insensitive to the time required to obtain planning approvals. The very rush for approvals which the government created at this time would probably have backfired later when the necessary parliamentary approvals were sought. Realizing the public's sensitivity over planning issues, the government commissioned two reports. The first was prepared by Economic Consultants Limited and entitled *The Channel Tunnel—Its Economic and Social Impact on Kent* [4]. It was published in 1973 and was not helpful to the tunnel. It concluded that while employment in south-east Kent would rise from 70,000 to 96,000 without a tunnel, the tunnel would create a further net employment increase of 3,000 to 6,000. The second was the *United Kingdom Transport Cost–Benefit Study* prepared by Coopers & Lybrand [5]. Despite the general wariness, if not to say weariness, of cost–benefit studies it was felt that a precedent had been set, and it had to be repeated, although hopefully on a smaller scale.

The rail link was still causing concern. Two strategies were considered: the high investment strategy cost £145 million (£105 million when discounted to 1973). This was designed to enable trains to travel between London and Paris in 3 hours 40 minutes. It required large sections of new track most of which would be parallel to the existing track. The low investment strategy cost only £15 million as for most of its length it used existing track. British Rail considered that this would have limited capacity and would prove 30 minutes slower than the high investment strategy. However, this would have created problems as the Anglo-French Treaty required that there should be a minimum journey time between London and Paris in order to provide competition with the air services. Thus, the highspeed rail link was, at least formally, an essential addition to the tunnel.

The report on the cost–benefit analysis was published in early June 1973 just after the report from the tunnel companies. However, the debate continued, particularly with the Chamber of Shipping. In August 1973, the government published a White Paper [6] which stated: 'Her Majesty's Government, having given most careful consideration to all aspects of this complicated question believes that the Channel Tunnel would accord with our national interest.' It added, perhaps unnecessarily (although it might have helped the political realities at that time): 'The government recognizes, however, that certain of these advantages would be gained only if the potential for development of through rail services was fully exploited.' It then declared 'that a high quality railway between the Tunnel and London and the provision for through services from provincial centres is essential for the success of the project'.

Phase I of the project was completed in June 1973 but Phase II did not commence until the following November. This five-month intermediate period was used to negotiate, agree and finalize the various documents needed for Phase II to start. In particular:

—the Anglo-French Treaty between the two governments concerning the tunnel was signed;
—agreements Number 2 between the governments and the companies were signed;
—the British Government issued a White Paper recommending the construction of the tunnel;
—the two companies issued Placing Memoranda for the raising of the phase-equity capital.

Perhaps the most difficult matter to agree was the equity remuneration formula which would govern the division of any equity surpluses between the equity shareholders and the governments, who saw themselves as the true equity risk takers. The equity capital was true risk capital in that it did not receive any dividends unless equity surpluses were earned. However, the shares were far removed from normal ordinary shares; they were really a type of cumulative, participating preferred stock. Interestingly, in the light of what ultimately happened, almost as much attention was given to what would happen in the event of termination as the event of successful completion. A complex set of provisions were agreed to cover three possibilities of abandonment:

—Abandonment by one or other of the governments: equity capital already raised would be repaid with a premium of 190 per cent for the original founders' shares, 40 per cent for the Phase II shares if abandonment happened before the raising of the Phase III shares, and premiums varying between say 30 and 190 per cent for all shares thereafter.
—Abandonment by the companies: basically the equity would be lost.
—Joint abandonment: between 50 and 90 per cent of the equity already raised would be repaid according to the class of equity, provided that the governments went ahead at a later date.

It was difficult to explain this package to the sophisticated institutional investors of Phase II and there was some real concern on the marketability of the Phase III shares to the public at large. Nevertheless, the Phase II capital was successfully raised despite a Labour government being in power in the United Kingdom.

Phase II commenced with some nervousness over the rapidly deteriorating economic situation caused by the recent OPEC major oil price increases, which caused some redefinition of the economic studies. The whole project team was working well and gearing up towards full construction. The engineering works were being used as a test for the procedures and controls which would be used during the main construction. The engineering design was moving much more into the detail stage, especially for the rolling stock and terminals where there was close cooperation between the marketing and traffic people and the engineers.

A comprehensive public relations exercise got under way and over half of the Members of Parliament were given detailed presentations in groups of five to ten. There were many other presentations given, especially in Kent. A parliamentary Select Committee was set up. On balance, this went well for the tunnel despite formidable opposition from its opponents. There was growing nervousness amongst the bankers over the prospects of successfully raising the Phase III equity, but in the main, most people working on the project had increasing feelings that the worst was over and that the tunnel would actually be built.

The five-fold increase in oil prices caused the traffic forecasts to be reviewed in detail. The price changes helped rail travel considerably, especially when compared with air. The immediate effect of the change, before allowing for any resultant impact on economic growth, would be to reduce total cross-channel traffic by about 9 per cent, but increase travel through the tunnel by about 11 per cent.

The much more difficult task was to estimate what effect the change in the price of oil would have on the prospects for long term economic growth in Britain and on the Continent which, of course, was a crucial parameter in the traffic-demand forecasts. No one could provide convincing advice.

Agreements Number 2 were signed on 17 November 1973 and the contracts for the Phase II works were signed a day or so later. Construction work commenced in the last week of November 1973 on both sides of the Channel. The objective of the work in Phase II was to drive a short length of the service tunnel from each coast in order to gain experience of actual tunnelling beneath the sea with full-face tunnelling machines. In the United Kingdom, it was planned to spend as little as possible on the access works to the test drive. In France, the decision was taken to construct an inclined adit to service all the tunnel drives both landward and seaward. The French faced an additional complication in that their work had to pass through the fractured, water-bearing Upper and Middle Chalk layers.

In November 1974, the British Government announced that it would not proceed with the high-speed rail link because of its cost. The tunnel companies were informed by the governments of the abandonment of the tunnel on the very day the tunnelling machine on the British site was due to be started. A case was made for the driving of 250 metres of the tunnel with the machine. This was agreed to by the government and the drive was successfully completed.

Why was the project abandoned? This is not entirely clear, even to this day.

In the summer of 1974, British Rail announced their revised estimate of the capital cost of the proposed new high-speed rail link between London and the tunnel. The revised estimate was £330 million in 1974 (the previous estimate having been £130 million). After the initial shock, it was realized that the new estimate was more in line with the likely costs of the proposed scheme and that the previous estimate was an understatement. (There is some doubt, however, as to whether the estimate need have been quite so high.[3]) The two governments and the tunnel companies were, of course, concerned about this dramatic increase in costs. The British share of the tunnel and terminal costs was £235 million, so the high-speed link in Britain was going to be by far the most expensive item.

The legal position was quite clear. Under the Anglo-French Treaty and Agreements Number 2 the British Government was required to authorize and support British Rail in providing a new high-speed rail link. The Agreements Number 2 also made it clear that the governments had to make good any shortfalls in the revenues of the tunnel if the road and rail infrastructure, as defined in the third Schedule, had not been provided by the time the tunnel became operational. The forecast revenues earned by the tunnel from rail passenger services in the first year of operation were about one-third of the total revenues. Nowhere in the Treaty or Agreements were there any clauses which allowed either of the governments to avoid their obligations to provide the defined rail infrastructure. Thus, in the Treaty and Agreements, signed in November 1973, the British Government had, for all practical purposes, signed a blank cheque regarding the high-speed rail link. If the tunnel went ahead, then either the link was to be built or the revenues made good.

To the new Labour Government entering office in May 1974, the prospect of having to fund several hundred million extra pounds for the rail works associated with a privately funded 'European' project in 'Tory' South East England was not one about which it could wax enthusiastic. Certainly many in the trade union movement were against the project. Just what was said in Cabinet will not be known for some time but the indications are that the Minister responsible, Anthony Crosland, although intellectually a supporter of the project, did not feel that it justified his championing. Thus, in November 1974, the British Government announced that it would not proceed with the rail link due to the large and unexpected increase in the estimated costs. The government proposed that the programme be delayed for one year while the matter was reconsidered. It was also announced that the Anglo-French Treaty would not be ratified by the British Government by 1 January 1975, as required by the Agreements.

The Agreements stated that failure to ratify the Treaty within 20 days

---

[3] The £200 million (150 per cent) rise in British Rail's estimate was due to inflation, environmentally mandated additions, changed technical specifications and underestimation. British Rail could practically have reduced this figure if the technical specifications had been reduced. A study by a British Rail team in fact got the budget down by £100 million to £230 million but this budget was never officially accepted by the British Rail Board nor by the government.

of the due date would be regarded as abandonment by the government concerned. The companies held discussions with the British Government during the period November 1974 to January 1975 to see if there was an acceptable basis which would avoid abandonment. The companies argued, with some strength, since their compensation terms were not ungenerous, particularly in the then prevailing economic conditions, that they had raised £7.5 million between them on the basis of Agreements Number 2 and had to protect the interests of their shareholders. Nevertheless, they were prepared to negotiate a new basis which would enable the project to continue, provided that their shareholders did not suffer as a result of the change brought about by the government.

Unfortunately neither party was prepared to relinquish its basic position and so on 2 January 1975 the British Channel Tunnel Company formally served notice on the British Government that failure to ratify the Anglo-French Treaty by the due date would be in breach of Agreements Number 2 and would constitute abandonment by the government. They would be left with no alternative but to invoke the relevant penalty clauses.

The British Government issued a statement on 20 January 1975 making it clear that it was not prepared to enter into the undertaking requested by the companies. Thus the project was abandoned.

OVERALL SUMMARY

The Channel Tunnel was a political project. Born of political will, it died of political indifference. Had the Labour Government not been elected, or had it supported the project more actively, the tunnel would almost certainly have been built successfully, in time, in budget (bar exchange rate variations), at a profit, to just about everyone's satisfaction.

In between its birth and its demise, its political premise became muddled; as a result, so did its financing. To the City, putting equity into a project that had yet to be built and which was going to be operated as a regulated public-sector enterprise entailed some quite specific risks against which protection was required. For example, the City ensured there were good termination clauses in the Agreements. British Rail had no real commitment to the project, and indeed saw it as a diversion of time and much needed finance. The British Channel Tunnel Company's project management failed to recognize sufficiently the threat this indifference posed. When, to their dismay, British Rail realized the tunnel might go ahead, they prepared a 'high investment' scheme with a generous budget. The coincidence then of an election, with the new government preoccupied with other matters, transfixed with money problems, unsympathetic to the project, meant that approval of the project could not be given within the time that the international treaty required. Even then the project might have been saved had there been someone to save it. But, critically, it was not really in the interests of the members of the British Channel Tunnel Company to propose that the project continue. Their shareholders were better served receiving a certain, not immodest return on investment than in proceeding with a project whose commercial basis was still unclear and risky.

All the talk of organization challenges, engineering, environmentalists, the French, etc., ultimately pale behind this flaw in the project's structure and its purpose, a flaw only revealed by the unfortunate concatenation of events just described.

REFERENCES

1. *Proposals for Fixed Channel Link*, 1963.
2. Warnock, G., 1979.
3. Hall, P., 1980.
4. Economic Consultants Limited, 1973.
5. Coopers & Lybrand, 1973.
6. *Channel Tunnel, The*, 1973.

Chapter Three

Concorde

Concorde is one of the most technically advanced aircraft ever built and is the only commercial supersonic airliner in public service. The development 'represented a continual struggle to reconcile two entirely different design requirements, sustained supersonic flight and subsonic approach' [1]. All the aircraft's systems requirements represented considerable advances in their design state. For example, the engine had to be converted from a military standard into 'a civil engine capable of sustained supersonic power with acceptable direct and indirect operating costs' [2]. The basic requirement was to carry passengers across the Atlantic safely and supersonically through the world's air traffic control systems. This was achieved.

In the immediate post-war years, civil aviation developed at a very fast rate. Two of the principal goals of aircraft designers were the achievement of higher speeds and of increased safety. The world's first gas turbine powered commercial airliner, the de Havilland Comet, first entered service in 1953 and suffered the tragedies of structural failure which led to its removal from service and redesign. Later in the decade it re-entered service and was followed by the Boeing 707 and the Douglas DC8. These aircraft operated just below the speed of sound and represented an increase in speed of a factor of about two over the large, four-engined, propeller-driven aircraft which they replaced. To continue the progress as measured by the increase in speed, the next logical step was to look to the development of supersonic transports. Aircraft designers in the United states, the USSR and the United Kingdom were at that time giving considerable thought to this challenge. In France, the successor to the Caravelle was also being contemplated, with a supersonic version, the Super Caravelle, a strong runner. The Comet disasters were fresh in everyone's mind and development plans for a supersonic aircraft development in the Western world were formulated against that background experience.

In the United Kingdom in October 1956, Anthony Eden's government called a meeting of seven aircraft companies, four engine companies and the government departmental representatives to discuss the subject. It was agreed to form a committee to research further and carry out the design studies on supersonic transport aircraft. The formation of this committee, which became known as the Supersonic Transport Aircraft Committee (STAC), represents the important first step in the development of Concorde.

All the UK aircraft companies, the government establishments, the Air Registration Board, the National Physical Laboratories, and the College of Aeronautics at Cranfield, pooled their knowledge and resources to carry out the research and critical examinations to determine whether a supersonic transport was feasible.

By 9 March 1959 the STAC had done sufficient work to show the feasibility of a supersonic transport and recommended that two detailed design studies should be undertaken by the industry. One study was for a long range aircraft to carry about 150 passengers non-stop between London and New York (3,500 miles) at a speed of about Mach 2.0. The second study was for a smaller aircraft with a stage length of about 1,500 miles, a seating capacity of about 100, and a cruising speed of about Mach 1.2.

Broad estimates were made by the STAC of the likely operating costs for a range of speed of aircraft. This showed that the optimum speed would be about Mach 2.0 and that the costs (pence per short ton per statute mile) would be 30–50 per cent higher than for the modern subsonic airliner. This 'surcharge' for a further increase in speed in excess of a factor of two over the latest generation of gas turbine aircraft was considered reasonable. Their estimate of the likely market was that in 1970 a 'total demand for between 150 and 500 supersonic aircraft could arise' [3].

The STAC report dealt with aircraft noise and stated that the noise level should be kept below that of the noisiest gas turbine aircraft. It was proposed, therefore, that the noise should be limited to a figure equivalent to 103 decibels for unsilenced contemporary jet engines.

Aircraft flying at speeds in excess of the speed of sound generate a sonic boom at ground level, the intensity of which is dependent on the shape, height and speed of the aircraft. It was recognized that such bangs might be unacceptable in areas of dense populations, and if this were the case then acceleration to supersonic flight might have to be delayed until the aircraft was over the sea.

It was concluded that the aircraft should be constructed using conventional aluminium as the basic structural material and that the numerous technical problems which were considered in detail were soluble 'without excessive economic penalties' [4]. The development costs were estimated for both the aeroplanes, and with new engines and 20,000 hours' flight proving, came out below £100 million each (Mach 1.2 at £78 million; Mach 1.8 at £95 million) [5].

The committee recommended that development should proceed immediately on both aircraft with the stronger recommendation for the long range aircraft cruising at not less than Mach 1.8 and carrying 150 passengers. The step into supersonic passenger flight was recognized as a 'substantial' step forward which would require an unprecedented amount of proving flying.

POLITICAL BACKGROUND AND THE TREATY

The French aviation industry was backed by the French Government, whose policy was to expand France's industrial capacity. Compared with the United Kingdom, France had limited technical supersonic knowledge and resources but was determined to make progress as fast as it reasonably could and acquire the technology and resources to bring it into a leading position in world aviation.

The Conservative Government under Harold Macmillan, as had already been the case in previous years, had determined to become part of the EEC and was anxious to demonstrate its willingness to contribute to the development of European technical progress. The design study contracts which were placed on the British Aircraft Corporation (BAC) and Hawker Siddeley called for the companies to examine the possibility of collaborative arrangements with either French or German companies. As a result, discussions took place in April 1960 between members of BAC and a group from Sud Aviation (France). In parallel, Bristol Siddeley Engines had discussions with SNECMA of France and signed an inter-company agreement in November 1961 to collaborate on the development of an engine suitable for supersonic transport.

In December 1961 British and French ministers met in Paris to discuss Anglo-French collaboration on a supersonic transport and asked BAC and Sud to formulate the outline of a joint project. A year later, on 29 November 1962, the UK and French Governments signed a treaty for the joint design, development and manufacture of a supersonic airliner.

The treaty was very brief and was comprised of seven articles. These can be summarized as follows:

(1) Equal sharing of responsibility and costs covering development and production.
(2) Approval of the inter-company agreements on airframes (BAC and Sud dated October 1962) and engines (Bristol Siddeley Engines and SNECMA dated November 1961).
(3) The medium and long range aircraft should form the basis of the joint undertaking.
(4) Integrated British and French organizations of airframe and engines should be set up.
(5) A steering committee of officials from the two countries should supervise progress and propose necessary measures to ensure the carrying out of the programme.
(6) The medium and long range versions should receive equal attention and the integrated British and French firms should make detailed proposals for carrying out the programme.
(7) The date of the agreement was the date when it became operative.

There was no break clause in the agreement, which was an internationally registered treaty without precedent. Additionally, there were no specific performance requirements laid down for the aircraft and no financial limits, since at that stage of the feasibility/design studies any detailed specification would have been an impediment in the broad thrust to achieve a supersonic transport.

Technical proposals, management structures and programmes were included in a number of annexes to the treaty. The programme included the construction of two prototypes and one preproduction aircraft of each type. It was assumed that the rate of production would be three aircraft per month and that the first aircraft off the production line would be used to obtain certification. All testing activities would be carried out in parallel in both countries. The outline programme was:

Second half 1966—first flight of first prototype aircraft.
End of 1968—first flight of first production aircraft.
End of 1969—certificate of Airworthiness.

The financial estimates, which were the best that could be constructed at that time and were based on wide ranging assumptions concerning the solution of outstanding technical problems, were:

Airframe	£95.3m
Engine	£39.9m
Total	£135.2m

These figures did not include:

—allowance for inflation or changes in exchange rates;
—costs of series production.

Table 3.1 shows the division of the work between the two countries:

Table 3.1   Division of work between United Kingdom and France

System	United Kingdom	France
(1) Aerodynamics	Design and test on engine air intakes and nozzles	
	Deicing General performance calculations	All other aerodynamics not covered by United Kingdom
(2) Strength and aero-elasticity	Calculations of critical speeds under three-dimensional aerodynamic loading	Load calculation and load distribution
(3) Structures	Front part of the aircraft. Engine nacelles, including air intakes, mounting and gas exhaust	Front section of the wing, the centre of the fuselage
	Rear section of the fuselage, the fin and rudder	Elevons and landing gear
(4) Systems	Engine, fire warning and extinguishing systems	Hydraulics and flying controls including the automatic pilot and stabilizers
	Fuel system	
	Electrical generation and distribution	Radio and navigational systems
	Oxygen system	Generation and control of air-conditioning
	Thermal and sound insulation	
	Circulation and distribution of air in the cabin	
	Cabin thermal characteristics	
(5) Weight and centre of gravity	Weight estimates would be prepared by the companies directly responsible for the particular components	

When the Labour Government was elected on 15 October 1964 its first estimate of the national balance of payments deficit which it faced was £700 million. This problem was discussed between Prime Minister

Harold Wilson and his Cabinet colleagues, George Brown and James Callaghan, and the latter two were charged with drafting a White Paper, covering proposed savings including cancellation of prestige projects, for consideration by the Cabinet. Four aircraft projects were considered to be prestigious—Concorde, TSR2, P1154 and HS681.

The draft White Paper avoided naming specific projects under review, but between the Cabinet's discussion of the aircraft and its presentation to Parliament, the passage relating to prestigious projects was made much stronger. The change resulted in pressure from the United States whose government was shown a draft of the White Paper and who was being asked to help with the balance of trade deficit problem [6]. The US administration wished to have reference to a specific economy in the aircraft sector. Consequently a change was made to insert a statement to the effect that the government 'had already told the French that it specially wished to examine the Concorde project'. In view of the shortness of time this was further amended and in the event it was announced that the Minister of Aviation, Roy Jenkins, was going to Paris shortly to discuss a re-examination of Concorde with his French opposite number. The French Government were finally advised of the announcement very shortly before it was made in the House of Commons and when Jenkins made his visit some two days later he was received without enthusiasm. Jenkins presented the French delegation, headed by the Minister of Transport, M. Jacquet, with the British position and Jacquet insisted that his government would wish to discuss the proposal and would reply as soon as possible.

The French replied on 13 November and, having said they were ready to review Concorde at any time, saw no particular reason to review it at that point in time. They also made reference to the treaty and the fact that it was registered at the Hague Court.

The Cabinet submitted the reply to the Attorney General, who gave his opinion that if the United Kingdom pulled out France would sue through the Hague International Court for a sum of money of about £200 million. At that time it was believed that this would exceed the sum of money required to complete the project.

The Cabinet then considered the situation and attempted a compromise reduction in the programme—first, to drop the building of two preproduction aircraft, and second, to limit the activity to development; the French rejected both approaches. At the beginning of January 1965, the Cabinet decided to continue the programme to avoid being taken to the International Court and to improve their chances of being admitted to the EEC. Jenkins again visited Paris and informed Jacquet of the decision and then announced in the House of Commons that the Concorde review had been completed and that following exchanges with the French Government the Labour administration 'stood by the Treaty obligations into which the last government had entered' [7].

Throughout, the French Government appeared resolute in their determination to develop Concorde and to carry through the re-establishment of their aircraft industry on the base of the latest technology.[1] It seems that they never had any doubt that the project was not commercially viable, but regarded it as the vehicle whereby their industry could be resuscitated. The British Government, on the other hand, would have preferred to cancel, but in the light of cancellation costs and the profound effect it would have had on international relations, decided to continue the project and 'review its economic potential' from time to time.

The P1154 and the HS681 were cancelled in February 1965 and on 5 April the TSR2 was also cancelled [9]. Some eight months later the select committee under Sir Edmund Plowden set up to examine the aircraft industry strongly advocated European collaboration on all future major aircraft projects and further indicated a reduced level of government support in the future for the aircraft industry [10]. This policy, which has had vast ramifications, has in the main indeed been followed and has resulted in the steady growth of cooperation in Europe and, for example, the creation and establishing of the strong and successful operation of Airbus Industries.

During the period under which the Plowden review took place, there was intensive lobbying by the industry and the trade unions. It was perhaps relevant that Anthony Wedgwood Benn, the Minister, was the member for Bristol West in which constituency was the headquarters design centre and manufacturing organization of the aircraft company most involved in the project.

Summarizing, the Concorde project started as a genuine desire to make the next technological step in the development of civil aviation which at that time was identified as developing a commercial supersonic capability. It became a joint project with the French to share costs and thereby assumed a political mantle for good or ill which allowed it to survive the pressures for cancellation. Undoubtedly this political overlay had immense repercussions on the management of the project and its development programme.

[1] Both Feldman and Hayward, however, note that the French considered cancellation of the project on several occasions but did so with less publicity [8].

THE DEVELOPMENT

By the beginning of the development phase BAC had decided that the project should concentrate exclusively on the long haul transatlantic version. The French, on the other hand, were primarily interested in building a supersonic short haul replacement for the Caravelle.

Two years were spent in attempting technically to satisfy these two differing requirements with the maximum use of common design and equipment. However, it eventually became obvious that there was no market interest in the medium range aircraft and this was abandoned in 1964 and both companies concentrated all their efforts to produce an aircraft capable of flying, with a commercial payload, from London and Paris to the east coast of the United States of America.

There followed many months of intense design activity in which the various technical problems were attacked and solved. The underlying problems of drag, weight and thrust were dealt with against the dominating background of safety. Some systems were redesigned several times, especially the engine intakes and exhaust systems. Considerable effort was deployed on silencer development and ultimately the noise was reduced to what were considered to be acceptable levels for take-off and landing.

Several major innovations were undertaken. For example, the electronic control systems for the air intakes and engine were originally analogue systems. During the course of the development, it was decided to go to an integrated digital system which proved very successful. This, in the early 1960s, was a bold innovative step which has now been followed by all modern designs.

All technical information, that is, design data, calculations and test results, were examined by the two companies and, although this procedure meant that in some cases there was duplicated effort, in general it was beneficial, especially in establishing uniform standards of design excellence and, not least important, of safety.

Design work proceeded to achieve sufficient performance to meet the target specification. There were at least four weight-saving exercises which were extremely important since the weight of supersonic aircraft is, if anything, more critically important than in subsonic transport aircraft design.

The ground and flight testing programme from inception had been recognized as having to be a comprehensive series of combined environmental tests to prove the inherent safety of the aircraft. The rigs that were developed to simulate thermal and load characteristics to be encountered in operation were major engineering undertakings in their

own right. Although the scale of testing envisaged in the original estimates was beyond any previous scale, it is unlikely that the costs associated with this part of the programme were fully estimated and they
inevitably contributed significantly to the overspend of the original
budget.

The flight test programme of any new aircraft is indicative of the new
developments which have been incorporated in the conceptual design,
and at any time progress achieved gives a direct measure of the development status of the new plane. The Concorde flight test programme was
no exception and because Concorde represented a large step forward
in design Mach number for civil aircraft, the programme was always
conceived on a large scale and was, in fact, increased by the demands
of the Civil Aviation Authority who needed adequate information on
which to issue a full Certificate of Airworthiness.

The development programme involved seven aircraft: two prototypes
and two preproduction and three production aircraft. It was assumed
there would be 1,935 flying hours for development, 795 hours for
certification and 1,500 hours for route proving, giving an overall total
of 4,230 flying hours.

By 1969, when the flight programme detail was compiled, the key
dates had become:

Summer 1969—first supersonic flight.
Spring 1970—first Mach 2.0 flight.
1973—airline service.

This programme, which was very different from that contained in the
first STAC report, took into account the tremendous amount of testing
which had been carried out on the ground rigs and of course, was some
four years later than envisaged when the treaty was signed.

The essential ingredients of the programme were to explore margins
of performance and prove that the basic design could be flown by an
airline pilot safely and well for the comfort of the passengers. The
prototype aircraft were heavily instrumented and recordings made of
thousands of measurements throughout each flight. These results were
analysed and where necessary modifications were designed and introduced to widen flying limits and improve the handling capability of the
aircraft.

The first flight of the French prototype 001 took place on 2 March
1969 and 002 first flew from Filton (Bristol) to Fairford on 9 April. The
following diary gives a summary of the progress:

1969	1 October	001 achieves Mach 1.0
1970	25 March	002 achieves Mach 1.0
	1 September	002 makes first flight on UK west coast test corridor

	4 November	001 achieves Mach 2.0
	12 November	002 achieves Mach 2.0
1971	January	One hundredth supersonic flight
	(24 March	American SST cancelled)
	13 May	001 makes first automatic landing
	June	Flight test time reaches 500 hours. Bench and flight testing of engines reaches 10,000 hours
	August	Flight clearance for Olympus 593.4 engine. One hundredth Mach 2.0 flight
	20 September	01 first preproduction aircraft rolled out at Filton
	17 December	01 first flight Filton to Fairford
1972	February	02 structurally complete at Toulouse
	12 February	01 exceeds Mach 1.0
	18 May	1,000 hours total flying logged by 001, 002 and 01
	2 June	002 begins sales demonstration flights to Middle East and Australia
	10 August	01 returns to Filton for modifications including Olympus 593 Mk 602 power plants and production standard air intakes
	28 September	02 rolled out at Toulouse incorporating all the latest modification standards
1973	10 January	02 first flight
	22 January to 24 February	002 hot and high airfield performance trials at Johannesburg
	23 February	02 flies Toulouse to Iceland and returns in 3 hours 27 minutes (equivalent to Paris–New York)
	3 March	02 flies equivalent Frankfurt–New York in 3 hours 38 minutes
	15 March	01 returns to Fairford after extensive modification
	(3 June	Russian production supersonic TU144 crashes at Le Bourget)
	18 September	02 leaves Paris for United States (opening of Dallas/Fort Worth Airport)
	26 September	02 flies Washington–Paris in 3 hours 33 minutes—a record
	6 December	First flight of 201 (first production aircraft)
1974	7–19 February	02 low temperature trials Alaska
	13 February	202 (second production aircraft) first flight Filton to Fairford
	19 July	United Kingdom and France agree an initial batch of 16 production aircraft
	7 August	202 hot weather trials Bahrain
	12 September	Flight testing reaches 3,000 hours
	21 October	One thousandth hour of supersonic flight
1975	31 January	203 first flight
	26 February	01 flies to Nairobi via Cairo for tropical icing trials

27 February	204 first flight
28 February	202 certification trials at Madrid
28 May	Special category of Certificate of Airworthiness by Secrétariat Générale l'Aviation Civile (SGAC) for 203 to start endurance flying
9 June	203 starts endurance flying
30 June	Special category of Certificate of Airworthiness for 204 awarded by Civil Aviation Authority
7 July	204 starts endurance flying
2 August	203 completes endurance flying
9 October	French Certificate of Airworthiness granted
25 October	205 first flight
5 November	206 first flight
5 December	British Certificate of Airworthiness granted

This diary of achievements shows that after the 1969 programme was issued there was a further slip of three years on the date of the first commercial airline flight, which in the event was on 24 May 1976.

Table 3.2 shows a summary of the actual flying hours which were achieved by all pilots, including the Civil Aviation inspecting pilots who participated to the full throughout the whole programme. The total number, 5,494.89, represents an increase of just under 30 per cent of the estimated programme which was made in 1969.

Table 3.2   Total flying hours

Development and certification:		
Handling	570.54	
Performance	791.64	
Structures	153.60	
Internal noise	17.35	1533.13
Power plant:		
General	242.14	
Engine intakes	419.28	661.42
Systems:		
Autopilot flight control systems	287.24	
Air conditioning	57.37	
Deicing	212.27	
Radio and others	190.29	
External noise	67.45	814.62
Route Proving:		921.36
Other flying:		
Training	323.50	
Demonstrations	319.54	
Meteorological/environmental	38.35	
Miscellaneous	882.97	1,564.36
Total		5,494.89

The following is a summary of some of the design parameters.

Maximum taxi weight	412,000 lb
Maximum take-off weight	408,000 lb
Maximum landing weight	245,000 lb
Typical empty weight	175,114 lb
Typical payload weight	25,000 lb
Maximum operating Mach number	2.02
Maximum operating stagnation temperature	127 °C
Landing gear extension and retraction speed	270 kts IAS
Flight altitude limit	60,000 ft
Ground	−1,000/+10,000 ft
Temperature at sea level	−54 to +49 °C
Capacity	100 passengers
Range	3,545 nautical miles

PRODUCTION

With any large aircraft the necessary financial decision to go into production and to start to invest money in production tooling, assembly jigs, support gear and test equipment has to be taken a number of years in advance of the scheduled date of the first delivery. This was so with Concorde and, when in 1968 the decision to proceed with production was taken, the companies concerned were, for a number of reasons, unable or unwilling to find the necessary finance to meet the costs. The UK Government, therefore, decided to fund production costs in the United Kingdom and the necessary legislation was passed in the House of Commons to enable this to be done. This cumulative figure for production and in-service support up to 1982 was £464 million.

As the programme proceeded and the purchase options held by the airlines lapsed it became clear that only a small batch of aircraft would ever be made. The decision was therefore taken in the mid 1970s to limit this batch to sixteen, with spares which were ordered to appropriate levels. Production stopped when that level was reached. The last aircraft, No. 216, Registration G.BFKX/G-BOAF, was delivered to British Airways on 12 June 1980, bringing their fleet up to six aircraft.

THE MANAGEMENT ORGANIZATION

Now that the development of Concorde has been described in outline, let us look at the organization and management which achieved the technical success the plane undoubtedly ultimately represented.

The treaty signed by the British and French Governments established the management organization which was to start the Concorde project. Essentially there were six organizations—two governments, two airframe manufacturers and two engine manufacturers—with no one authority in absolute control. The concept was one of management by committee and design by consensus (see Figure 3.1). The chairmen of the Directing Committee and Management Board changed each year and alternated between British and French officials.

The Concorde Directing Committee (CDC) was comprised of senior civil servants from both countries and included the official project directors and Treasury representatives from both countries. This Committee provided the link to the highest level in both governments and gave advice to the responsible ministers. Below the CDC was the Concorde Management Board who implemented the decisions of the CDC and in general were responsible for the day-to-day running of the project in so far as this concerned governments. Its members were fully engaged on the project.

The working groups were made up of members of the aircraft establishments (RAE and NGTE)[2] together with representatives from the four principal firms and other authorities (such as the Civil Aviation Authority), where appropriate.

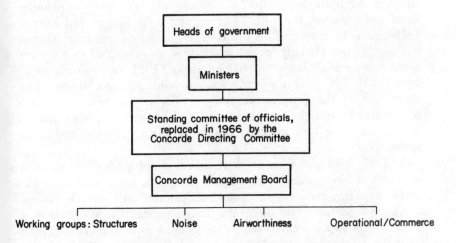

Figure 3.1 Concorde Treaty Management Organization

[2] The Royal Aircraft Establishment (Farnborough) and the National Gas Turbine Establishment.

The management structure the industrial partners used was similar to that of the officials:

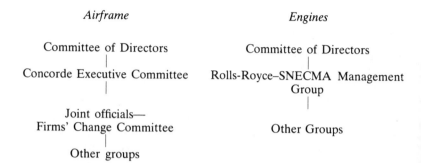

Airframe	*Engines*
Committee of Directors	Committee of Directors
|	|
Concorde Executive Committee	Rolls-Royce–SNECMA Management
	Group
|	|
Joint officials—	
Firms' Change Committee	Other Groups
|	
Other groups	

There was a technical 'group of six' who reported to the senior technical managers (directors) in BAC and Sud and generated the drive and coordinated technical activities in both companies.

Major schedule networks were generated in 1964–5 when the development tasks had been defined (under eighteen headings, four of which related to project control).

The fourteen work tasks, having been defined, were programmed and costed in each country. This greatly facilitated progress since for the first time a common approach was generated between opposite numbers. Additionally, for the first time costed programmes were monitored and reported, using PERT (Programme Evaluation and Review Technique). In practice PERT was never used as a real management tool and at the working level bar charts were generated in a format which was generally understood. The use of PERT was formally abandoned in 1972 because it proved to be unreliable and unworkable. 'The sheer size of the programme, the number of technical unknowns it contained, and the conditions of its trans-national management system, put it beyond any conventional problem of control and monitoring' [11].

By 1965, both governments were aware of the probability that the project had been underestimated and this produced a reaction in the decision making progress which can be illustrated quite simply. Having identified a particular problem, the design engineers would propose a modification which would then be considered by the officials (experts from the establishments). The natural reaction of the officials was to require more information whilst the natural inclination of the designers was to press forward quickly. These different approaches often led the project team into a situation where they had to decide the extent to which the contractor's costs were admissible.

It is easy to see that supervision of this type was time consuming, enervating and costly. The greater the governments' concern, the tighter the attempted supervision and monitoring; this led to a spiralling level of intrusion.

At the same time, there were problems involved in the participating companies working together. Each set of engineers had to learn to work with an opposite number—of an essentially different (Anglo-Gallic) temperament. Everything was questioned and nothing was assumed. The result was that people were much more cautious than usual and examined their proposals and calculations carefully to make sure they were not subsequently found to be in error. In all probability this general approach was, overall, good for the project, since both sides learnt from each other.

The French views of the problems of collaboration with the British working on Concorde were given by R. Beteille in 1969 [12]. They may be summarized as language (what a pity we don't all speak Latin!), temperament (as reflected in a tendency to understate or overstate a case), the NIH (not-invented-here) syndrome, and a desire not to 'lose face' either in the company present or with their absent senior colleagues. 'Committees, meeting with wide audiences, co-ordination bodies and so forth can be harmful. As far as possible co-operation must be done on a man-to-man basis, where things get done' [13].

CONTRACTS AND DEVELOPMENT COSTS, 1962–78

The initial contracts let by the British Government were 'cost plus fixed fee' but it was the government's intention that the firms would at some stage make a contribution to the launching costs. Both the French and the British Governments spent considerable time in trying to introduce acceptable incentive clauses but all four major firms showed a marked reluctance to move to accept a risk-bearing contract.

In 1968 a limited incentive scheme was eventually introduced. Manufacturing costs were reimbursed and profit rates were reduced when costs exceeded a percentage of an agreed target. If the target was exceeded by 15 per cent or more the contractor received a fixed fee. The target figure was increased when approved design changes increased the manufacturing costs. This scheme was not accepted by the engine manufacturers on the grounds that most of the problems arose due to design problems over which Rolls-Royce or SNECMA had neither responsibility nor control. (Rolls-Royce had acquired Bristol Siddley Engines in July 1966.)

Table 3.3 presents the development cost estimates up to 1978, by which time the aircraft was in regular service with both British Airways and Air France. This table simply illustrates the increase in costs over a period of 16 years. The cost of inflation, exchange rates and devaluation between them amount to over half (57 per cent) of the increases. The remaining 43 per cent can generally be attributed one way or another to underestimation of design problems, testing requirements and additional costs brought about by collaboration. These latter themselves amount to an increase, over the original figure on which the project was started, of a factor of approximately 2.5.

In production the agreements which were signed committed the manufacturers to accept a share in the risk after the first 20 aircraft had been produced. In practice this number was never reached and costs and a management fee were paid, although an incentive contract was negotiated for the last three aircraft that BAC produced.

APPROVAL FOR FLIGHTS INTO WASHINGTON AND NEW YORK

The struggle to obtain approval for scheduled Concorde flights into America began in February 1975 when letters of application were sent from British Airways and Air France to the Assistant Administrator International Affairs, and the Federal Aviation Authority (FAA) in Washington. Each letter requested an amendment to their airline operations specifications to allow them to operate a scheduled service into Washington (Dulles) and New York (Kennedy).

Under the US Environmental Policy Act, the approval procedure was thought to be a lengthy process, and hence there was a decision to make the application early, when proving flights were still to be completed. Data were supplied to the FAA and a draft Environmental Impact Statement (EIS) was published in March 1975. Public hearings were held in April in Washington, New York and Sterling Park, Virginia. Having acquired more information, the FAA prepared and released in November 1975 a final EIS in which it was stated that a public hearing would be held in Washington on 5 January 1976.

The decision of the Federal Aviation Administrator (John Coleman) was published on 4 February 1976 and gave permission to British Airways and Air France to conduct limited scheduled commercial flights into the United States for a trial period not to exceed 16 months. It

Table 3.3 *Increases in estimates to completion (all figures in £m)*

Year	Design changes	Under estimate	Delays	Exchange devaluation	Others	Inflation	Total increase	Cost to completion
1962								150–70
1964	45					65	110	275
1965					50		50	325
1966¹	39	80				56	175	500
1969	90	40		40	20(50)	90	230	730
1970	35				20	40	95	825
1971	10		15		20	15	60	885
1972	25	15				45	85	970
1973		10	20	30	5	35	95	1,065
1974							5	1,070
1975				15	(39)	50	26	1,096
1976		(9)		21		46	58	1,154
1977					(13)		(13)	1,141
1978					(4)		(4)	1,137
1979					(8)		(8)	1,129
Totals	244	136	35	106	1	442	964	
% increase	25.3	14.1	3.7	11.0		45.9		n x 7

¹ The figure quoted was a lumped figure for design changes and inflation and has arbitrarily been split in the same ratio as for 1964.
Source: Major Projects Association and Knight [14].

allowed each airline two flights a day into and out of J. F. Kennedy and one a day into and out of Dulles.

The decision was extraordinarily complex and involved environmental, technical, safety and international considerations. The document analyses each point and shows that, whilst there were some questions where it was impossible to be numerate, in other cases the environmental effect would be negligible.

The owner of Dulles Airport is the FAA so that flights into and out of Dulles could start immediately once preparations had been completed. The first commercial flights to Washington from Paris and London started on 24 May 1976.

The New York Kennedy Airport is run by the Port Authority of New York and New Jersey and in March 1976 this authority passed resolutions banning Concorde from Kennedy. British Airways and Air France filed suits against the authority and there then began a long legal battle which the Port Authority eventually lost. Commercial scheduled flights to New York began on 22 November 1977 some 18 months after the first flight to Washington.

Noise measurements were made round Dulles on the 618 flights in the first year of operation. The noise levels were consistent with the EIS predictions: Concorde was twice as noisy on take-off and the same on approach as the noisiest subsonic jets.

Air pollution was less than expected and there were no traffic control problems. The measurements at Kennedy produced similar results.

The FAA made their usual deep examination of the design data on the aircraft and having asked for and obtained some small modifications granted an FAA Certificate of Airworthiness on 9 January 1979.

There was considerable opposition by the environmentalists and other lobbies, but the careful appraisal that was carried out which resulted in a reasoned, undeviating line of action achieved the right of entry. The governments' ministers, officials and their advisers, together with the companies' representatives, all played their roles in a combined effort to ensure the success that was achieved. It is obvious in retrospect that here was a clear demonstration of the strength available when numerous parties combine to achieve one goal.

THE AIRLINES

When the Supersonic Transport Aircraft Committee was first set up in 1956, the British airlines (BEA and BOAC) were asked to contribute.

They did so, and the airlines and the International Federation of Airline Pilots and the British Airline Pilots' Association continued, with other overseas airlines, to participate in the programme over the whole period of development.

The appraisal made by BOAC in 1972 showed that with projected scheduled flights to New York, Johannesburg, Sydney and Tokyo for the year 1977/8 they would make a loss of about £9 million. In addition, the airlines were concerned that an additional cost due to the loss of passengers on their subsonic aircraft would be incurred. This was not included in the direct operating loss figure given above. It can be seen, therefore, that from the beginning the airlines were not enthusiastic about the commercial prospects of Concorde. However, BOAC remained enthusiastic about the aircraft and continued to concern itself with how to operate the aircraft profitably.

The first twelve aircraft were reserved by the British and French Governments for their national airlines and Pan American was the first foreign airline to sign an option, for six aircraft, on 3 June 1963. Many other airlines followed this lead, with BOAC and Air France converting their reservations into options so that by May 1964 sixteen airlines had signed options for a total of seventy-four aircraft. All the options were dependent on BOAC and Air France confirming their orders and this took place on 28 July 1972 when they ordered five and four aircraft respectively.

The finance for the BOAC purchase was to be provided interest free by the government until an operating profit was achieved. The cost of each aircraft complete with spares and back-up equipment was £23 million.

Following the 28 July orders the critical date for converting the options of the various airlines of the United States of America into firm orders was 31 January 1973. On that date Pan American and TWA announced that they had decided not to take them up. In March the sales option system was abandoned.

Only Braniff, other than British Airways and Air France, operated an independent Concorde service and that had a limited life, from 12 January to 1 June 1979. During that time a subsonic service between Washington and Dallas/Fort Worth was operated.

The reasons for the airlines not taking up their options were the high capital cost of the aircraft against the number of passenger seats (100) and the restrictions imposed on overland supersonic flying due to the sonic boom. The combination of these reasons (with, now, the increased price of fuel) made the aircraft commercially unacceptable.

British Airways Concorde Division was formed in November 1974 and consisted of three executives and two secretaries. The aims of the

Figure 3.2 Concorde assembly
Source: *British Aerospace*

Figure 3.3 Concorde taking off
Source: *British Airways*

division were to determine the right schedule, the right quality of in-flight service and the right price, backed by punctuality and speeded-up ground service. These have in fact been achieved.

Eventually the capital purchase costs were written off by the British Government and the five unsold production aircraft were 'sold' for nominal sums to the two airlines on the agreement that the operating profit would be shared on a 4:1 basis between the British Government and the airline. British Airways now have seven operational Concordes. However, on the 31 March 1984, the airline paid £16.5 million and the prior arrangement was cancelled. With this latest agreement, the airline retains the operating profit and is responsible for all expenditure to maintain the aircraft in service. This includes the normal maintenance operations, payments to British Aerospace, Concorde Support Division and payments to the Royal Aircraft Establishment, Farnborough, for analysis of structural fatigue tests (which have been completed to an equivalent aircraft life of 20 years).

In 1977 a deal was agreed between British Airways and Singapore Airlines, which was complicated by alternative negotiations being carried out simultaneously between the two airlines. A joint BA–Singapore Airlines service was operated for about 18 months to Singapore. The agreement with Singapore Airlines was biased heavily in their favour and subsequently the route proved to be a heavy loss maker for British Airways and was cancelled.

Services have continued across the Atlantic and have been, and still are, very successful with a load factor in excess of 60 per cent. An analysis of traffic figures across the Atlantic shows that after the introduction of Concorde more than 50 per cent of the business was new business and was not a transfer from British Airways subsonic jets. Indeed, there are statistics which show that after the introduction of Concorde, British Airways' share of the transatlantic business increased.

Special flying techniques have been evolved to minimize take-off noise, and in 1981 noise regulations were violated in the United States on only 1.5 per cent of the take-offs (compared with 3.6 per cent of transatlantic subsonic aircraft take-offs). These figures have been maintained and no out of the ordinary problems exist with the airport authorities.

The Concorde Division of British Airways is now operating as a profitable division, including normal overhead charges and the cost of continuing technical support referred to previously. The current flight schedules and traffic across the Atlantic, together with charter flying, can be used as a basis to show that, had the airline paid the £115 million for their seven aircraft, with normal accounting practices the write-off would have been completed and profitability reached in approximately year 12 of the aircraft's operation.

The aircraft with the highest number of flying hours is at a figure just below half of its tested life, which means that the fleet will be in service up to the turn of the century. The annual British Airways revenue is about £100 million, and there appears to be no reason why the divisional profitability of about £15 million per annum should not continue and it may well increase as the heavy cost of the support programme decreases.

The operational staff of the Concorde Division consider the aircraft to be an unqualified success in that its flying characteristics are excellent and its reliability extremely high. They point out with some pride that it is the only commercial high technology project in the world conceived in the 1960s which will still be in operation into the twenty-first century. In general discussions with British Airways staff, it was noted that the Concorde programme had laid the foundations for European collaboration in the development of large civil aircraft. Without it, Airbus Industries would not have been possible and the European aircraft industry would not have reached the standards of excellence it has attained today.

Other major spin-offs include a number of features which were novel in Concorde and are now exported by the European industry to the rest of the world, such as tyre pressure warnings; carbon disc brakes; high quality, high performance hydraulics; and specially toughened Triplex glass. In general, equipment firms engaged on the Concorde programme benefited from the forced advance in this technology and were able to capitalize on it when competing for similar systems in new military aircraft like the Tornado.

OVERALL SUMMARY

The Concorde project was conceived as a technological advance which would give the European aircraft industry a leading position in the world. This it has done.

The costs of developing a supersonic transport were beyond the financial resources of the industry and therefore government funding had to be obtained. The British and French Governments both saw advantages in a collaborative project and agreed on a joint project.

The project thus was based on the confidence and design ability of the aeronautical engineers (in government service and industry) and the national ambitions and plans of the politicians. It suffered from an inefficient management committee structure, inappropriate contracting and controls, excessive stages in prototype development, and the challenges of major technical advances, all in an environment of unprecedented inflation. In spite of this unattractive base, the project succeeded in producing an aircraft which is unique in the skies and which is now, after skilful financial manoeuvering, being operated profitably by the Concorde Division of British Airways.

Concorde can be seen as the foundation of the new and thriving European commercial aircraft manufacturing business and the beginning of the end of ineffective contract and management systems. Basically, the project was more successful than unsuccessful in that it succeeded in all aspects other than in development time and cost; it produced a graceful aircraft operating on a regular scheduled service with an unequalled reliability record and with important broad technological benefits to the European aerospace industry.

The project, which cost the British taxpayer £500 million in 1970 £ sterling, will always be a controversial one, at least until a few more decades have passed and it can be seen in a wider perspective. Perhaps then it will be possible to decide whether the widespread effects of Concorde on the European aircraft industry can justify the vast investment in a plane which carries a few privileged passengers across the Atlantic each day.

REFERENCES

1. Hayward, K., 1983.
2. Ibid.
3. Supersonic Transport Aircraft Committee, 1959.
4. Ibid.
5. Ibid.
6. Wilson, A., 1973.
7. Ibid.
8. Feldman, E. J., 1985b; Hayward, K., 1983.
9. Williams, G. *et al.*, 1969; Wood, D., 1975.
10. *Report of the Committee of Inquiry into the Aircraft Industry*, 1965.
11. Hayward, K., 1983.
12. Beteille, R., 1969.
13. Ibid.
14. Knight, G., 1976.

Chapter Four

The Advanced Passenger Train[1]

In 1962 Sir Brian Robertson, the Chairman of the British Transport Commission (subsequently the British Railways Board), decided to centralize the various research units which existed in the four regions and asked the new centralized research organization to study and modernize the various technical equipments in operation in the railway systems. It was decided that the new laboratories would be located at Derby, adjacent to the main line to London, and they were formally opened three years later. In 1964 Stanley Raymond was appointed the Chairman of the British Railways Board which was then comprised of a number of full-time executives including engineers (electrical, mechanical and signals), the accountant and a number of outside part-time directors. Up to the early 1960s the Board's limited development policy was dominated by the edict that speeds on British Rail would be restricted to less than 100 miles per hour, which was the principal factor in determining journey times. With the growth of the motorway systems, however, and the increasing additional competition from the airlines, the Board was forced to abandon its speed limitation and generally look forward to finding means of safely and reliably reducing passenger journey times between city centres and speeding up its freight traffic.

Dr Sidney Jones, who had been recruited from industry to head up the new research organization in 1962, was later invited to join the Board in 1967. Dr Jones's prior long experience in research in the government's Royal Radar Establishment and his recent experience in industry introduced a new element of independent thinking into the well established, long experienced railway executive. He recruited a team comprised of scientists and engineers, only a small number of whom came from British Rail's engineering organization.

---

[1] The story of the Advanced Passenger Train is described by Williams, Boocock and King, and Boocock and Newman [1].

Dr Jones has commented that

> the greatest problem that [then] existed was that of introducing modern
> technology into an established industry. In trying to modernize a traditional
> industry two problems emerge:
>
> (i) the level of technical understanding in the established industry is very
>   poor and
> (ii) the attitudes of minds are extremely different from those in the high
>   technology industries and there is a big resistance to change [2].

This, then, was the background against which the research department started, for the first time in the history of the railways, to develop
a programme of long term research.

It was well known at that time that the dynamic behaviour of the
steel wheels riding on the rails was one of the speed limiting features
of the existing rolling stock. Additionally, the costs of wheel maintenance were high. Therefore, one of the first problems to be tackled by
the new research organization was to establish a complete theoretical
understanding of the dynamic behaviour of a coned flanged set of
wheels riding on a steel rail with a view to increasing the critical speeds
at which instability sets in. The experimental investigation and mathematical analysis was carried out by Dr A. Wickens and a successful
mathematical model was constructed. The validity of the model was
checked in the laboratory using new and used tyres. As a result a
suspension was designed for a high-speed freight vehicle and the model
indicated that for this suspension design the critical speed would be
reached at 140 miles per hour. This was confirmed by laboratory roller
tests and subsequently reconfirmed in practice on the track. This experimental success led to the construction of a small number of prototype
vehicles which were run in excess of 100,000 miles and demonstrated not
only the improvement in stability desired, but, additionally, a significant
reduction in maintenance requirements. This research was applied to
new rolling stock and successfully introduced into service in 1967 in
both high-speed and commuter passenger trains [3].

The significance of this technological advance was that new concepts
of high-speed vehicles could confidently be considered in the knowledge
that the speed of the steel wheel riding on a steel rail was no longer a
limitation. Additionally, this successful piece of research gave the
research team the confidence to consider a completely new concept in
railway engineering which became known as the Advanced Passenger
Train (APT). Other important aspects of railway engineering were also
being investigated in the Research Centre, e.g. signalling, the track, and
the design of lightweight coaches. There was by 1965 an accumulation of

preliminary research results which could be applied to future generations of trains.

The Beeching Report [4] recognized the competition of the motorway and aircraft modes of transport and in defining the role of the railways emphasized the importance of meeting the demands of the intercity travellers over distances of 100–500 kilometres. It thereby underlined the recognition that, in order to be successful in this competitive market, journey times would have to be reduced. Unlike Japan, where the new Tokaido Line was built and brought into operation on 10 October 1964, the United Kingdom had an established network of railways; the possibility of building new straight tracks was therefore ruled out because of the practical considerations of cost and the time taken to acquire new land over which the track could be laid.[2] Therefore, the basic requirement was to achieve higher speeds on existing networks.

The Research Centre's design aims for the APT were summarized as follows:

—It had to operate on existing tracks, with existing signalling systems, in the established physical environment (clearance, stations, tunnels, urban environment, etc.) and not violate any of the safety or environmental standards set by existing equipment.
—There should be a speed increase up to 250 kilometres per hour (155 miles per hour).
—It should be capable of taking curves at an increased speed of 40 per cent over the existing equipment.
—Passenger comfort should be maintained.
—The cost per seat mile should be similar to that of existing equipment.

An examination of British Rail's major routes showed that about half the length is made up of curved track and half of this is of relatively small radius. In order to obtain a significant reduction in journey time in addition to increasing speeds on straight tracks, it was considered essential to increase the speed on curves. Since curving speeds are in the main limited by passenger comfort, it was proposed to maintain passenger comfort by tilting the passenger car body by means of an active roll suspension system.

The roll system was conceived to tilt the coach so that the effect of the centrifugal force on the passengers at higher speeds would be

---

[2] The French Train à Grande Vitesse (TGV), which was the first European high-speed train, ran on straightened and relaid track between Lyon and Paris only. The line opened from Suthenay to Verigny, a distance of 169 miles, on September 1981 with the first commercial TGV in service at a maximum of 100 miles per hour. The full service from Paris to Lyon, a distance of 265.5 miles, commenced on 25 September 1983, the journey taking 2 hours to complete.

reduced to that normally experienced in conventional coaches when travelling round bends at 'normal' speeds. The normal speed retardation on a bend is set to allow a cant deficiency of 4.5 degrees, and an active tilt system which tilted the coaches as a function of speed could in effect double this angle and thereby for the same passenger comfort level allow an increase in speed of 40 per cent on curves.

Other innovations were necessary to achieve the overall requirements in the bogies and suspension, and in the braking system, the structures, and the aerodynamic and transmission systems. Each of these areas was considered and a programme was drawn up which envisaged three phases.

(1) An experimental phase for research and development proving the novel technical concepts. Included in this was the design development and testing of the Advanced Passenger Train (Experimental), APT(E).
(2) A prototype phase to integrate all novel features into a total train design and to prove technical, operational and commercial performances in a limited public service, APT(P).
(3) A production phase to consolidate all developments into a final train design for series production and fleet operations, APT.

In 1966 the proposal to build a single APT(E) in the Research Centre, representing the first phase of the above programme, and estimated as costing £3 million, was put to the British Railways Board by the Director of Research. The proposal was not well received by the established railway engineers on the Board, but after considerable debate it was agreed that if the finance for it could be found from sources other than British Rail then the Board would endorse the programme. There followed three years of promotion and lobbying during which the Minister of Transport, John Peyton, visited the research laboratories and became a supporter of the project. Richard Marsh later became Chairman of the British Railways Board and in 1968, with the Department of Transport providing 50 per cent of the relatively small additional funds required for the APT(E), a 5-year programme, incorporating the design aims given above and costing £3 million, was approved.

Nearly three years had thus been spent in promoting the APT concept; the project would not have been started but for the perseverance of the Research Director. The Board remained doubtful, with the mechanical and electrical engineers being strongly opposed and the enthusiasm of the team engaged on the project in the Research Centre matched only in the passenger department. This dichotomy of views on the prospects of the project led to an instability which was not conducive to rapid progress towards the practical realization of the concept of the APT(P).

APT(E)

Special test rigs were built in the laboratories to enable extensive testing to be carried out on all the novel systems. The principal rig was a brake dynamometer which simulated train masses travelling up to the maximum speed envisaged of 250 kilometres per hour. Additionally, a section of disused track between Milton Junction and Edwalton, 22 kilometres in length, was refurbished and prepared for use as a test track.

The first experimental vehicle to be constructed was a Power-0-Power formation as a two-car articulated train to test the coach tilt, suspension and bogie mechanisms. It first underwent track trials in the autumn of 1971 and was used extensively in the development of the coach tilt system.

It was decided that the APT(E) should be powered by gas turbines. There were two power cars, one at each end, and two trailer cars, instrumented to test the suspension and tilt mechanism. Four Leyland gas turbines driving Houchin 400 hertz alternators generated the driving force in each power car. This propulsion system was designed entirely for the experimental train and was necessary to allow trials to be conducted on tracks which had not been electrified.

On 16 December APT(E) was unveiled and six months later, after completion of the detailed installation of the instrumentation and control systems, the train began its braking trials as a necessary preliminary to running on the test track. This was scheduled for 28 June 1972, but the one traction motor which had been connected to the driving wheels proved inadequate to move the train. The next day, 29 June 1972, an additional motor was connected and the train moved under its own power for the first time.

Four drivers and three inspectors were given a one-day course on the train and were then given practical demonstrations on the vehicle. They then took part in the commissioning which included, as is usual in highly instrumented complex systems, the removal of numerous defects.

On 25 July 1972 the train was taken to Duffield at a speed of 25 miles per hour, at the end of which run clearance was given, in spite of numerous instrumentation faults, to take the speed up to 50 miles per hour (80 kilometres per hour). At the end of the run the media met the train and the first wave of publicity was released.

The train was blacked by ASLEF, the Associated Society of Loco-motive Engineers and Firemen, the train drivers' union, as part of the controversies on double manning and additional pay for drivers of high-speed vehicles. The ASLEF blacking included a complete ban on any movement of the APT(E). In November a decision was taken by the management to move the train into the locomotive works, by using a diesel shunter driven by an inspector to push the train into the shelter of the works. This action, which saved the train from considerable potential damage by unnatural exposure to the elements, provoked ASLEF to call a 24-hour general strike the next day.

During the period of union negotiation, an extensive modification programme was carried out with considerable assistance from British Rail Engineering. To comply with the Railways Board settlement with the unions, additional seats were included in the driving cab, which had been designed for one-man operation. The modified APT(E) began further trials on 9 August 1973, just a little over a year after the train had been immobilized by union blacking.

During the experimental testing period numerous silly faults occurred. There were problems with horns which jammed on, doors being open whilst the train was moving, and false 'steps down' warnings. Whilst conceptually these were trivial and unimportant they fed the scepticism of the 'established'[3] and critical railway engineers. Then, significantly, there were failures of the tilt and brake systems which were at the heart of the new concept, and these led to considerable development work to produce reasonable practical engineering solutions to the problems.

All this time, the experimental train, which was highly instrumented with automatic recording of all significant technical parameters, was controlled by a system of verbal relays drawn from the past. The system was that the trial supervisor passed instructions on the intercom to the field trial representative in the rear cab. He then restated them to the inspector in the front cab, who instructed the driver. The train super-visor's deputy, who heard the instructions on the intercom, was with the driver but no shortening of the chain of communication was allowed.

The train started its scheduled programmes of testing on 20 August 1973; on 21 September it achieved 100 miles per hour on the Dalby test track. Early in October 1973, 125 miles per hour was reached, and later, on 10 August 1975, a speed of 152.3 miles per hour was attained.

Considerable data were accumulated on all the novel systems under

---

[3] The use of the term 'established engineers' is meant to define the traditional railway engineers who had been in the railways system for considerably longer than the new recruits in the research department.

test and on the basic problems of traction adhesion and vehicle dynamics. These data, which were analysed by the research department, proved to them the feasibility of an APT.

The cautious approach of the British Railways Board, which could be interpreted as hostile, persisted, and an independent critical analysis instituted on the viability of APT was conducted by the Chief Executive of the Board. This took some six months during which time consideration was given to the question of who should design and build the APT(P) (prototype) if approval were given to proceed. Eventually it was agreed that British Rail's engineering organization should be responsible and that members of the research teams should be transferred into that organization to ensure a good line of communication between the research and engineering organizations. On 2 October 1974 the British Railways Board authorized the design and construction of three APT(P)s with the Department of Transport's financial support. The costs, which included the cost of special depots in Glasgow necessary for maintenance of trains initiating journeys there, amounted to approximately £50 million.

In parallel with the APT, the British Rail Engineering Department had in 1971 embarked upon another high-speed rail programme, the High-Speed Train, using diesel–electric traction, in which existing technology was extended to provide what was initially considered to be an interim solution to the requirement to reduce journey times on the intercity routes. The progress on the High-Speed Train (HST) was rapid; it was originated by the established engineers and it was strongly supported by them. It advanced through the prototype phase and successfully entered commercial service in 1976 as the InterCity 125 operating at speeds up to 125 miles per hour [5].

APT(P)

The basic design requirements of the APT(P) were not changed from the original concept, which included a speed capability of 250 kilometres per hour and increased curving speeds made acceptable by a coach tilting mechanism. The operational requirement was for a train comprising twelve passenger coaches and this necessitated the use of two power cars, positioned centrally, each with 3 megawatt electric traction. The train was conceived to operate on the main line west coast route and collected electrical power from overhead supply lines using a single pantograph.

The essential new features in the design were associated with the aerodynamic shape and surface smoothness, an articulated train configuration resulting in fewer bogies, active tilting mechanism, advanced lightweight bogie suspension, lightweight coaches, hydro-kinetic braking supplemented at low speed by auxiliary friction brakes and the transmission of 750 kilowatt drive to each powered axle in such a manner as to meet low targets for unsprung mass and bogie mass to be achieved.

In 1977, approximately three years after authorization had been given, the first power car started trials using one of the redundant HST prototypes for its motive power. During the three years all the P designs of the novel features were rigorously tested in the laboratories and subsequently endurance tested to establish the life of critical components.

The first prototype train was marshalled early in 1979 and with two power cars and two three-car trailer rakes. One of these rakes was fitted out to monitor and record comprehensively all the important characteristics of the new train. Delays were produced by industrial disputes and the main series of performance tests did not take place until mid 1979 and carried through into 1980. In December of 1979 a new high-speed record of 250 kilometres per hour was established. The second APT(P) was commissioned in late 1979 and committed to an extensive programme of driver training. The third train, completed in the spring of 1980, was used on an extensive programme of endurance running between Glasgow and London in a pre-operational training and reliability testing phase. On one journey during this phase, when VIPs were being carried as passengers, an axle broke while the train was travelling at 200 kilometres per hour. The breakage caused the derailment of an articulated bogie but the train was successfully brought to a halt with no injury to any passenger and only minor damage to the track. All three trains were withdrawn for a complete investigation to be made to establish the cause of the failure. This proved to be due both to deficiencies in design and to poor assembly procedures, which as a result were revised, and the trains restarted their trials in mid 1980.

During the trials numerous problems were identified and remedial designs were incorporated in the equipments. In particular a satisfactory fail safe, closed loop tilt system was difficult to realize. The so-called Mark III system, however, proved to be an effective solution and an independent supervisory tilt failure detecting device was introduced to lock the vehicle in an upright attitude when failure occured. The vertical ride quality was made better by engineering changes to improve the dynamic characteristics of the train, but at this time the noise levels at the ends of the coaches were still in excess of the design criteria

Figure 4.1 APT(P)

Photo: *British Rail*

The trials showed that the track loadings from the APT(P) at a cant deficiency of 9 degrees were almost identical to those from the HST with a deficiency of 4.5 degrees. Similarly, the hydrokinetic braking under adverse track conditions was shown to achieve the same braking distance from a speed of 210 kilometres per hour as the HST from 160 kilometres per hour.

The Board decided to open on 7 December 1981 an inaugural Glasgow–London–Glasgow passenger service three times a week, and the first train completed the journey at an average speed of 95.1 miles per hour including one stop, two minutes inside the time that had been scheduled.

In the national press, the *Express* on 8 December 1981, reporting the inaugural run, commented that the train was 'one minute early and fourteen months late' and that the unique tilt 'made a few people feel queasy'. The *Financial Times* on the same day reported the train as achieving a journey time of 4 hours 13 minutes 59 seconds[4] and a passenger carrying record speed of 137 miles per hour. *The Times* was

---

[4] Shortest scheduled journey time in 1985 is 5 hours 11 minutes (leaving Glasgow 0905).

critical of the ride over parts of the track—'it was like driving over cobbles until south of Motherwell'—and raised questions as to why the train did not reach its design speed. The *Telegraph* highlighted the fact that the APT 'limped into Glasgow 28 minutes late after returning from its record breaking run'. There had been a tilt failure which 'spilt drinks and food across the floor and jammed electrically operated doors'. There was extensive BBC coverage on both radio and television and this was continued over the next few days as the train failed on its journey or failed to run.

On the 10 December 1981 the *Telegraph* reported that 'the accident prone train' had failed again and the *Express* gave details of the brake failure which led to 60 passengers having to be transferred to a 'local train'. The unfortunate saga continued and on 24 December 1981 the Transport Secretary announced in the House of Commons that the APT would have to prove itself in commercial service before the government would put up money for a fleet.

It was planned that a daily APT service between Glasgow and London would be started after 11 January 1982. The conflict between the unions and the British Railways Board over pay and conditions resulted in a strike which started on 12 January and was not settled until 18 February. There was considerable criticism of the Board by the media and a period of negotiations with the unions. It was in this environment that the British Railways Board withdrew the APT(P) and was forced to re-examine its policy with regard to the future of its high-speed equipments.

A reassessment of the business requirements of the west coast main line has led to a reduction in train length which allows a return to the more flexible arrangement of a single driving car at one end of the rake. New driving cars are being acquired for the east coast main line and conceptual designs exist for the IC 225, which is the production version of the 140 miles per hour (225 kilometres per hour) driving car due to be in service about 1990.

The April 1984 issue of the British Rail house journal says in an article on InterCity sector management:

Despite the absence of government approval for east coast mainline electrification, InterCity planning still assumes that the future lies with electric rather than diesel traction. Even so, the last two years have been marked by vacillation in traction policy.
    APT is clearly a non-starter in its present form, having survived less than a week when placed in revenue service in December 1981 [6].[5]

---

[5] Government approval has now been given.

OVERALL SUMMARY

The APT project failed not because the technology was too advanced at that time—it was in fact only medium/high technology—but because the project involved introducing that technology into an old established engineering organization whose conditions and practices were long out of date. Whilst the prototype APTs have been scrapped, much of the technology base which was used in that concept has found application in the more modern British Rail rolling stock and systems.

The APT project came into being with considerable opposition from established Board members, and without restructuring the Board and the research team it would be difficult to formulate a different management approach which would avoid that project-destroying environment. It could be argued that the project should not have been started or that the reasearch organization should have stuck to its mandate and not stretched this mandate to include a new concept for a new era of rail travel. Perhaps the results of the research should have been made available for application by the established engineers (as in practice happened in the High-Speed Train). It is probable that without the spur of APT, HST would not have appeared until a number of years later and this would have meant a further fall in British Rail traffic.

Even though the APT can be classified in no other way than as a failure, some of its effects were good and some of its more innovative features may yet come into public use by the end of this decade. Additionally, the research department which was built up during the early life of the project is now a well established and well respected part of British Rail, closely integrated in the new British Rail management structure.

REFERENCES

1. Williams, H., 1985; Boocock, D. and King, I., 1982; Boocock, D. and Newman, M., 1976.
2. Communication to the authors.
3. Jones, S., 1975; 1977.
4. *Reshaping of British Railways*, 1962.
5. Wickens, A. H., 1983.
6. 'Sector Management', 1984.

Chapter Five

The Thames Barrier[1]

The need for the Thames Barrier arises from three circumstances associated with the site and growth of London: the development of the low lying areas adjacent to the tidal Thames for commercial, industrial and residential purposes; the steady rise in high water levels in the estuary with the passage of time; and the sporadic occurrence of storm generated surges in the southern North Sea.

The rise in sea level is estimated at about 1.5 millimetres per year. Over a period of 1,900 years, this accounts for the rise of mean tide level at London Bridge of 2.85 metres. In addition, the tidal range is increasing for several other reasons: there has been an increase of 7.3mm in the high water level over the last 110 years; geologic settlement of south eastern England, due to the disturbance of the equilibrium of the tectonic plate on which the country lies, accounts for about 1.5 millimetres per year; the remainder is the result of changes in the configuration and shaping of the embankments of the Thames.

The surge tides factor introduces an element of chance in predicting high waters. High surges in sea level are generated far out in the Atlantic Ocean when a deep depression moves on a north-easterly course, as commonly happens.[2] Provided the movement of the depression continues in a north-easterly direction, there will be no problem for the east coast of England. Occasionally, however, these depressions take an easterly course, passing to the north of Scotland, and then turn south-east, passing over northern Germany. This brings a 'hump' into the northern North Sea. An area of high pressure will

---

[1] Much of the story of the Thames Barrier is described in greater detail in the delightful and informative book *The Thames Barrier* by Stuart Gilbert and Ray Horner [1].

[2] The low air pressure which exists at the centre of the depression raises the level of the sea by 10 millimetres for every millibar of air pressure below the average figure. Sea level at the centre of a deep depression may therefore be raised by some 300 millimetres. The dynamic effect of the movement of the depression amplifies the height of the surge which is further enhanced by passage from the deep water of the Atlantic to the shallower water of the Continental Shelf.

normally exist to the west of the depression and the steep pressure gradient will cause strong northerly winds to blow on the western flank of the depression. The drag of these winds on the surface of the sea will push the hump to the south into the narrowing funnel formed by the east coast of England and the west coast of the Continent. The Straits of Dover are too narrow and shallow to allow the large volume of water to pass into the Channel and so the water piles up. A 300 millimetres hump in mid Atlantic may amplify to 600 millimetres by Wick, increasing to over a metre by Forth. Two metres may be attained by Humber and as much as 4 metres has been recorded at Southend on the rising tide.

In a disastrous flood in February 1953, the sea level at Southend was raised by 2 metres. Some 64,750 hectares of farm land were flooded together with 24,000 houses, 200 major industrial premises, 320 kilometres of railway, twelve gasworks and two electric power stations. Over 300 people were drowned as well as much livestock. The parapet walls of the Houses of Parliament were lapped. The probability of similar or higher water levels being reached is estimated as 1 in 50 in a year.

This threat of flooding obviously created strong political pressure. The government appointed a departmental committee, the Waverley Committee, to examine the danger. The committee reported in 1954 that the idea of a barrier be urgently examined. Sites were suggested and initial design ideas developed by two firms of consulting engineers, Rendel, Palmer & Tritton and Sir Bruce White, Wolfe Barry and Partners. Concern was expressed by the Port of London Authority that there be a single unobstructed opening of not less than 1,400 feet. This complicated the design requirements considerably. As a result, by 1965, when there was another high surge tide, the Waverley Committee recommendation had got nowhere.

In 1966, Sir Hermann Bondi, an eminent astronomer, mathematician, government scientist and sometime Master of Churchill College, Cambridge, was asked to review the flood threat. Professor Bondi concluded that a serious flood in London would be 'a disaster of [a] singular and immense kind' and that it must not be allowed, particularly since the ability to prevent it existed [2]. He suggested that a less expensive barrier than that proposed to date should be studied. This was now feasible since containerization had reduced traffic to the Port of London dramatically. Professor Bondi recommended that three sites be considered in detail: a barrier around Dagenham, a barrier around Woolwich or a barrage upstream of the Surrey Dock entrance (Figure 5.1). (The term 'barrier' was applied to a structure which normally allows a free flow of the tide and passage for shipping but which could be closed when necessary to prevent a high surge tide flooding London.

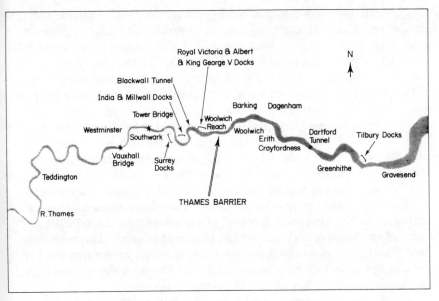

Figure 5.1 Location of the Thames Barrier

A 'barrage' would be a structure stopping the tidal flow at all times and only allowing flow seaward through the structure.)

SITE SELECTION

Once Professor Bondi had submitted his report to the government, the Greater London Council (GLC), which had been created in 1965 and had statutory responsibility for flood protection of London, pressed the government to take action. The government responded by inviting the GLC to undertake an urgent investigation into the three suggested schemes. The GLC agreed on the basis that the government paid half the cost of the investigation, and said that they proposed to consider the problems of strengthening flood defences downstream of the proposed structure and other sites and methods of flood protection as well. There was an element of confrontation between a Labour Government and a then Tory Greater London Council in this, which was not unhelpful in getting the barrier project initiated. The GLC also made it clear that the investigation was to be undertaken with a view to resolving the complex issues in the shortest possible time, and that a firm decision would be taken and put into effect at the conclusion of the investigation.

Navigational, oceanographical, meteorological, groundwater, pollution, siltation, amenity, civil engineering, and cost of delay to shipping, working parties were set up. Political direction was organized through a policy committee, chaired by the Parliamentary Secretary of the Department of the Environment, with representatives of the Department of the Environment, the Ministry of Agriculture, Fisheries and Food, the Hydraulic Research Station, the Port of London Authority, Trinity House, the Chamber of Shipping, the Essex and Kent River Authorities and the GLC. A steering committee chaired by the GLC's Director of Public Health Engineering, with similar representation, was responsible for the detailed direction of the investigation. The working parties were all chaired by the GLC's project manager, Ray Horner.

The first requirement was an assessment of the flood risk and an estimate of the long term increase of high waters in the tidal estuary and of the possible changes in this rate in the future. The main task for the navigation working party was an appraisal of the number and size of openings for shipping for barrier structures at the various sites, or locking facilities in the case of barrage proposals.

By the late summer of 1969, the stage had been reached where a first report of the studies could be published [3]. The report recommended further studies concentrating on barrier schemes at the Woolwich and Crayfordness sites. In fact it was evident at this stage that the choice lay between a barrier at the Woolwich site—proposals for a drop gate with a 120-metre and two 46-metre openings with towers 92 metres high were well developed (see Figure 5.2)—and the raising of flood defences throughout the estuary to the required standard. The raising of flood defences throughout the whole estuary to Teddington Weir and beyond, although quite practical, was politically and environmentally unacceptable. The barrier was the 'modern solution' and as such appealed to both the government and the Greater London Council. The problems of ensuring that a barrier was closed without any possibility of failure were brushed aside at this stage. A barrage would not have this problem, but this solution was ruled out as a result of the Hydraulic Research Station assessment that siltation problems would be unacceptable. In May 1970, the Minister of Housing and Local Government, Anthony Greenwood, expressed his preference for a proposal to site a drop gate barrier in the Woolwich–Blackwall Reach area and invited the GLC to proceed with studies on such a project. In the meantime, however, he requested raising the banks as an interim measure. Ultimately 216 kilometres of bank were raised 0.5 metres[3].

---

[3] Rothwell *et al.* discuss the contract conditions used for this urgent work [5].

Figure 5.2 Artist's impression of Woolwich barrier
Source: *Gilbert and Horner, and Thomas Telford Publications [4]*

In late 1969, the Port of London Authority announced the closure of the Surrey Docks. It was evident that closure of the West India and Royal Docks would come in a few years. The need for a large central opening thus appeared to have reduced dramatically. Attention now focused on one preferred site at Woolwich Reach. The barrier proposed had one 135-metre central opening and two of 61 metres, all three openings having drop gates: but then one of the staff of Rendel, Palmer & Tritton working in the joint engineering consultancy team came up with the idea of the rising sector gate. This gate rotates up from the river bed to close the opening between the piers.

This is accomplished by securing each end of the gate, which is segmental in cross-section, to large disc-like structures pivoted at their centres. Rotation of these wheels causes the gate to move in a circular arc from its open position in the bed of the river to the closed position between the piers [6].

The rising sector gate was simple and robust and could be closed within a few minutes (Figure 5.3). In addition, the piers could be reduced in height. This meant less opposition to the project by planners and public,

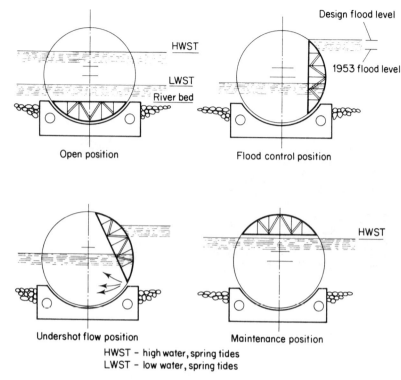

Figure 5.3 Barrier gate in four positions
Source: *Gilbert and Horner, and Thomas Telford Publications [7]*

as had occurred on the Eastern Scheldt scheme in Holland[4]. The final scheme comprised four 61-metre openings[5] and two 31-metre openings, all with rising sector gates, and four 31-metre openings with simpler radial gates.

In December 1970, the Secretary of State for the Environment, Peter Walker, approved this proposal. The GLC then promoted a Private Bill in Parliament to obtain the powers necessary to construct the Barrier. Rendel, Palmer & Tritton were appointed as the consulting engineer for the detailed design and project supervision in 1971. The

---

[4] The initial proposals and works to close the estuaries of the south-western part of the Netherlands, following the disastrous flooding of 1953, utilized barriers, but because of the ecological disruption this would create, in destroying wetlands and through siltation and the build-up of heavy metals and chlorinated hydrocarbons, this method was changed in 1974–6 to a more innovative barrier design [8].

[5] A 185-metre wide navigable channel was a concession to the navigators to compensate for the loss of the large central opening.

Bill was passed in August of 1972. The Bill was unopposed as a result of the efforts made to meet objections and to modify the proposals to gain as wide support as possible. This was essential in the circumstances since opposition to the Bill could have caused considerable delays. Some additional costs were incurred, but there was really no alternative in the circumstances. The choice of a barrier (which could be converted to a barrage at a later date) illustrates this point. A decision to build a barrage (a more reliable flood defence) initially would have generated considerable opposition from both navigation authorities and environmentalists. The involvement of many organizations in the working parties and the widespread publicity given to each stage of the project were all factors in the final stage of an unopposed passage of the Barrier Bill through Parliament.

FINANCE

Upon passage of the Barrier Act, responsibility for the barrier within the government passed to the Ministry of Agriculture, Fisheries and Food (MAFF). MAFF was concerned, of course, with the impact of flooding upon farming, but essentially the decision to give responsibility to MAFF was one of financial convenience: a government grant of 75 per cent could be obtained under MAFF whereas the Ministry of Housing and Local Government, the alternative possibility, would have had difficulty in allocating a grant for anything over 40 per cent of the project budget.

The finance for the barrier followed the normal GLC practice for major projects. Initially, the investigation stage was treated as a project in its own right. At the feasibility stage, estimates were prepared for the various schemes. Once a decision had been taken on the selected scheme, detailed estimates were prepared with expenditure forecast and grant income estimated for a period of five years ahead. These figures were used by the Treasurer for his financial plan to raise the necessary money. Before a contract of any size was let, a report was submitted to the Public Service Committee and authority to spend was sought. Any possibility of overspending on any particular section would be reported as soon as foreseen. Capital estimates were updated each six months as the project moved forward. As regards inflation, the GLC practice was that this was not allowed for on any single project, but dealt with as a council-wide exercise by the Treasurer in determining his financial plan for rate precept and borrowing.

All expenditure on which grant aid was claimed was subject to a further detailed check by the engineers and accountants of the Ministry of Agriculture, Fisheries and Food. As a condition of grant aid, all variations over £50,000 had to have prior approval by the ministry. Below this figure, *post facto* sanction could be given.

DESIGN

With the Act passed, there was considerable pressure to get the project under way. Detailed design began in earnest. While the detailed design of the civil, mechanical and electrical work was carried out in the consultant's office, continuous liaison was necessary with the GLC's Department of Public Health Engineering, the department responsible for the project, and with the Department of Mechanical and Electrical Engineering which had the responsibility for the equipment standards. The GLC Architect's Department had been nominated to work with the consultant but this link was separate from the control relationship. The Architect's Department was responsible for securing the approval of the Royal Fine Arts Commission of the scheme.

The piers had to be as narrow as possible, to reduce obstruction of the waterway, consistent with overall stability and ability to house the electrical equipment and operating machinery. When the main dimensions (65 metres long, 11 metres maximum wide and 5 metres wide at the waisted section adjacent to the gates) were determined for the main piers, the machinery had only been designed in outline; space had therefore to be left for the equipment.

Early scheduling work by the consultants demonstrated that economic construction and efficient utilization of the heavy equipment necessary for the project, coupled with the Port of London Authority's navigational requirements—one 122-metres wide channel or two 61-metre openings—required a two-phase, sequential construction. Construction periods for the foundations of individual piers were critical and so a number of alternative designs were prepared in outline. In the event, two of these were included in the tender documents but all tenderers submitted their main tender on the basis of the conventional heavy sheet piled brace cofferdam.

The scheduling work also showed that if the project was to be constructed to a reasonable time scale, the sills between the piers needed to house the gates in the open position and to provide the water cut-off below the gates, would have to be pre-cast elsewhere and floated into position. Each of the four big sills was 60 metres long by 27 metres wide by 8.5 metres high and weighted just under 10,000 tons. Incorporated in the sills were twin 3-metre diameter subways providing access between the piers and carrying the duplicated power and control cables and service pipes. Constructing these to a high degree of accuracy, placing them and then connecting them to the piers was to prove a major project activity.

The detailed design was started whilst many of the equipment requirements were still undetermined and before all the model and investigation results were available. As a consequence changes had to be made to the drawings and there was thus some delay in their production. Fortunately, this delay did not hold up the contractors.

CONTRACTUAL ARRANGEMENTS

The Thames Estuary is one of the areas in the United Kingdom where major projects are, or at any rate were at this time, especially liable to run into labour problems. Consideration was given at an early stage to what might be done to reduce the risk of these problems arising. Discussions were held by Rendel, Palmer & Tritton with both the Federation of Civil Engineering Contractors and the Engineering Employees Federation on methods of handling the contracts and to find out if there was a basis for a site agreement for labour conditions. A site agreement was not favoured. The possibility of the main contractors having informal discussions on labour problems off the site was also explored. When the main contracts were placed, the consultants attempted to promote such discussions. Some were held, but generally the contractors were unwilling to enter any regular and semiformal procedure for them. The GLC was aware of the action the consultants were taking, but as a public sector employer it was very wary of the consequences of being known to be involved in any labour matters.

Alternative contractual arrangements were reviewed. The primary options were to have a number of separate contracts or one major contract with specialist subcontractors. Based on their previous experience, Rendel, Palmer & Tritton recommended that the work should be split into a number of contracts. It was thought this would allow greater control and a quicker start on site. Considerable use was made of nominated subcontractors.

The design office work was consequently phased with the intention of letting contracts at the right time to fit in with the overall project schedule. The main contracts were for preliminary site clearance, rebuilding the south bank river wall and preparing the site for main contractors, diversion channel dredging, main civil works in the river, dredging maintenance of navigational channels, machinery, shore works and buildings, gates, services (piped and electrical) and equipment supply, and amenity works. Some of these contracts had associated separate supply contracts for equipment. Of these contracts, the civil was the largest.

The GLC was concerned that it should be aware of its major financial commitments before proceeding beyond the letting of the preliminary contracts. Accordingly, although it was not essential for schedule purposes to place the contracts for the gates and machinery at the same time as the main civil works, all three tenders were sought and appraised before the latter was awarded. For the civil works the forms of contract were the Institution of Civil Engineers' Conditions of Contract (4th Edn) with minor modifications to suit the GLC's requirements. For the electrical and mechanical works (including the gates contract) the forms of contract were based on Institution of Mechanical Engineering Form A, but as substantially modified by the GLC.

Tenders for the three main contracts were invited during 1973. This was at the time that the labour unrest which the Heath Government was having to face was approaching its peak. Consequently, none of the tenderers was prepared to accept the full risk of dealing with potential labour and supply cost problems on contracts which were to extend over many years. This was particularly so in the case of the civils tenderers because the civils conditions of contract are more onerous than the electrical and mechanical conditions as regards responsibility for the costs and effects of labour disputes.

CIVILS CONTRACT

Bids for the civils work were received in November 1973. As a consequence of the labour unrest, only four consortia from an invited prequalification list were prepared to tender. Of these, one required a negotiated contract and one would only carry the work out on a 'cost-plus' basis. The other two submitted *bona fide* tenders based on priced bills of quantities but even these were so qualified as regards labour that they could hardly be regarded as 'firm' tenders. Accountability in the public sector requires that tenders should be as unqualified and as firm as possible. However, negotiation, as distinct from clarification of a tender, is also subject to severe restrictions. Consequently, the consultants were authorized to talk with the two consortia at senior level to endeavour to negotiate terms which might be acceptable to the tenderer, but at the same time to preserve a 'firm tender' situation, particularly as regards responsibility for labour. They reported to a small GLC team as negotiations proceeded. It was only in the later stages of the negotiations when the pattern of an agreed contract was emerging that the GLC became directly involved in the negotiations.

The contract was finally awarded in July 1974 to the consortium CTH comprising Costain, Tarmac and Hollandesche Beton Maatschappij. The key terms of the contract were:

—reimbursement to the contractor for the effect of inflation to cover that element which is not reimbursed by the Baxter formula;[6]
—a side letter which required that the contractor should take responsibility for the first 21 days of labour disruption in each of the first two years and that at the end of two years the contract should be reviewed in relation to excessive inflation and the cost of industrial relations disputes;
—the contract would be reviewed at the end of the two years at which point it could be terminated on a cost with minimum profit basis as set down in the contract.

A Joint Venture Board was established in which Costain, as sponsor contractor, provided the chairman. Costain was also to act as liaison between the Joint Venture Board and the project manager and to provide the head office organization.

The structure of the Joint Venture Board (Figure 5.4)—with two directors from each of the three companies, each company having one vote—proved an effective means of administering the project and of establishing satisfactory relationships with the client, the Greater London Council, and with Rendel, Palmer & Tritton.

The project was conducted as an autonomous business with staff seconded from the separate companies working in a fully integrated relationship. The individual companies were represented at senior level in the management of the project with the project manager appointed by Costain, the deputy project manager appointed by Tarmac and the assistant project manager appointed by Hollandesche Beton Maatschappij (HBM). Staff involved in man management, planning, design of temporary works, engineering and other administrative duties such as

---

[6] The Baxter formula is used on civil engineering projects to adjust for inflation. The Baxter formula assumes a certain proportion of materials, labour and other cost items and calculates an average cost adjustment for the project as a whole as the price indices of these items change.

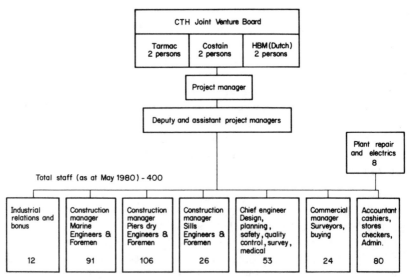

Figure 5.4 CTH Joint Venture Board
Source: *Major Projects Association*

accounts, surveying and commercial matters amounted at the peak period of the project to some 400 persons. In all company matters relating to personnel, duties on site, career development, discipline, etc., they referred to their respective senior company representative.

In view of the constraint of minimizing interference to the river and of avoiding drainage and siltation problems, only some 30 per cent of the cross-section of the river could be cut off. The pier structures were constructed *in situ* inside cofferdams built in the river. The sills which span between the piers were constructed in pre-cast concrete form in a large dock on the north side of the river. When the piers had progressed sufficiently, the sills were removed from the dock and lowered into position between the piers. This sequence of construction imposed considerable difficulties. The piers and sills had to be constructed separately to extremely demanding tolerances and the sills then placed in position between the piers to exceptionally high standards of accuracy. The major difficulty of marine civil engineering works is to get the heavy equipment to the point at which the work is to be carried out (in as economical a fashion as possible). Access jetties and working platforms were constructed of tubular piles driven into the river bed from floating piling frames on pontoons, with suitable bracing, with roadway slabs to support cranes weighing approximately 100 tons and capable of carrying 100-ton loads. This work progressed initially from the south bank towards the middle of the river with protection provided by dolphins and a mid-river fender to guard against the impact of shipping.

The cofferdams required a level, clean chalk surface before the 5-metre-thick concrete foundation base could be placed; the specifications for the preparation of an acceptable formation were extremely demanding.[7] Initial methods failed and had to be considerably improved. Since the formation had to be prepared with the cofferdams full of water (in order to overcome the uplift water pressures) many innovative methods had to be used. Airlift techniques had been used previously, but this branch of hydraulics had to be further developed before the requisite approval criteria could be attained.

Other difficulties were encountered in achieving a stabilized pressure relief system to deal with the uplift in the cofferdams. To overcome upward pressures, concrete had to be placed in the foundation base to the piers, whilst the cofferdam was filled with water. A complicated system of 'tremie concrete' was used. The volume of concrete in the largest pier constructed by underwater methods was 6,500 cubic metres; the work was carried out in a period of about four days with the site operating on a 24-hour basis [9]. Once this operation was begun, it had to be continued until completed to ensure that the foundation base was homogeneously constructed. The operatives were aware of this; as a result they exerted some industrial muscle over payment for this work. Ultimately this led to a severe labour dispute, culminating in strike action, as is described below.

During the first two years of the project, from 1974 to 1976, only some 50 per cent of the scheduled work was achieved, mainly due to technical difficulties and industrial relations problems. A continuation of the work at that rate would have extended the project to an unacceptable length. It was thus realized in 1976 that it would be impossible to fulfil the planned schedule unless both day and night shifts were fully operational. (Later in the project, and as a consequence of further industrial action, it became necessary to introduce three 8-hour shifts in order to keep to schedule, as will be described shortly.) During the first two years, inflation soared to around 25 per cent. There had been a long learning period in dealing with some of the technical problems.

---

[7] In later stages of the project, the Larssen 6 Sheet piles in the cofferdams were replaced by Peine piles. Having considerably greater strength than the Larssen 6 piles, the Peine piles enabled a reduction in the number of intermediate strutting frames and thereby minimized the problems on the removal of the chalk shoulders which had occurred in the piers on the south bank. This allowed the excavation and preparation of the formation of the cofferdams to be accelerated and reduced the work load for platers and welders on the manufacture of the strutting frames. If used at the beginning of the project, the Peine piles would have speeded up the programme. However, they were of German manufacture and were not available at the outset of construction.

Labour productivity had been low and there had been many minor disputes on working conditions and rates.

When the time came in 1976 to make the review at the end of the first two years, it was obvious that major changes would be necessary if the contract was to proceed satisfactorily. Neither the GLC nor MAFF, nor the consultants, were at all happy with progress. The labour situation was very unsatisfactory but in the prevailing industrial climate there was a limit to what CTH could do to improve it. The consortium changed the director responsible for the project and the project manager. This change of senior personnel was beneficial in the longer term but the effect was inevitably slow in becoming evident.

Consideration was given to terminating CTH's contract but this was not considered viable because of the delays and extra cost it would incur; anyway, a new contractor might experience the same learning problems CTH had. It was ultimately agreed to assist the consortium make better progress by making the following changes to the contract:

—payments for the first two years were increased so that the contractor was not in a loss making situation;
—measured rates were increased;
—lump sum payments were to be made for the next two years to cover the cost of labour dislocation, with provision for a formula adjustment if agreement could not be reached on the subsequent lump sum payment;
—minimum loss/excess profit limitations were introduced;
—monthly cash advances were to be made to limit overdraft requirements.

From this time on, neither party had the option to withdraw from the civils contract.

At the beginning of the project, the site operated a 12-hour day shift with a 12-hour night shift. The day shift was intended to be fully operational on all trades and to be the major productive unit, the night shift having only a limited production input. Employing labour on the basis of day and night shifts of 8 hours with normal overtime of 4 hours gives effective continuous working for 5 days a week, but this is not a satisfactory basis over a long period—many operatives were not prepared to work more than a 40-hour week, certainly without receiving considerably greater pay; and in any case, labour was using the overtime working period as a weapon to force concessions on pay. Other tactics were also being used to secure increased payments. This continuous guerilla warfare was placing a severe demand on top management. The importance of timely completion of the project was recognized by all, including labour. In fact, in the early stages of the project there were difficulties in establishing work on a productive basis and it proved necessary, though regrettable, to pay reasonably high levels of standing bonus. This was one of the causes of discontent which later led to hard bargaining on bonus deals, when the technical problems had been resolved and higher productivity was possible.[8]

CTH's new management realized the limitations of the two 12-hour schemes and hence proposed there be three 8-hour schemes. This was immediately approved by the GLC, MAFF, the consulting engineer and the unions (who saw the benefits of the extra employment three shifts would create). Unfortunately the operatives saw instead that much of their bonus pay would disappear. Negotiations became bitter and frustrating with the operatives now also demanding termination payment of the kind paid on the nearby dock closures. The operatives had realized that continuous working was essential for the underwater concrete processes. The working rule agreement gave them the option of working a 12-hour day shift and night shift with the mandatory requirement that they must work a minimum of 40 hours a week. Overtime was therefore optional. The operatives decided to increase pressure by taking industrial action to limit the working hours to an 8-hour day shift and an 8-hour night shift, thereby making it impossible to carry out the underwater concrete pours.

The Joint Venture could not concede to the termination payment system in view of the costs involved and the effect on other sites. It was also felt that the three 8-hour shift system was strategically essentialy. CTH therefore resorted to the Civil Engineering Conciliation Board and achieved a ruling that the operatives would be required to work on the three 8-hour rotary shift system. Contract labour then struck, staying on strike for two months. Eventually the men returned to work but

> there was, however, a feeling of resentment by the labour force, and the proposal to add half an hour overtime per shift (to facilitate) handover between teams was not accepted. This was a considerable handicap and the problem was not solved until the 1979 agreement on bonus payments [10].

Nevertheless, production on site now improved to the point where there could be some degree of confidence in achieving the schedule.

The three shift system involved further recruitment on a large scale.

---

[8] Eventually, bonus schemes were devised for all trades but the multiplicity of the schemes and the varying earnings caused dissension, later resolved by devising an all-embracing scheme in which all operatives were paid the same amount of bonus per hour with production measured against the target programme.

The number of operatives rose at peak from 490 to some 1,550; with 450 subcontractors, a total labour force approach 2,000. In view of recent experiences, the most careful controls had to be applied. A balance had to be made between the risk of potential industrial relations problems and the individual's ability to do the work. In consequence, careful off-site interviewing procedures were established.

In 1978, the GLC were still dissatisfied with progress. A near flood in January 1978, unpredicted by the warning system, put the civil engineering works at risk. It also caused sufficient concern in Parliament that the Minister of Agriculture, Fisheries and Food, John Silkin, was moved to request informally if progress on the Barrier could not be expedited, 'even at the risk of spending a little more money' [11]—a suggestion willingly taken up by the GLC. With some difficulty the Port of London Authority was persuaded to accept navigation through only one 61-metre opening in the partly constructed works and this gave the council the opportunity of negotiating directly with CTH to secure a reduction of the estimated time to completion by some 18 months. CTH used the requirement for the changed programme to secure payment terms which were significantly improved over those which the 1976 review provided. The conventional form of contract was to be operated in parallel with a target cost-shared saving form to be introduced with effect from January 1979 until completion of the project.[9] From this time, CTH undertook all risks on the project and the profit element was converted into a completion time incentive payment to be paid in full if the August 1982 completion date was met.

These targets were, of course, negotiated after the contract had been running for four years. There was thus extensive knowledge available on basic problems, plant requirements, labour productivity, etc., and this made it not too difficult to arrive at reasonable targets. To have done this earlier would have been a more difficult exercise. Both the time and cost targets were met: the contract was completed ahead of time and well within the overall cost. The contractor earned his full bonuses.

At the same time, an agreement was made with the unions known as the 'Green Book Deal', the most important point of which was an incentive scheme for operatives if the work achieved certain stages by specific dates, linked with the operatives' acceptance of the planned redundancy policy. The milestones were reached, the redundancies were accepted and, apart from the minor problems of rearranging the

---

[9] A target cost of £165 million with the provision of profits or losses up to 5 per cent shared was agreed, the target cost being calculated at January 1979 prices, subject to an indexed (Baxter) adjustment.

labour on changed shifts, work proceeded without difficulty. This was a considerable achievement in that, as noted, at peak some 2,000 operatives were employed and almost 400 staff. The 'Green Book' agreement achieved a saving of a minimum of one year, and possibly a maximum of two years, for an assessed payment of one month's cost of running the project at the peak period. The agreement was achieved as a result of a postal ballot of all the operatives. The scheme was based upon payment of a unit share of £X with the value of each unit share equalling £500. An additional two weeks' payment was in lieu of notice on termination (Table 5.1).

Table 5.1   The 'Green Book' stage payments scheme

Labour force	Date	Labour force leaving, approx.	Labour force remaining, approx.	Payment of shares each value £500	Total payment to operatives
1,400	July 1979	Nil	1,400	One	
1,400	April 1980	300	1,100	One	2X + 2 weeks £1,000 + 2 weeks
1,100	July 1980	300	800	One	3X + 2 weeks £1,500 + 2 weeks
800	Sept 1981	350	450	One	4X + 2 weeks £2,000 + 2 weeks
450	Jan 1982	50	400	One	5X + 2 weeks £2,500 + 2 weeks
400	April 1982	150	250	One	6X + 2 weeks £3,000 + 2 weeks

Source: *Major Projects Association*

On 31 December 1978 there was another near flood. Everyone's resolve to complete the project quickly was reinforced.

When the civils contract became fully 'cost plus' Rendel, Palmer & Tritton, assisted by a firm of accountants appointed as independent auditors, became responisble for a detailed check of all contract expenditure. This also involved being kept informed of the contractor's proposals and actions on labour negotiations. CTH remained responsible, having regard to its target requirements, but the risk of having expenditure disallowed from its costs if the consultant judged any such expenditure as improper or unreasonable exercised restraint on its payments to labour.

The reporting methods adopted by CTH to meet these requirements were on three levels. First, the project manager reported directly to the consulting engineer's representative on site who also held regular monthly meetings on all aspects of the works. Second, formal meetings were held, quarterly, by the GLC, the consulting engineer and the Joint Venture directors, to consider progress and the overall direction of the project in financial terms. Third, management meetings were held by the CTH staff with their opposite numbers in the consulting engineer's team at which more specific details of the works were discussed.

CTH provided method statements for the consulting engineer before work could be begun. Approximately 60 per cent of the volume of the civil engineering work was concerned with the design, procurement and carrying out of temporary works involved in construction of jetties, working platforms, cofferdams, sill lowering mechanisms and such like. Some 7,000 drawings were produced on site. Quality control of production was carried out with the consulting engineer. (Many aspects of the works were executed in conditions that allowed no possibility of the removal and correction of defective work.)

Critical path networks were produced to support the programmes prepared by the various section managers. A computer based, resourced and costed network system was introduced to the site at the beginning of the project as a method of management control. As a management tool, the project cost model proved to be far too cumbersome and was dispensed with towards the end of 1976. Manual methods of critical path network translated to bar charts were used, with resource requirements imposed on the programmes. The main virtue of the system was that speedy amendments could be made. It had been hoped to use the project cost model system of computer control to facilitate the levelling of labour resources. It also proved too cumbersome, however, and the exercise was carried out manually. With 30 different trades to be assessed, the scale of this exercise was considerable. In the circumstances prevailing during the contract period, recruitment and redundancy requirements had to be very carefully calculated since statutory notification of redundancy and subsequent recruitment of similar trades became an important feature of the industrial relations machinery.

A project budget was used by the Joint Venture Board. After the 1978 contract changes, this budget was provided for the client and his accountants and progressively monitored.

The major problem in creating an effective control system with a staff of this size, bearing in mind the added difficulties of staff seconded to a joint venture from parent companies, was in fact a human one: leading the team in a demonstrably positive manner that could be seen by all to be fair and impartial. Difficulties occurred with the staff from time to time due to the imbalance of payments between personnel paid on a salary basis and those paid according to the working rule agreements with additional payments for overtime, condition monies, bonus, transportation, etc. Supplemental agreements were made with the staff to recognize this problem, but in general the operatives were paid more than the more highly skilled and highly qualified salaried staff. Overall, the management structure of the contract worked extremely well.

MACHINERY AND GATES CONTRACTS

Contracts for machinery and gates were awarded in July 1974 and October 1974 respectively. The lowest tenders for both contracts were submitted by a consortium of Davy Lowy Ltd and Cleveland Bridge & Engineering Company Ltd—the Davy Cleveland Bridge Consortium. They were substantially qualified only in respect of inflation in excess of 25 per cent.

Although the philosophy was that interaction between contracts should be dealt with by the consulting engineer, it was recognized that the intimate relationship between the gates and machinery contracts could produce complex situations, particularly if there were delays. As both contracts were secured by the same consortium, it was decided that the two contracts should be contractually linked. This was done, although the negotiations were long and tedious, primarily because of the requirement for adherence to key dates (to which were attached liquidated damages) for completion of particular sections of the work. The situation was further complicated because some of the final running tests and combined tests were also dependent on other contractors installing services.

The fabrication of the gates on Teesside went slowly, but as the main civil works were delayed this was not of major consequence. Even then the completed gate sections had to be stored at the fabrication yard until the site was ready to receive them.

The initial stages of site erection had technical and managerial problems. The gate erection work required the use of two 800-tonne floating cranes, such as are used for North Sea oil rig work (Figure 5.5). These had to be scheduled well ahead, and because of the delays to the site works the GLC had to undertake financial commitments to ensure the availability of the cranes at the time they were required.

The placing of the first gate went according to plan (Figure 5.6), but the initial attempt to place the second 61-metre gate on pier 7 failed— the links could not be connected as it did not prove possible to position the two heavy-lift cranes with their 1,200-tonne load in a tidal current with sufficient accuracy. Nevertheless, the operation was attempted

Figure 5.5 Heavy-lift cranes lifting gate end
Source: *Cleveland Bridge & Engineering Co. Ltd*

Figure 5.6 Placing the first gate leaf, 14 December 1981
Source: *Cleveland Bridge & Engineering Co. Ltd*

again the next day. This time, perhaps because of a slight swell, the gate landed too heavily on the jack head, which fractured. Unfortunately, the cranes now had another assignment and had to leave. In addition, it was necessary at this point to switch navigation channels between piers 7 and 8 to let CTH proceed with sill installation on piers 6 and 7. To avoid delaying the programme, it was decided to store the gate at the Royal Docks while a new method of installation was devised and CTH got on with the civil works. The delay in installing the gate was nearly a year but because of the rearrangement of the schedule the effect on the overall completion date was negligible. Problems were also encountered on the gate leaf between piers 6 and 7: a labour dispute in the docks prevented the docking of the barge carrying the gate. The installation programme had again to be rearranged.

The Davy Cleveland Barrier Consortium had not qualified their tenders in respect of labour problems except as already mentioned. The high 'bonus' payments on the civils contract inevitably led to demands for similar payments by their labour. That some concession had to be made in the interests of completion was accepted by the GLC. Supplemental agreements with the consortium were therefore made to permit some reimbursement to the contractor of such extra payments. In the negotiations on both the extra cost of the very large floating cranes and the additional labour payments, care was taken to tie the contractor to completion of certain works by specific dates. The contractor received modest bonuses for such completion. The GLC considered that the concessions made were worthwhile to improve the chances that the consortium would finish on time and thus the extra money paid to CTH for the accelerated programme would not be wasted.

CLIENT RELATIONSHIP

The GLC Department of Public Health Engineering had the direct responsibility for the barrier project. The consultant reported to that department through a number of formal links as well as on a day-to-day basis as circumstances required. The formal links included monthly reports, monthly coordination meetings, site coordination monthly meetings, quarterly financial reports, and variation order approval and claim reports.

Because the project was 75 per cent grant aided by MAFF, all matters relating to increased cost had to be passed by the GLC to MAFF for agreement, in theory, prior to their being committed or agreed with the contractor by the consultant. At times of major contract negotiations, either at tender award or when supplemental agreements were needed, the council's Controller of Operational Services and the Legal Department were involved in the decisions. Finally, at times of major crisis, discussions were held with the Permanent Secretary of the Ministry of Agriculture, Fisheries and Food. Then, from time to time, behind the scenes, GLC politicians and government ministers joined the action. On most of these occasions the consulting engineer was brought into the discussions.

The Department of Public Health Engineering and the particular team in that department were recognized by all parties as the basic client command centre. Whilst the department was closely involved with the activities of the consultant, it was very careful not to interfere with the contractual role of the consultant as engineer for the contracts. Representatives of the department were regularly present at the progress meetings with the contractors, but only in the role of observers. This was particularly important when contractors' labour matters were being discussed as the GLC was concerned not to get embroiled with the unions, whose members were also employed directly by the council.

In 1979, the Ministry of Agriculture, Fisheries and Food was concerned about the rising and high level of costs and the delays and, after discussion with the GLC and the consultants, appointed a Thames Barrier Advisory Team to provide high level, independent advice on the progress of the project. This group comprised an experienced civil engineering contractor, an industrial engineer and a trade unionist. The team talked regularly with all the main organizations involved, including unions, but did not have any executive function. They recommended that the GLC should appoint a person with wide powers to control the project and have responsibility for decisions. Because of the liability which public accountability creates, it was not possible for this to be done. However, the GLC thought that there was some merit in having contacts with the contractors other than through the consultant in his formal role as engineer and accordingly required the consultant to appoint a senior person as project director. The person appointed was the consultant's associate in charge of the barrier project, his place as project leader being taken by his deputy. He had a roving commission outside the role of the engineer, primarily to investigate and make recommendations to the GLC on developing situations ahead of contractual decisions. Not unnaturally, he was much concerned with labour relations. Although the project director remained under the control of the partner who was in charge of the project, care was taken within the consultant's office to keep his role distinct from that of the project leader.

In the GLC, all major matters required committee approval. Chairmen of the committees were from time to time directly involved in major negotiations with the contractors. This was particularly the case in 1978 when negotiations were held with CTH over the modifications to the programme and contract conditions necessary to complete the project.

FINAL COSTS AND SCHEDULE

As already noted, the GLC budgeted the project on the basis of current costs—no allocation was made for inflation. The schemes of the early 1960s were estimated to cost £13–18 million. The barrier itself was priced in October 1973 at £110.7 million. The civil engineering component of this, it must be remembered, had been heavily qualified. At completion, the barrier cost about £440 million. It is reckoned that some 70 per cent of the £329.3 million 'overrun' was due to inflation, 5 per cent due to design enhancements, 10 per cent due to construction difficulties not covered in the contract, and 15 per cent due to poor productivity, whether caused by industrial relations problems or poor management or both [12]. Virtually all the contract cost overruns occurred on the civil construction contract.

Construction work took almost twice as long as expected: seven and a half years (plus six months mobilization) compared with the four years planned initially. The preconstruction period, of course, had also been subject to extensive delays.

OVERALL SUMMARY

The Thames Barrier is an impressive, in many ways beautiful, piece of engineering (Figure 5.7). Building it required construction skills of a high order. The barrier has prevented flooding and in so doing saved lives and immense financial loss and physical damage; that is, it is well worth its cost.

Over and above these facts, which deserve the fullest recognition, there are two questions that remain to be answered in evaluating the success or failure of the project: should it have taken so long to have got construction under way; and should the cost and duration of the construction have been so much greater than initially planned?

Figure 5.7 Thames Barrier
Source: *Greater London Council*

Had London been flooded between 1959, say (allowing reasonable time for construction after the Waverley Report), and 1982—a not improbable occurrence considering the likelihood was estimated at 1 in 50 per annum—there is no doubt that many people would have criticized the delay in starting the project. The reasons for the delay have been fully described; procrastination over issues of long term importance is an unfortunate trait of governments (and individuals).

As to the issue of project overruns, it is probably the case that, given the institutional setting in which the barrier was built, they could not have been much reduced. This setting included inflation, the (local) labour relations climate and the traditional way of working imposed by the ICE form of contract and the lack of real, proactive project management typical of local authorities in the United Kingdom: their unwillingness (or inability) to delegate decision-making authority to a single 'project manager'.

REFERENCES

1. Gilbert, S. and Horner, R., 1984.
2. Bondi, H., 1967.
3. Greater London Council, 1969.
4. Gilbert, S. and Horner, R., 1984.
5. Rothwell *et al.*, 1975.
6. Gilbert, S. and Horner, R., 1984.
7. Ibid.
8. Angremond, K. d' and Kooman, D., 1986.
9. Grice, J. R. and Hepplewhite, E. A., 1983.
10. Gilbert, S. and Horner, R., 1984.
11. Ibid.
12. Ibid.

Chapter Six

Heysham 2 Nuclear Power Station and the AGR Programme

Ours is a nuclear age. The story of how society has developed nuclear power for a peaceful purpose—for the commercial generation of electricity—is one of hope, of the most optimistic kind, and frustration, of resistance and accommodation. Mistakes have certainly been made; lessons have been painfully learnt. The United Kingdom's Advanced Gas Cooled Reactor (AGR) programme represents that story in its fullest. Heysham 2, along with Torness, is the latest of the AGRs, representing a major effort to 'learn and get it right'. At the time of writing, late 1986, they are both nearing completion. They may be the last AGRs to be built.

To understand Heysham 2 it is necessary to go to the beginning of the nuclear power story and to look at the enormous challenges the programme offered and the decisions and mistakes that were made.

THE MAGNOX AND AGR PROGRAMMES

After World War II, the nuclear efforts of both Britain and the United States of America were dominated by military considerations. It was not until the early 1950s that the possibility of using nuclear reactors to generate electricity was considered. In 1953 the decision was taken to build a plant at Calder Hall, Cumberland. The plant was to be used for making plutonium (for military purposes) and to generate electricity. Using a design developed by the UK Atomic Energy Authority (UKAEA), the plant used natural uranium with graphite moderators cooled by carbon dioxide—a reactor type known as magnox. In the United States, on the other hand, the first power station, at Shippingsport, a prototype 60 megawatt (MW) plant, begun in 1953, used pressurized water as the reactor coolant, a technology transferred directly from the US nuclear submarine programme [1]. An alternative reactor technology was also developed in the United States, that of allowing the water in the reactor to boil and using the steam thus formed directly to drive a turbine—the Boiling Water Reactor (BWR). This reactor type was developed at the Argonne National Laboratory. A small experimental plant of 5,000 KW came on stream in February 1957, about a year before Shippingsport. These differences of gas versus water and relatively civilian versus strongly military origins have had a marked influence on the different ways in which nuclear power developed in the United Kingdom and the United States.

The United Kingdom's First National Nuclear Programme of 1955 envisaged some 1,500 to 2,000 MW of nuclear capacity being installed over a 10-year period. One year later the plan had been upgraded to 5,000 MW. In 1960, the forecast was 5,000 MW by 1968, being provided by eight magnox plants built by the Central Electricity Generating Board (CEGB) in England and Wales and one by the South of Scotland Electricity Board (SSEB). Station size varied from 275 MW to 1,200 MW. Table 6.1 summarizes the key project histories of the eight English stations. It was decided in both countries, after considerable lobbying (in the United Kingdom at least) by the electrical/mechanical manufacturers, that nuclear power plants would be built by private enterprise. In the United Kingdom, it was proposed in 1954 that the heavy electrical plant manufacturers should form consortia with the boilermakers. Five consortia were formed in 1956. Of the nine magnox stations built in the United Kingdom, two consortia built three stations each and the remaining three consortia built one each.[1] In the United States, BWRs were the first reactor type to be built commercially: the BWRs were built by General Electric, the first commercial plant, 5,000 kW, being for Pacific Gas and Electric in 1956 at Vallecitos. Westinghouse was the contractor for the first Pressurized Water Reactor (PWR), San Onofre, which was begun in 1963. Babcock & Wilcox and Combustion Engineering both got orders for PWRs three years later in 1966.

By this time Britain's magnox programme was moving towards completion and a successor reactor design was being sought, for both technological and economic reasons [2]. A Cabinet committee, the Powell Committee, had met to review the future pattern of nuclear power early in 1962. It was now evident that the magnox stations were costing more than had been forecast, though it was hoped that future

---

[1] It is considered by some that if any single decision is to be questioned as having brought the later achievements of the early nuclear power programme into disrepute, the decision to form so large a number of consortia has to be first choice.

Table 6.1 Summary of achieved programme dates for magnox nuclear stations (first units in each station)

	Start main foundations		Synchronization		Construction period to synchronization		
	Intended programme*	Actual	Intended programme*	Actual	Target months	Actual months	Overrun months
Berkeley	n/a	Jan 1957*	n/a	Jun 1962	n/a	65	n/a
Bradwell	n/a	Jan 1957*	n/a	Jul 1962	n/a	66	n/a
Dungeness A	Jan 1961	Nov 1960	Sep 1964	Sep 1965	44	58	14
Hinkley Point A	n/a	Sep 1957*	Jun 1962	Feb 1965	57	89	32
Oldbury	Jul 1962	Jul 1962	Jun 1966	Nov 1967	47	64	17
Sizewell A	Jul 1961	May 1961	Jun 1965	Jan 1966	47	56	9
Trawsfynydd	n/a	Jul 1959*	n/a	Jan 1965	n/a	66	n/a
Wylfa	n/a	Apr 1964†	Sep 1968	Jan 1971	53	81	28

n/a – not available.
* 'Start main foundations' date not available, and 'start preliminary site work' used instead.
† Since the original table was printed, a 'start main foundations' date has been identified, and this is now quoted instead of 'start of preliminary work'.
Source: Central Electricity Generating Board.

stations would be cheaper. The number of consortia had now reduced
to three (see Figure 6.1). A UKAEA/CEGB working party—the Joint
Assessment Panel—was formed to evaluate the reactor types then available: the United Kingdom's standard magnox reactor, an advanced gas
cooled reactor (AGR) developed by the UKAEA, the Canandian
Heavy Water Reactor and the US BWR (the PWR, not yet being
commercially available, was not considered a candidate). The evaluation was necessarily somewhat artificial: there were next to no 'real'
data on operating efficiency since none was yet in use and difficulties
arose over agreeing discount rates.

By mid 1963, the Joint Assessment Panel's deliberations had proved
inconclusive: there was little difference in cost between the AGR, BWR
and CANDU. Indeed, there was little obvious cost advantage even
over fossil fuels. With some reservations, then, the CEGB decided to
opt for AGR technology (which contained the gas coolant experience
gained from the magnox programme). Just prior to the Powell
Committee finalizing its report to Cabinet, however, the CEGB was
approached by General Electric (the US BWR contractor) who
proposed to offer, in conjunction with Bechtel, basically fixed price
bids for the construction of BWR stations. As a result of this offer, the
Joint Assessment Panel decided to leave the decision to the Cabinet,
but to recommend that while an invitation to bid for AGR stations be
issued, British firms should also be allowed to bid for water moderated
reactors of proven design. It was also suggested that the construction
programme did not need more than two consortia. A White Paper a
few months later (April 1964) proposed a programme of 5,000 MW for
1970–5, with one possible additional station in Scotland.

The first of the second generation of UK nuclear power stations was
to be Dungeness B. The CEGB issued tender inquiries in April 1964.
There had by then been considerable discussion between the CEGB
and the UKAEA. As a result, it had been agreed that, because of the
substantial differences in technology between the magnox reactor and
the AGR, the first commercial AGR should be a scaled-up version of
the prototype at Windscale (Calder Hall), which was a 33 MW reactor.
The Nuclear Power Group (TNPG) consortium, considered by many
to be the best managed of the three consortia then remaining, had been
working on the AGR since 1962. TNPG now froze its AGR design.
The English Electric/Babcock & Wilcox/Taylor Woodrow consortium,
however, decided to upgrade its magnox technology rather than scale
up the Windscale design. The United Power Company (UPC), the third

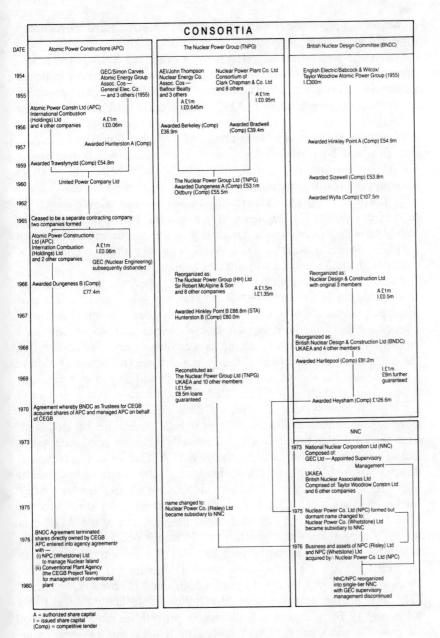

Figure 6.1 *Amalgamations of the nuclear consortia*
Source: *Monopolies and Mergers Commission [3]*

consortium, meanwhile, was in the process of breaking up: only a token proposal was being prepared.

Given the new terms of reference, in mid 1963 TNPG decided to prepare a BWR bid in addition to their AGR bid since they believed that the BWR reactor would be cheaper. The UKAEA then persuaded Atomic Power Constructions (APC), the successor to UPC, to consider bidding. This APC did, submitting a last minute proposal in February 1965 using a 36-pin design[2] which had just been developed by UKAEA, though crucially in outline form only. TNPG's bid was based on the UKAEA's existing 18-pin design: 36 pins allowed better space utilization in the pressure vessel and promised more efficient on-load refuelling. There were vigorous complaints against this last minute use of the new 36-pin design [5] (Figure 6.2), though the bid advantage in fact hardly proved decisive. In the final analysis, the cost difference between TNPG's BWR bid and APC's AGR was less than 7 per cent— considered to all intents and purposes negligible.

There now occurred what has rightly been called 'the most important single decision in the entire AGR programme' [6]. It had been hoped that open competition would obviate the need for a political decision. Unfortunately this did not happen. Instead, the bids based on American and British nuclear reactor technology were evenly matched, even after the last minute development of the 36-pin design. The future of atomic energy in Britain, and the part the UKAEA would play in that development, stood in the balance. The CEGB made it clear that they would not stand behind APC in the event of difficulties with their design. The steering committee evaluating the proposals (made up of engineers from the CEGB and the UKAEA) ultimately recommended acceptance of the AGR bid, but only after noting that APC must hire a technical director knowledgeable in AGR design and after expressing concern over the insufficiency of detailed information in the tender. After further discussion the CEGB endorsed the decision. In May 1965 the Minister of Power, Fred Lee, presented the selection of the AGR as a 'jackpot' representing the 'greatest breakthrough of all time' (doing so, as did the CEGB afterwards, with the aim of presenting the AGR in the best light for international commercial reasons [7]). In September 1965, a contract was awarded by the CEGB to APC for £79.9 million. (The total project cost was to be £106 million; load fuel date was to be 1 January 1970.) Dungeness B ultimately proved the most unhappy of all power station projects undertaken in Britain, for reasons to be

---

[2] The fuel assembly unit comprises a fuel stringer and a fuel plug unit. The fuel stringer comprises fuel elements, each of which contains fuel pins of uranium oxide encased in stainless steel [4] (see Figure 6.2).

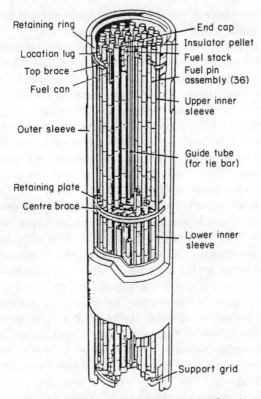

Retaining ring
Location lug
Top brace
Fuel can
Outer sleeve
Retaining plate
Centre brace

End cap
Insulator pellet
Fuel stack
Fuel pin
assembly (36)
Upper inner
sleeve
Guide tube
(for tie bar)
Lower inner
sleeve
Support grid

Source: Central Electricity Generating Board

*Figure 6.2 One of the eight 36-pin fuel elements
in a fuel stringer*
Source: *Central Electricity Generating Board*

described shortly: the project was not completed until 1983, some £140 million over budget.[3]

During the final discussion with APC on the award of its contract for Dungeness B, the CEGB began discussions with TNPG for the second AGR power station, Hinkley Point B. To maintain schedule with the Second Nuclear Power Programme, which planned 8,000 MW of capacity by 1975, the second AGR contract had to be placed by July 1966. The English Electric consortium, being preoccupied with Wylfa,

---

[3] At constant prices: approximately £300 million over budget if inflation is included. It is worth noting that the BWR competing bid offered by TNPG, using a design developed in large measure by General Electric, was subsequently built by General Electric at Oyster Creek in the United States, and that this project too suffered significant problems and overruns.

a magnox station, was not yet ready to bid for Hinkley Point B. TNPG, on the other hand, had a large and competent workforce but a work programme which was nearing completion. Following a similar proposal from APC, TNPG agreed a bid price approximately 10 per cent less than Dungeness B. Although this was exceptional, negotiations proceeded on this basis. There was maximum competition from suppliers. On 13 March 1967, a contract was awarded to TNPG for £89.387 million (the total project cost, including work by CEGB and initial fuel costs, to be £108.228 million). Because of the unfavourable national economic situation, the start date was delayed until September 1967. TNPG then won Hunterston B in open competition by offering a repeat of Hinkley Point B.

Thus by early 1967 the Second Nuclear Power Programme was effectively launched. The consortia arrangements, however, were not yet stable. To be viable, each consortium had to have at least two power stations under construction. There were now great stresses on APC and NDC (the successor to the English Electric consortium—see Figure 6.1). NDC therefore decided on a bold technological leap to gain competitive advantage: it situated the boilers in pods inside the concrete pressure vessel instead of adjacent to the reactor as in previous AGRs. Boilers were, therefore (in theory at least), replaceable, thus offering considerable benefits over the TNPG design in which boilers which became defective could only be replaced if there was a very expensive shutdown. In addition, NDC made every effort to prepare a low cost bid. NDC was awarded Hartlepool in October 1968 on the basis of outstanding technical merit and price. Two years later, on 30 November 1970, BNDC (NDC's successor) was awarded a contract for Heysham 1, to be built as a repeat of Hartlepool. In 1969, however, the Nuclear Inspectorate questioned the effect of this boiler arrangement on the pressure vessel integrity. As a result, in 1970 it was decided to change from single to double boiler closures and to add secondary and tertiary shutdown devices. As a result, approximately two years' delay was incurred and project costs rose £40 million, with additional increases in related contracts.

As will be apparent, during this period considerable changes had been occurring in the organization of the consortia. During the 1950s and 1960s, there had been substantial alterations in the business performance of British boilermakers. Demand was showing signs of easing considerably; overseas work was less plentiful; at home, labour militancy was affecting all companies. By the end of the 1960s, all but Foster Wheeler had joined one of the three nuclear power consortia. Meanwhile, the CEGB had been looking at the possibility of there being just two consortia. This ultimately became a matter of public concern. In October 1967, a parliamentary select committee recommended that there be just one organization for the design and construction of nuclear power station boilers, that the consortia should be phased out ('the Generating Boards should regard themselves as free to place orders for nuclear stations in the same way as they do for other types of power stations' [8]) and that the UKAEA should become more commercially aligned where appropriate. In 1967, the Industrial Reorganization Corporation (IRC), with Hartlepool now awarded to BNDC, recommended that there be two nuclear consortia—TNPG and BNDC. The UKAEA joined both these consortia in 1968/9 (see Figure 6.1).

Unfortunately, a valuation by Coopers & Lybrand of APC's work-in-progress on Dungeness B, which showed that serious problems were emerging on the station, now complicated the process of merging the consortia. Several technical problems were in fact being experienced on Dungeness B[4] but the most serious at the time was that severe distortions to the liner of the pressure vessel had been discovered. This should have meant that there would be a major hold-up in the installation of the boilers; however, there was a separate delay on the boilers since an acceptable design had not yet been developed for them. These problems effectively prevented the merger of APC into TNPG. The IRC now changed its objection to redistributing the UKAEA's resources and proposed that the UKAEA join the only body capable of effectively absorbing the Authority's resources, namely TNPG, which was accordingly reconstituted in 1969.

By late spring 1969, the CEGB had been forced to intervene on Dungeness B and tried to take control of APC. Throughout 1969 and early into 1970 the CEGB pursued this course, attempting to wrest control of APC from Fairey Engineering and International Combustion by terminating APC's contract and extracting maximum penalties. Unfortunately, through their boilermaker, APC had substantial leverage over the CEGB as International Combustion had contracts for the boilers for the Kingsnorth and Fiddler's Ferry coal power stations. The governement then suggested that the CEGB consider cancelling Dungeness B. The merchant bankers N. M. Rothschild were asked to investigate this option: this they did and concluded that the project was too far advanced for it to be financially worthwhile to be abandoned. The CEGB, who had been trying to persuade BNDC, the other principal nuclear power consortium, to take over the project, now reluc-

---

[4] The problems encountered by Dungeness B in particular, and the first generation AGRs in general, had their origin in the scale of engineering on, and the lining and insulation of, the large prestressed concrete pressure vessel: this technology was not addressed in the Windscale AGR.

tantly recognized that they themselves would have to take responsibility for it. On 11 September 1970 the CEGB bought APC for £1. Babcock & Wilcox took over the boiler contract in the spring of 1971. Substantial financial penalties were extracted from Fairey and International Combustion. BNDC supplied senior management to the project early in 1972.

With the purchase of APC's stock for £1 by the CEGB in 1970, the two-consortia arrangement came formally into effect. In 1973, BNDC was reconstituted as the National Nuclear Corporation, which had a 35 per cent shareholding by the UKAEA, 35 per cent by British Nuclear Associates[5] and 30 per cent by GEC, who executed supervisory management responsibility. In 1976, TNPG (now named the Nuclear Power Co. (Risley)) and the National Nuclear Corporation merged to form a single tier National Nuclear Corporation, with GEC's supervisory role terminated. (Figure 6.1 summarizes the consortia history.)

HINKLEY POINT B AND THE RUN UP TO HEYSHAM 2

The contract for Hinkley Point B was placed in March 1967. As already noted, initiation of project work was delayed until September 1967, for national economic reasons. Contract completion was then scheduled for 1 December 1971, with full load for Unit 1 by 1 July 1972. In fact, full load was not achieved until June 1976, almost four years late.[6]

Hinkley Point B was, as the second AGR, supposed to learn from the experience of Dungeness B. Before very long, however, it had overtaken Dungeness B and become a prototype plant. The situation thus soon developed where considerable development work had to be undertaken during both design and construction to deal with problems which were not evident in the early project stages. This had indeed happened on the magnox programme but there problems had yielded relatively quickly to research and development. The AGRs, however, with their more advanced technical features and more compact designs, encountered more elusive problems. There was consequently a need to do considerable but unexpected development work. There was substantial difficulty in obtaining timely design information on a sound basis of adequate testing. In order to keep to schedule, many decisions had to be taken on the basis of engineering judgement, in the most complex

[5] Taylor Woodrow Construction, Clarke Chapman John Thompson, Babcock & Wilcox, Sir Robert McAlpine, Head Wrightson & Co., Whessoe, and Strachan & Henshaw.

[6] Fuel load on Dungeness B, Heysham 1 and Hartlepool was not achieved until 1983.

engineering environment, with test work continuing in parallel with manufacture and construction on a confirmatory basis.[7]

The original cost of Hinkley Point B had been estimated in 1966 at £96.119 million; the final cost was £144.531 million, an increase of £48.412 million, or 50 per cent. Design changes constituted some £25 million of this cost increase: of this, £5.8 million was due to fundamental changes and £19.2 million to the modifications and development needed to bring the basic plant design to revised standards. Some £10.7 million was due to underestimation and £13.7 million to inflation. There were no significant construction problems or delays. Most of the major problems arose during work on the reactor and during commissioning. The primary problem areas are shown in Table 6.2.

Table 6.2   *Primary problem areas at Hinkley Point B*

	Schedule Delay	Cost Increase (£m)
Pressure vessel insulation and corrosion modifications	2 years approx.	8.3
Main gas circulators	9 months	0.327
Fuel assembly plug units	11 months	4.457

Briefly, the nature of these technical difficulties was as follows.

Pressure vessel insulation   During the contract, TNPG proposed replacing the original insulation scheme, of stainless steel foil and mesh, with a mineral-based fibre blanket secured in position by cover plates. This was accepted as satisfactory subject to testing, which was done in parallel with manufacture. During erection, however, problems arose in the distortion of the cover plates and relaxation of the insulation blanket. Tests confirmed the problem and a stronger design had to be developed.

Corrosion modifications   Evidence arose twice during the project of potentially serious corrosion of steel in the hot CO_2 environment. On the first occasion, in 1971, evidence came from the magnox stations and resulted in an intensive design, procurement and construction exercise to examine in detail all fixings and joints within the pressure circuit at Hinkley Point B. Material specifications were also modified and every fixing and joint had to be examined non-destructively. On the second occasion, data from the national working party on corrosion

---

[7] Hunterston B, meanwhile, was proceeding very closely behind Hinkley Point B. With an almost identical design (it had no computer and a different electrical emergency supply system) it tended to learn from Hinkley and 'catch up'. There thus arose a clash of priorities between the two stations which required resolution at the highest level. This resulted in Hinkley Point B being given definite priority so that some plant originally destined for Hunterston was despatched instead to Hinkley Point B.

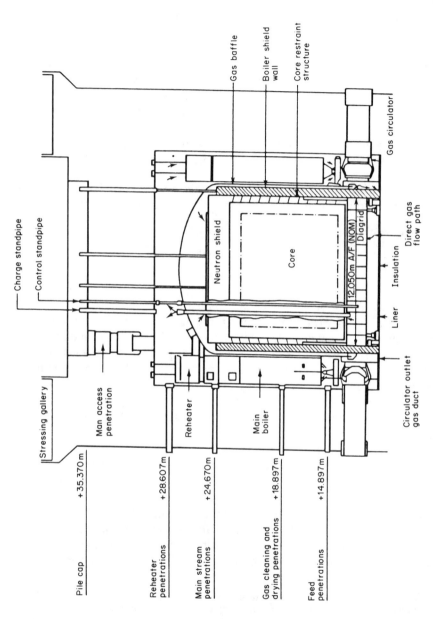

Figure 6.3 Vertical section through Hinkley Point B reactor pressure vessel

indicated potential problems with 9 per cent chrome steels. Action therefore had to be taken to divert gas from cooler regions of the reactor to protect such steels.

Gas circulators The drive motors had to be uprated on three occasions due to the availability of new data and to changed design. The circulator dome support was found to be inadequate and had to be redesigned. Seals on the circulator lubricating oil had to be improved to prevent leakage and subsequent carbonization.

Fuel assembly Several of the fuel stringer gag units failed during commissioning due to vibration problems and this component had to be redesigned. Rectification involved the removal of all the fuel from the reactor, modification and fuel reloading.

Hinkley Point B was managed initially by the CEGB's Midlands Project Group, which was based in Birmingham, but was moved to Barnwood, Gloucestershire, when the formation of the board's Generation Development and Construction Division was finalized. A single comprehensive contract had been let to TNPG for the complete station on a design, manufacture, supply and erection basis. Project management of the plant was thus largely in the hands of the consortium. Relations between the CEGB and TNPG were good; TNPG were considered responsive and efficient. Labour relations were in general good: the area is not militant, nor indeed were the times—there was a lot less strife in the industrial relations climate in the late 1960s and early 1970s than half a decade later; TNPG set up, at the CEGB's request, an Employers' Coordination Committee, meetings of which all contractors on site were invited to attend along with the CEGB.

The financial strength of the consortium, or rather the lack of it, affected the project, partly in TNPG's negotiations with suppliers (who were financially much stronger) and partly through the enormous financial and schedule risk, should the consortium fail. The former became increasingly difficult as inflation cut into suppliers' liquidity and as the negotiations to consolidate TNPG into NNC developed. As a result, the CEGB had to assist TNPG in their negotiations with a number of suppliers. This pressure on TNPG, which was operating basically on a fixed price contract, was exacerbated by the lack of further orders in prospect. Additionally, the lack of future orders prevented the consortia providing guarantees which the CEGB were seeking.

In 1970 the government requested an ex-Treasury official, Peter Vinter, to decide which nuclear system Britain should build next. Vinter's committee concluded that it had been set the wrong question and that the real one was how the nuclear industry should be structured to ensure success. Vinter recommended stronger, more streamlined consortia.[8] As a result, the government was instrumental in setting up the National Nuclear Corporation (NNC) with £10 million capital in 1973 to take over BNDC's commitments, TNPG being incorporated later, in 1976. A watchdog body was also set up known as the Nuclear Power Advisory Board.

By 1972 the CEGB had decided that, in view of the delays in the construction programme, it could not at that time proceed with further AGR orders. It accordingly advised the government that the next nuclear orders should be for PWRs, arguing that this would enable the United Kingdom to benefit from the extensive experience then available in PWRs. In the event, however, Eric Varley, the new Secretary of State for Energy, decided in 1974, on the advice of the Nuclear Power Advisory Board, that the next generation of nuclear reactors would be neither AGR nor PWR but SGHWR—Steam Generating Heavy Water Reactors—a reactor design developed by the UKAEA. This reactor was considered to be the very best design internationally available and to offer good export opportunities. No commercial design yet existed, however, and the source of fuel was uncertain: it would most probably have to come from Canada. Further, the costs of the reactor proved extremely difficult to establish.

After considerable public, often unhappy, debate, it gradually became accepted over the next few years that the SGHWR would be too costly. In 1976, the UKAEA formally concluded that the SGHWR had little prospect of satisfying the United Kingdom's long term nuclear power requirements. The government therefore requested the NNC to develop a thermal reactor assessment study. A study by the CEGB, the 'Thermal Reactor Strategy', which was derived from the NNC's thermal reactor assessment and was delivered to Anthony Wedgwood Benn, the new Secretary of State for Energy, in 1977, concluded that the SGHWR option should be abandoned on the grounds of technical immaturity, economics and safety. The decision as to what the United Kingdom's next reactor type should be was now reviewed in an atmosphere of the fiercest debate and lobbying. Sir Arnold Weinstock of GEC was considered the main force behind the PWR lobby, supported by Sir Kenneth Berrill, head of the Central Policy Review Staff, and Sir Kenneth Keith of Rolls-Royce. Anthony Wedgwood Benn and Sir Francis Tombs, Chairman of the Electricity Council, favoured the AGR. The Prime Minister was thought to favour the PWR [10]. The CEGB's 'Thermal Reactor Strategy' noted that although problems were

---

[8] As with the Powell Committee a decade earlier, the Vinter Committee's recommendations were shrouded in commercial secrecy and took a considerable time to emerge in a public form, so sensitive was the issue [9].

still being encountered with three of the AGRs, Hinkley Point B and Hunterston B had now been commissioned and that operating experience was becoming available. The PWR was considered an attractive alternative but it could only be properly evaluated once it had been designed to UK safety requirements, received the statutory authorizations (which would probably mean a public inquiry), and built. All this would take many years, perhaps as many as ten. If a further nuclear order was not placed in Britain during the next few years, the UK nuclear industry, which by then had not received an order for almost ten years, might very well decline to the point at which, should it ultimately be decided to keep the AGR capability, it would no longer be there to keep. The 'Thermal Reactor Strategy' adopted by the government, therefore,

—endorsed the CEGB's long term need for nuclear power;
—proposed that an option of a proven alternative reactor system be developed for the United Kingdom;
—proposed that the reactor type be either PWR or AGR, depending on the board's further experience of the two types.

Since there was need for additional capacity, since the AGR was the only reactor immediately available for licensing in the United Kingdom, and since the industry needed a new order to provide continuity, the CEGB accordingly proposed that a new AGR station should be ordered, based on limited modification of Hinkley Point B. The CEGB would meanwhile proceed with design work on a PWR station with a view to statutory approvals being sought around 1982. (This became the proposal for Sizewell B.)[9]

In January 1978, the Secretary of State announced his acceptance of the CEGB's 'Strategy', but added crucially, and contentiously, that all future orders beyond those indicated would 'be a matter for decision at the appropriate time'. The government, Benn made clear, wished to keep the future options on reactor type open [11]. Benn's policy was reaffirmed when the government changed in 1979 and David Howell became Secretary of State for Energy. The AGR station in fact was two stations: approval was also granted in 1978 for a virtual replica of Heysham 2 to be built by the SSEB at Torness.

---

[9] In the early 1970s, Arnold Weinstock, on behalf of BNDC, which held the PWR licence, set up a small working party to develop an independent reactor strategy. This group strongly endorsed the CEGB's 'Thermal Reactor Strategy' with the exception that the licensor be Kraftwerke Union, not Westinghouse, on the grounds that they had more competence and knowledge of complete station construction, as A/E's, and because the German approach to safety was more comparable to the UK approach than was the American. Unfortunately, arrangements between GEC and the Germans were not considered sufficiently suitable by GEC for this recommendation to be adopted.

HEYSHAM 2

Considerable thought had been given during the 1970s by both the boards and the consortia as to how the problems of the first generation of AGRs could be avoided in the next phase of nuclear power station construction. The NNC had enhanced the AGR design to satisfy new safety and seismic standards. The operating margins had been improved and the pressure vessel diameter had been increased so that there was now more room around the boilers [12].

The CEGB was well aware of the criticisms levelled against its project management performance on other (conventional) power station projects. There had been a succession of high level reports,[10] all making more or less similar points: too many technical changes, too many delays, low productivity, inappropriate contract policies. The board's own analysis concurred with most of these criticisms. In addition to the issue of better phasing the board's ordering pattern with the supplier's work loads, it focused on technology and design management, contract strategy, project management and industrial relations. The board's proposed philosophy now encompassed:

—standardization of design wherever possible and firm control of design changes during the project;
—discrete upgradings of technology, introduced only at reasonably long term intervals;
—maintenance of stable relationships with suppliers where appropriate (e.g. replication), but competitive bidding where new features were involved;
—the use of design contracts where possible in order for the board to manage the development of design;
—the use of firm price contracts where appropriate, with appropriate incentives for timely completion;
—increased attention to the quality of bidder's management;
—improved quality of management at site level;
—greater discipline at site on industrial relations on the part of both unions and management;
—consideration of site agreements;
—greater discipline amongst and between contractors over industrial relation matters.

---

[10] The 1969 Wilson Report, the 1970 NEDO report on large sites, the 1976 NEDO report comparing nuclear plants and other large projects with overseas performance, and the Monopolies and Mergers Commission [13].

This last point, of discipline between the contractors, was tied to the question of the arrangement under which the project was to be managed. Should the CEGB engage a management contractor to manage the work on site, possibly employing all the site labour, or should the CEGB, perhaps in association with the NNC, manage the project directly? And if this latter, how would discipline amongst all the contractors be assured? (It should be remembered that the CEGB was at this time experiencing terrible labour difficulties on its Isle of Grain oil fired station—the site was closed for an extended period in 1976: the situation continued to be very unsatisfactory into the early 1980s, as it was also at Littlebrook D and Ince B.)

The question of the best role for NNC was, of course, intimately bound up in the question of how best to organize Heysham 2 (and Torness). Initially it was proposed that the NNC be the turnkey contractor for the nuclear island, but the CEGB were concerned that NNC did not have sufficient share capital for it properly to accept liability for the nuclear island. As the Monopolies and Mergers Commission noted, even the NNC accepted that ultimately the CEGB would have to bear most of the project risks (as it ultimately had done on its first four AGRs), and in the United States of America, too, even the much larger nuclear steam system suppliers were unable to give guarantees of station performance [14]. In 1979 a Joint Supervisory Board (JSB) was set up for Hartlepool and Heysham 1 comprising CEGB and NNC staff: full information on technical and engineering progress and expenditure was made available to the CEGB and presented to the JSB. Contract authorization was also subject to JSB approval. The NNC were awarded the design contract in 1978 and firm price turnkey bids were prepared by the NNC for the two stations following an inquiry to this effect from the two generating boards in March 1979. In December 1980, however, following sustained pressure from the CEGB, the NNC became a single tier company. In September 1981, the NNC's role was further restricted when it was proposed that the NNC should act as the boards' agent for the nuclear island, rather than as a contractor, with the boards being responsible for the balance of plant and the overall direction of their projects. Finalization of this decision took until September 1981. By that time, the pressure vessel liner contract had been let by NNC to Whessoe. This contract had therefore subsequently to be novated to the boards.

In order to reduce design changes and their impact on manufacture and construction, it became the CEGB's policy to have all design work completed by contractors before any manufacture of hardware began. Nuclear power projects typically require a significant design input from the manufacturers. The CEGB therefore pressed for, and got, many manufacturers to accept design contracts prior to their hardware contracts. Manufacturers had been reluctant to do this in the past since they were reluctant to commit their design teams if they were not guaranteed the follow-on manufacturing work; their depressed order books at this time changed their attitude to accepting design contracts.

There proved to be relatively little difficulty in persuading the contractors to bid fixed price. This had in fact been normal practice before the 1970 NEDO report [15] recommended reimbursable contracts for erection; also, it was generally accepted that the technical risks were at this time a lot better understood, and indeed much smaller. Needless to say, the contractors' vision of the margins required to provide adequate cover for these risks differed from the CEGB's and there were some tough negotiations.

A relatively new contractual innovation was applied to seven or eight of Heysham 2's contracts: the key date procedure. If a contractor does not achieve his scheduled progress by the contractual key dates, a substantial stage payment is withheld. The key date concept was introduced as a more immediate and effective incentive than the threat of liquidated damages. Its incentive arises in two ways. One is the obvious one of withholding stage payment. The other is that the key date procedure requires directors from the CEGB, the NNC and the contractors to meet at approximately six-monthly intervals to review progress; if this is not satisfactory, the contractors' directors must report to their main board that payment is being withheld. In this way, senior management involvement in the project is guaranteed. Withholding has been invoked on three or four occasions on Heysham 2 and has proved effective.

Several new organizational arrangements were introduced to increase industrial relations discipline. The CEGB had been taking an increasingly interventionist role in order to improve construction during the 1970s—a move in line with the tenor of the various public reports on industrial relations. For Drax, the CEGB required all major contractors to agree to participate in a Management Group to coordinate the contractors' site industrial relations policies. Membership of a similar group was also a contract condition for the contractors on Heysham 2. A further innovation on Drax was the Joint Study Group, which consisted of representatives of the trade unions, contractors and their trade associations, and the CEGB. On Heysham 2 this coordination group was superseded by the Project Joint Council, formed under the provisions of the National Agreement for the Engineering and Construction Industry (NAECI), as shall be described shortly.

The CEGB's Generation Development and Construction Division (GDCD) sought Board sanction for Heysham 2 in April 1978. A project manager was appointed in February 1979. An early task was to build the project team. Though the GDCD had been at Barnwood since mid 1974, the project manager still had work to do to mould his project staff into an effective team. The creation of that team attitude proceeded in parallel with the development of new organization, management and control procedures. Those connected with Quality Assurance (QA) were of fundamental importance.

Quality Assurance is the management process of providing documentary evidence that quality standards, and the procedures necessary for achieving those standards, have been followed. QA and the regulatory environment are very closely interconnected. In the United States of America, regulatory requirements are promulgated by the Nuclear Regulatory Commission (NRC). The NRC is required to issue a licence for each plant before it can begin fuel loading; the licence is issued after the operator has demonstrated to the NRC staff that all regulatory requirements are in compliance. In the United Kingdom, the procedure is subtly different. The Nuclear Installation Inspectorate (NII), the regulatory body, does not write standards. Instead the operator—in the case of Heysham 2, the CEGB—must satisfy the NII that the plant is safe. The CEGB initiates safety criteria for acceptance by the NII from which guidelines are derived which are used in the preparation of the plant's safety case. The NII first approves the plant design and issues a licence to begin construction. The NII then monitors construction, and if it is satisfied that construction is in conformance with the licensed design, the plant may be commissioned. In general, this procedure, together with the simpler industry structure in the United Kingdom and the different state of industrial activity when Three Mile Island occurred, has led to much less 'regulatory ratchetting' in the United Kingdom than has been the case in the United States. This is not to say, however, that regulatory requirements have not been upgraded during construction. They were on the first AGRs, but largely because the designs were untested. There have been changes in NII standards during Heysham 2, but these changes have been proposed in a way which might best be characterized as regulatory dialoguing rather than ratchetting.

Quality Assurance arose as an important discipline in the nuclear industry first in the United States of America in the early 1970s. The NRC's QA requirement, promulgated in 1974 by the NRC in document 10 CRF.50 Appendix B, was fairly vague but became interpreted over the next few years to mean that basic management and engineering actions during the whole project process had to have formal documentary evidence to demonstrate that quality standards had been achieved. This requirement was enforced mandatorily in 1979 following Three

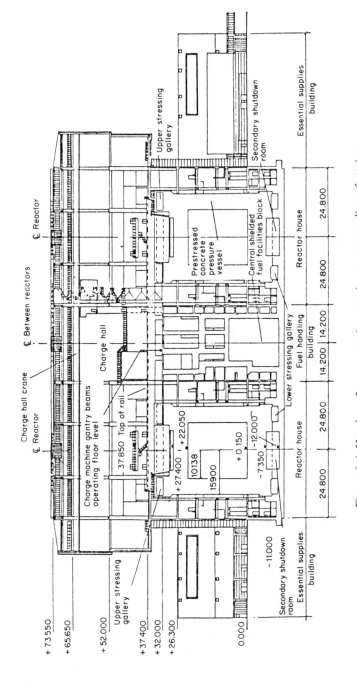

Figure 6.4 *Heysham 2 power station: section on centre line of station*

Source: *Central Electricity Generating Board*

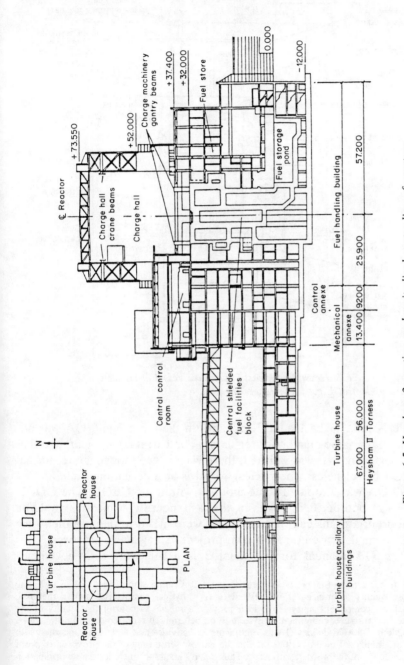

Figure 6.5 Heysham 2: section on longitudinal centre line of reactors

Source: *Central Electricity Generating Board*
For details of the reactor pressure vessel, see Figure 6.6

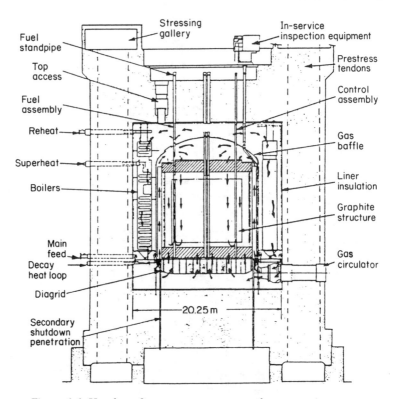

Figure 6.6 Heysham 2 reactor pressure vessel cross-section
Source: *Central Electricity Generating Board*

Mile Island. In the United Kingdom, on the other hand, QA was not
seen in the same mandatory regulatory context: it could be argued that
so long as the NII was satisfied, there was no need for separate, formal
QA.[11] Nevertheless, the nuclear world is an international one and by
1979 QA was a topic of some moment within the CEGB. The GDCD
at Barnwood decided, however, that a standard QA manual would be
inappropriate; instead, project teams were asked to prepare their own
QA manuals, based on their own project management practices.

The QA manual for Heysham 2 is a relatively slim document,

---

[11] In the United States, the Nuclear Regulatory Commission defines QA as including
'those quality assurance actions related to the physical characteristics of a material,
structure, component or system which provide a means to control the quality of the
material, structure, component or system to predetermined requirements'. In the United
Kingdom, BS 4778 defines QA as 'embracing all activities and functions concerned with
the attainment of quality rather than in the narrow sense only of the provision of proof
associated with the word "assurance". Thus quality assurance includes the determination
and assessment of quality' [16].

certainly in comparison with US QA manuals. Developing it, however, was a fruitful exercise requiring considerable attention from the team in the project's early stages. It is now well regarded by the team as something which makes explicit the essential basis upon which the project is managed. The NII has to be satisfied that the CEGB has acceptable QA procedures for the project. There is also a QA audit division within GDCD. There is a further, outside check in that at the NII's request the CEGB has contracted an independent firm (Lloyds) to 'quality control' selected contractors' QA on Heysham 2.

A second important early organizational task was achieving effective integration between the CEGB and NNC. The NNC accepted its new role of agent almost immediately, at least corporately. Apart from the difficulties of role change, the different bases upon which the CEGB and the NNC were organized created some difficulty. The CEGB team was organized on a project basis[12]; the NNC, on the other hand, was organized as a weak matrix. Despite these differences in orientation, considerable efforts were made in order to make the CEGB–NNC relationship a success.

Fifty per cent more programme time was allowed for Heysham 2 than for Hinkley Point B (Figure 6.7), resulting in a 78 months programme for the first unit. The project was, however, driven to a target programme of 75 months. The investment programme, used in the project appraisal to calculate the project's net effective cost [17], was 90 months.

The original strategy was that design would be completed before hardware contracts were let. Design was to have been completed by 31 December 1979 but work fell two months or more behind schedule. This was partly due to the problems of getting the required resources effectively mobilized sufficiently quickly, but partly since the amount of work involved in substantiating the design to the satisfaction of the NII was greater than anticipated, as already discussed. The original strategy did recognize, however, that some early material orders would have to be placed in order to meet the target commissioning date, and in fact early manufacturing did begin on gas baffles, diagrids and liners, boilers, charge machines and gas circulators.

Taylor Woodrow began preliminary site construction work in April 1979. There were some early 'trial of strength' labour disputes, which were firmly withstood, as was a more serious three week dispute in March 1981 and a five week one in May the same year. Taylor

---

[12] Additionally, the project was supported within Barnwood on a (strong) matrix basis in so far as resources were allocated to it from functional service units on an as-needed basis.

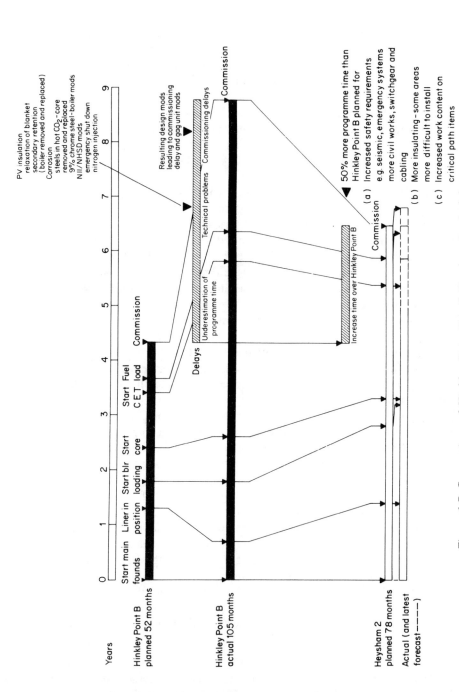

Figure 6.7 Comparison of Hinkley Point B and Heysham 2 schedules

Source: Central Electricity Generating Board

Woodrow, supported strongly by the CEGB and members of the Management Group, were absolutely firm in rejecting issues in dispute as being outside the working agreement. Finally, a meeting at the highest level between Taylor Woodrow and the union agreed to convene a panel of inquiry, which found for Taylor Woodrow. There have been virtually no labour problems on Heysham 2 since then other than a brief dispute over a (wrongly) suspected occurrence of legionnaires' disease (June 1984), some problems on developing a payment-by-results scheme for the cabling operatives and difficulty in introducing double day shifts. Double day shift was first used on Drax, where it was introduced as soon as a contractor began work on site. Double day shift is unpopular with the operatives, as it is fairly disruptive of normal social habits.[13] On Heysham 2, it was not introduced until March 1982 by which time Whessoe had already been working on site on a single shift basis for some months. Whessoe operatives resented double day shift and productivity was in consequence poor for some time.

The Management Group practice was established early in 1981 and got off to a good start. Off-site managers from all the major contractors together with the CEGB industrial relations (IR) officers on-site and from Barnwood, a representative of the Engineering Employers Federation and the NNC's industrial relations officer and construction manager meet under the chairmanship of the CEGB's project manager. The National Agreement for the Engineering and Construction Industry (NAECI) came into effect in November 1981. Heysham 2 was a 'nominated site'[14] and as a result a Project Joint Council (PJC) was established covering mechanical and electrical trades. This comprised ten representatives from the contractors, ten from the unions (three site shop stewards and seven local officials) and an independent chairman. The PJC endorsed a site agreement for the project. There is widespread consensus that the PJC has been beneficial. Discipline has been main-

---

[13] A typical double day shift pattern is 6.00 a.m. to 2.30 p.m. four days a week and 6.00 a.m. to 1 p.m. one day a week for the first shift, and 3.00 p.m. to 12 midnight four days a week and 2.00 p.m. to 7.00 p.m. one day a week for the second shift.

[14] Under NAECI certain large sites are nominated. A number of measures are contained under the agreement aimed at eradicating major labour difficulties, specifically:

—control of bonus payments nationally by establishing fixed limits within which incentive payments may fluctuate;
—increasing the proportion of basic rate to bonus pay in the weekly wage packet, thereby stabilizing earnings and reducing the impact of problematic bonus schemes;
—creation of dispute procedures and investigatory arrangements involving all parties interested in the project as a means of securing a rapid and effective resolution of the problems;
—promoting full consultation at all levels through the National Joint Council/Project Joint Council structures between the parties on all issues affecting individual projects and the engineering construction industry as a whole.

tained—in fact, the industrial relations situation on large construction projects throughout the country has improved dramatically since the introduction of NAECI. Just how much this is due to the rise in unemployment and the generally poor prospects within the industry is of course impossible to say; while undoubtedly a factor, so too, it is felt, is NAECI. On Heysham 2, the PJC has concerned itself primarily with the double shift—hours, cycle frequency, premiums. A measure of the improvement in industrial relations is that whereas 2,500 operatives were considered the maximum number that could be handled on-site from an industrial relations viewpoint in the 1970s, at Heysham 2 there have been 6,500 (4,000 of whom being in NAECI)—with virtually no problems. This is a remarkable achievement.

In September 1981, full financial sanction of the project was requested. Prior to giving this, a seven man senior audit team, drawn from the CEGB and NNC, was asked to review the project. The team commented upon two areas where the programme appeared under some threat and upon the overall 'design risk', but in general gave the project a favourable report. The two areas were the civils contract—in the CEGB's opinion, Taylor Woodrow had not manned their work at the speed that the programme required—and the pressure vessel liner and gas baffle—manufacture had been held up by the national steel strike in the spring of 1980 which had delayed Whessoe's work by three months; rescheduling of on-site work allowed this slippage to be recovered, however. The programme was compressed by bringing forward the lift-in date of the gas baffle to further compensate for these delays. The audit group were satisfied that basing the design on the 'known' Hinkley Point B design, coupled with the rigorous implementation of design freeze dates, brought the design risk to an acceptable level.

A special task force was set up by NEI Power Engineering with support from the CEGB, NNC and SSEB early in 1982 to tackle welding problems which were arising in the manufacture of the boilers. As a result, the programme schedule was maintained. Some problems in the design of the boiler supports and gas seals were experienced but in general manufacturing work proceeded on schedule.[15]

Perhaps the biggest threat to the construction schedule came in the pressure vessel. The pressure vessel liner was rolled into position in January 1982, just one week late. Shortly afterwards, Whessoe introduced double day shift work; as already described, this met with resistance from the workforce. Poor productivity was compounded by an

---

[15] A fuller description of the construction history of Heysham 2 may be found in a paper by S. F. Newey, Heysham 2's project manager, in *Nuclear Energy* [18].

Figure 6.8 View down roll-in track after the liner roll-in
Source: *Central Electricity Generating Board*

underestimation of the work required to be done and by under-resourcing. In addition, there was partial failure of one of the temporary supports during jack-down of the liner. As a result, concreting of the pressure vessel could not begin until four months after the scheduled date. Concreting then went slower than planned and progress now fell 22 weeks behind schedule. A rescheduling of the concrete pour sequence, however, allowed some of the progress to be made up. To compensate for the further loss of progress, construction activities were reprogrammed. Delays were experienced in the delivery of secondary shutdown pipework but these were overcome.

Special attention had to be given to ensuring that the boilers were installed on schedule, which meant overcoming problems experienced with defective welds, late release of design information and inclement weather. In fact, the boilers were installed in virtually only half the time anticipated due to the special efforts of all concerned, particularly NEI Nuclear Systems. Graphite laying of the core encountered difficulties in alignment which delayed the programme ten weeks or so. A major problem then arose in the vessel roof insulation. Hot spots were noted on Hunterston B and as a result new material stress codes had to be developed. This required the contractor, Darchem, to rearrange their work schedule but ultimately it did not affect the overall programme.

Guide tube erection in 1985 went extremely well and this allowed for much of the delay previously experienced to be made up. In January 1985, the work was four months behind the (75-month) target programme, by July only two.

Delays were experienced in pipework installation around the boiler (partly due to a company takeover and change in management), many of which have been largely 'scheduled out' by the NNC. These delays affected the start of proof pressure testing, the first of the combined engineering tests leading to commisioning.

A special task force was set up in 1984 to deal with the emerging problems and delays in the delivery and performance of computer hardware and software. Testing of the complex computer systems required extensive schedules of precise data, the provision of which took considerable resources on the part of the NNC and the CEGB. Despite this management attention, delays were still experienced.

Figure 6.9 Heysham 2 construction
Source: *Central Electricity Generating Board*

Temporary computer facilities therefore had to be used in order for commissioning not to be compromised.

Cabling, as a 'last in line' activity, was inevitably affected by the schedule disruptions, though work progressed as smoothly as possible, largely due to the Matthew Hall's good management. The cabling contract was managed using CADMEC, a computer system developed by the CEGB for the design, estimating, scheduling, installation measurement and payment for cabling work. Over 45,000 cables were laid on Heysham 2, about 50 per cent more than the initial estimates indicated. The growth in cabling was due to the increase in safety requirements, greater control and instrumentation requirements, and the greater use of computers.

Other computer systems used by the CEGB for managing Heysham 2 include SNAP (network analysis), SMART 2 (resource scheduling), computer aided engineering, quantity surveying, information retrieval, and drawing office records. A project financial evaluation system (PROVAL) and various statistical analysis systems were also used.

The overall programme was established in the very earliest stages of the project on the Project Master Schedule. Commitment dates were defined for key items: there were around 3,000 to 4,000 of these. Initially, work was planned by systems, then into contracts and then into plant. For commissioning, activities were again packaged by system. Interfacing was done by the project team at Barnwood. Since contracts were essentially fixed price, progress control consisted basically of monitoring the contractors' spend rates, usefulness of spend and completion date forecasts, with particular attention given to technical problems and resources being allocated, and changes, claims and dayworks issued.

Changes were controlled through an elaborate procedure designed to minimize the incidence of design change. Any proposed change had to be costed and its physical, schedule and financial effects on interfacing systems described; every technical officer in the project team[16] then had to sign his approval of the proposed change; after that, the project senior engineer signed his approval. Prices were sought by the CEGB from the contractor and the project manager was required finally to sign a variation form. NNC's procedure for proposed changes in the nuclear island, were similar, though they additionally required ultimate approval by the CEGB. This procedure worked well to keep changes to a minimum. Changes were largely confined to places where 'risk' had been put into the project (such as the pressure vessel roof following the 'hot spot' modifications mentioned above). Even with this heavy

---

[16] Civil, mechanical, electrical, control and instrumentation, drawing office, programming and computer.

control, however, there were still one or two changes which with hind-sight may not have been totally necessary and whose impact was not fully appreciated.

Commissioning occurs in two stages. First, individual plant is commissioned (under the review of the Plant Completion Committee); second, complete systems are tested (under the review of the Station Commissioning Committee). The NII is intimately involved in this second phase. Two areas of potential concern in licensing were fore-seen: one that the project documentation might not be ready in time; the other that the NII might not be able to assemble adequate specialist resources to meet the programme.

With the greater emphasis on documentation, e.g. in the new QA procedures and the CEGB's new completion and plant commissioning procedures, there was much greater demand on engineers' time in preparing the documentation needed for commissioning and operation[17] and NII approval (the 'Station safety report') than occurred on previous plants. In the event there was some delay in preparation of the 'Station safety report' for submission to the NII though this delay was in fact overtaken by three unforeseen problems, each of which created its own delay.

In mid 1985 engineers at Hunterston B noticed some cracking in the standpipes which pass through the concrete shield over the reactor. At the time these cracks, though important, were not considered critical. Studies were initiated to try to understand the cause of the cracking and to suggest possible resolution. Later, similar cracks were found at Hinkley Point B. It was thought at the time that the problem would not affect Heysham 2 because of slight design differences at the point where cracking occurred. By mid 1986, however, it became apparent that some modification to the fuel plug units on Heysham 2 would be required to overcome the problem and appropriate design and procure-ment activities were therefore initiated.

By this time the Chernobyl accident had occurred. Chernobyl has had a substantial impact on the public and its perception of nuclear power. Even though the design of the AGRs is quite different from that of the Chernobyl reactor, all parties concerned with the British nuclear industry were immediately extremely conscious of the need to pay particular care to ensure public acceptance of the safety of UK reactors. It had been normal practice for NII to examine the 'station safety reports' submitted to it and then, when satisfied, give consent for fuel loading and subsequently for raising power. Their consider-ations were recorded in an in-house report which was prepared

---

[17] Commissioning procedures, O & M instructions and life time records.

subsequent to granting consent. Following Chernobyl, this procedure was changed in that, first, though raising power is more significant from an engineering view, since the public might perceive fuel load as more crucial this stage was now given additional scrutiny by NII; second, it was felt that NII ought to have its in-house reports prepared at the time of fuel load and power raising and not subsequent to these acts.

By early October 1986 it thus looked as though these two events—the fuel plug unit modifications and the delays in NII approvals—would add three or four months' delay to the CEGB's internal programme, with start of fuel loading put back until early 1987. Unfortunately, at the end of October a new and potentially major problem emerged: fretting and rubbing of the control rod assemblies caused by turbulence in the cooling gas around the control rods. The configuration of the nozzles in the gas baffle had been changed from Hinkley Point B to facilitate weld inspection; as a result, the inlet ports on Heysham 2 were slightly different from those on Hinkley Point B. The design change was very small, and in fact had been considered too small for special rig tests, but the consequences to the built plant, with modifications probably required amidst a forest of tightly packed guide tubes, could be substantial. At the time of writing, November 1986, special working groups are studying the problem and its possible resolution. It is expected that Heysham 2's first reactor schedule will be delayed by about three months.

The original sanctioned budget for Heysham at March 1980 price levels was £1,169 million. The current estimate is that the project should be completed within 5 per cent of that budget (at March 1980 prices). Inflation to date has brought the project cost up to £1.8 billion.

Community opposition to the station has proved virtually non-existent. The local community welcomes the plant from a business viewpoint. Relations over Heysham 1 are good. There have been one or two expressions of concern from Lancaster University over potential pollution. A CEGB liaison committee meets on a regular basis to inform the local community of what is happening on Heysham 1 and 2.

OVERALL SUMMARY

The Prime Minister visited Heysham 2 on 1 November 1985. She was told that the success of the project was primarily attributable to four factors:

(1) the use of an established design which was then 'frozen';
(2) a definitive contract strategy with regard to the NNC and contractors and, within the CEGB, defined responsibilities and accountability;
(3) competent management in all areas (technical, organizational, etc.) and enthusiasm;
(4) firm management of industrial relations.

Heysham 2 is undoubtedly a more successful project than the first five AGRs. It is so very largely because of the less uncertain technology and better design and management (the unfortunate problem with the control rods being quite literally the exception which proves the rule). While it is difficult to make an economic case for the monies spent on the first five AGRs, as Henderson has shown [19], in so far as the second phase of AGR construction would appear to have only a modest budget overrun, of 5 per cent or so, Heysham 2 and Torness represent a much sounder economic case.

The contractual relationships on Hinkley Point B between the CEGB and TNPG were well defined, but less so between TNPG and the major contractors. This became increasingly awkward as the cost overrun mounted and the financial power of the consortium waned. On Heysham 2, the CEGB, supported by NNC, has been able to exercise rigorous management control over all the major contractors.

The board's technical management of Heysham 2 was generally on a par with that for Hinkley Point B. But importantly, the project management attitude was substantially more considered. The CEGB embarked upon Heysham 2 after a considerable amount of scrutiny of its approach to managing major power station projects. And with this base, the board was able to implement much more rigorous management than on previous nuclear projects. The emergence of the control rod problem only goes to demonstrate the need for the utmost care in managing such complex technology. The small design modification to the inlet ports was not rig tested which, with hindsight, it should have been.

While industrial relations was not a significant problem on Hinkley Point B, it was on many major projects in the 1970s. The lessons of joint management–union discipline, of rigorous enforcement of industrial relations policies early in the project, and of coordinated policies between contractors, appear abundantly evident.

The two critical industry-wide decisions discussed in this account of the AGR—the selection of the first generation reactor type (Dungeness B) and second generation (Heysham 2/Torness)—exhibit the worst problems of such major technical decision making: vested interests and fierce lobbying on technical grounds against vaguely formulated commercial and industrial management backgrounds, with the onus ultimately being put, unfairly, on politicians who clearly lacked the requisite technical expertise.

REFERENCES

1. Hazelrigg, G. A. and Roth, E. B., 1982.
2. Hannah, L., 1982; Williams, R., 1980.
3. Monopolies and Mergers Commission, 1981.
4. National Nuclear Corporation, 1981.
5. Hannah, L., 1982; Williams, R., 1980.
6. Henderson, P. D., 1977.
7. Williams, R., 1980.
8. Ibid.
9. House of Commons, 1967.
10. Williams, R., 1980.
11. Ibid
12. Newey, S. F., 1981.
13. Monopolies and Mergers Commission, 1981; National Economic Development Office, 1970, 1976; Wilson, A., 1969.
14. Monopolies and Mergers Commission, 1981.
15. National Economic Development Office, 1970.
16. Nuclear Regulatory Commission, 1984; British Standards Office, 1978.
17. Monopolies and Mergers Commission, 1981.
18. Newey, S. F., 1985.
19. Henderson, P. D., 1977.

Chapter Seven

The Fulmar North Sea Oil Field

No oil was extracted from the North Sea until 1975. By 1985, Britain's North Sea production was one of the largest in the world after Russia, the United States of America, Saudi Arabia and Mexico. The scale of expenditure—around £45–50 billion in 1984 terms—and management effort which has gone into developing the North Sea oil province is staggering.

Development of North Sea oil and gas was triggered by the United Nations Conference on the Law of the Sea in 1958 in which it was agreed that coastal states would have sovereign rights to exploit the Continental Shelf and in which the median line principle for the allocation of offshore acreage was established. In 1959 a giant onshore gas field was discovered at Groningen in northern Holland. Shell and Esso worked on a joint-venture basis for the development of this, and subsequent fields in the Netherlands. Later, Shell UK Exploration and Production—known also as Shell-Expro—was formed and employed as the vehicle for Shell's fifty–fifty participation with Esso, with Shell as operator, in exploration and production, in the UK sector. The first non-commercial, offshore oil discovery was in the Danish sector in 1966 and the first major discovery was made by Phillips Petroleum in the Norwegian sector at Ekofisk in 1969. A small field was also discovered in the UK sector at Montrose in 1969 but it was the discovery of the huge Forties field in 1970 and Brent in 1971 that established the United Kingdom as a major oil area and provided the impetus to the enormous development efforts of the offshore industry.

Since these first discoveries there have been some 35 or so fields developed [1], more or less in three phases (Table 7.1 and Figure 7.1). The first phase covered those fields developed in the early 1970s and was characterized by enormous uncertainties over physical conditions, design techniques and construction methodology, with development undertaken by an industry with little native experience in offshore work, particularly at the depths of the Central (300 feet) and Northern

Table 7.1 UK Central and Northern Basin fields: chronology and facilities

Operator/field Block number Water depth in ft(m)	Discovery to first production	Development[1] Time scale in months	Facilities
Amoco North West Hutton 211/27 492 (150)	1975 1983	96	One steel platform docked over 7 template wells, 20 inch oil export line to S Cormorant, 10 inch gas line to Western Leg
Marathon South Brae 16/7a 367 (112)	1977 1983	72	One steel platform, 30 inch oil export line to Forties C
BP Magnus 211/7a,12a 610 (186)	1974 1983	109	One steel platform, 7 subsea satellite wells, 24 inch oil export line to Ninian Central, 20 inch gas line to Brent A-Northern Leg
Philips Maureen 16/29a 318 (97)	1973 1983	127	One steel gravity-base platform docked over 19 pre-drilled template wells, concrete ALP/shuttle tankers for oil export
Conoco Hutton 211/27, 28a 485 (148)	1973 1984	130*	One tension-leg platform installed over 9 pre-drilled template wells and tied-back, 12 inch oil export line to NW Hutton
CFP Total Alwyn North 3/4a, 9a 442 (135)	1975 1987	144*	Two steel platforms, 12 inch oil export line to Ninian Central, 24 inch gas export line to Frigg TCP2
Sun Balmoral 16/21a, 21b 479 (146)	1975 1987	144*	One floating production platform, 8 satellite and 11 template wells to 14 slot pre-drilled seabed template/manifold, 14 inch oil export line to Braes-Forties pipeline
BP West Sole 48/6	1965 1967	16	Three platforms, 16 inch and 24 inch pipelines to Easington Terminal

98 (30) Shell/Amoco Leman Bank 49/26, 27, 28 125 (38)	1966 1968	28	16 steel platforms (+5 planned), 3 30 inch pipelines to Bacton Terminal
Phillips/Arpet Hewett 48/28, 29, 30, 52/4, 5 75 (23)	1966 1969	33	Five steel platforms, 2 subsea wells, two 30 inch pipelines to Bacton Terminal
Amoco/Shell Indefatigable 49/18, 19, 23, 24 98 (30)	1966 1971	63	Nine steel platforms, 30 inch pipeline to Leman Bank. 2 small platforms planned
Conoco Viking 49/12a, 16, 17 85 (26)	1965 1972	80	13 steel platforms, 28 inch pipeline to Theddlethorpe Terminal
Conoco Victor 49/17, 22 108 (33)	1972 1984	148*	One steel WH platform docked over 5 pre-drilled template wells, 16 inch pipeline to Viking B
Hamilton Esmond, Forbes and Gordon 45/8a, 13a, 15a, 20a 115 (35)	1969 1985	192*	Four steel platforms, 24 inch pipeline to Bacton Terminal, 10 inch and 12 inch infield pipelines
Shell Esso Sean 49/25a 105 (32)	1969 1987	221*	Three steel platforms (+1 future), 30 inch pipeline to Bacton Terminal

1 From discovery to first production.
* Estimated.
Source: Thomas [2]. Copyright SPE-AIME; first presented at the European Petroleum Conference, London, 1984.

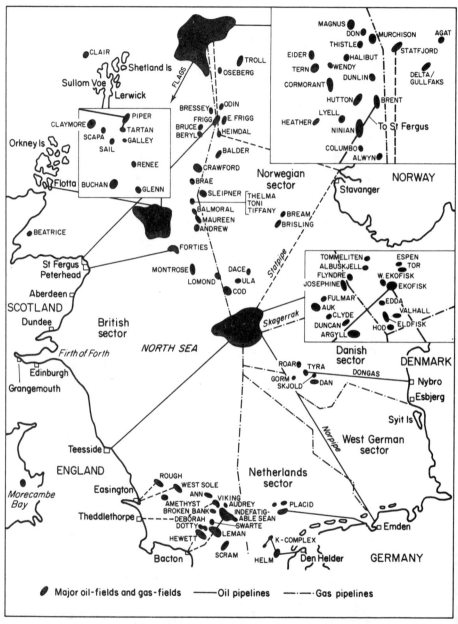

Figure 7.1 Oil and gas fields and pipelines in the North Sea
Source: *Whitehead [3] and Kogan Page*

(450 feet) basins or in environments of such hostility.[1] As a result, these projects experienced substantial overruns.

The second generation of fields, roughly those of the late 1970s and early 1980s, reflected the much greater experience of an industry that had tried and tested many methods in the preceding seven or eight years and had learnt much from manufacturing and installing such deepwater structures.

The third generation are those facing development in the late 1980s. The challenge now is one of bringing projects in with the minimum of unnecessary expenditure since the reduced price of oil is making the economics of these fields in many cases marginal.

THE DEVELOPMENT OF FULMAR

Block 30/16 in the UK sector of the Central North Sea was awarded in 1972 to Shell-Expro in the fourth round of licences (Table 7.2). The block is 194 miles east of Dundee where the water depth is 270 feet. The reservoir was discovered in November 1975 and was code named Fulmar. A project team was formed in July 1976 while further

Table 7.2   Licence rounds for UK offshore fields

Round	Area	No. of blocks offered	No. of blocks awarded
First 1964	North Sea	960	348
Second 1965	North Sea, Irish Sea Channel	1,102	127
Third 1970	North Sea, Irish Sea West Shetland	157	106
Fourth 1971–2	North Sea, Irish Sea West Shetland	436	282
Fifth 1976–7	North Sea, Irish Sea Celtic Sea, West Shetland	71	44
Sixth 1977–8	North Sea, North West Shetland, Western Approaches, West of Wales	46	42
Seventh 1980–1	Company nominated area of North Sea Government nominated area of North Sea, West Shetlands Western Approaches, Channel	—	42

Source: Brown & Root

[1] Waves of over 100 feet and winds of 150 miles per hour are experienced.

geological and seismic work was carried out. An appraisal well was tested early in 1977. The reservoir is located in Upper Jurassic sands at a depth of 10,000 feet. So good is the structure of the reservoir that it was possible, in July 1977, to declare the field commercial on the basis of the information provided by the single appraisal well. Ultimate recovery is estimated to be almost 427 million barrels of stabilized crude.

As is common in oil joint ventures, one of the partners, Shell, is responsible for the development work, the other, Esso, exercising only a review function within the joint venture. Shell-Expro is currently Britain's biggest private investor, having constructed, at the time of writing, 9 of the 43 platforms so far built for the North Sea: its capital expenditure in the North Sea over the past 20 years has been over £13 billion in 1985 terms. Shell-Expro's first field was Auk, a small field in the Central Basin [4]. In the same year, 1971, Shell-Expro discovered Brent, a giant field in the North Basin. In 1973 it discovered South Cormorant, also in the Northern Basin, and in 1973 Dunlin, next to Brent. In 1974 North Cormorant was found and in 1975 Fulmar, near Auk. Other Shell-Expro finds since Fulmar include the large Gannet field and Kittiwake in the Central Basin, and Eider and Tern in the Northern Basin. Figure 7.2 shows the position of these fields.

Fulmar was the first field to be developed following moves by the UK Government to control the rate at which oil could be produced. Between 1964 and 1975, exploration and exploitation of the UK North Sea fields were governed by the Continental Shelf Act of 1964. In 1975, the Petroleum and Submarine Pipelines Act and the Oil Taxation Act were introduced. Among items covered by the first Act were the establishment of the British National Oil Corporation and the requirement that licensees submit a programme of work for the development of a field which had to be approved by the Secretary of State for Energy before work could start. The Oil Taxation Act (enacted at the time of the second oil shock) introduced a selective tax on oil production known as the Petroleum Revenue Tax, or PRT.

PRT and this background of increasing government regulation had a direct impact on the way Fulmar was developed, in terms both of its broad strategy and specific design configuration. Under PRT, production was taxed at 45 per cent. No tax relief was allowed on interest charges on capital borrowed although to offset this an 'uplift' on capital invested of 75 per cent was allowed against the developer's overall tax burden. (Further, the first 1 million long tons per annum of production were allowed tax free for 10 years.) Since relief could additionally be obtained on capital invested under corporation tax, there was in effect a total uplift on capital invested of 90p in the £1.

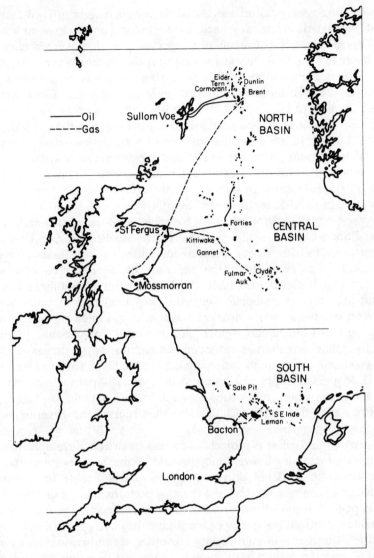

Figure 7.2 Major Shell-Expro Oil and Gas fields in the North Sea
Source: *Shell UK Exploration and Production*

This was a very considerable incentive to licensees to invest rapidly to develop fields quickly.

It was only natural therefore to move ahead quickly before amendments or restrictions might be applied by the government, which seemed increasingly likely in 1977, particularly given the exceptionally encouraging geological prospects and robust economics offered by the field. All oil field economics place heavy emphasis on Net Present Value (NPV); in conditions of regulatory uncertainty, such as were becoming apparent in late 1977, it was only natural that future revenue should be discounted even more heavily than would normally be the case.

In August 1978 there were indeed regulatory changes. The tax rate was increased to 60 per cent, the 'uplift' was reduced to 35 per cent and the 'oil allowance' was reduced from 1 million long tons to 500,000 metric tonnes. In addition, the practice of granting lifetime approvals for development schemes—i.e. no government restriction on production—was halted. All future development had to operate on the basis of staged approvals; only the fourteen commercial discoveries in operation prior to June 1978 were exempt.

Suggestions that there might be a change in government policy had caused Shell-Expro, along with other North Sea licensees, to indicate a reluctance to incur major financial commitments until these changes became known. To facilitate this situation, the Secretary of State for Energy, Eric Varley, had in 1977 provided 'assurances' that there would be no prorating of production until January 1986 or four years from the start of production, whichever was the later. Following agreement with the Gas Council and Amoco, licensees of the neighbouring block 30/11b into which Fulmar extended, on unitization,[2] a development and production programme was submitted to the Department of Energy on 31 May 1978. Approval followed on 2 June. Approval was given for about ten years' production, though in two sequential phases of approximately five years each. Fulmar thus became the government's first staged approval.

An early task of the project team had been the development of alternative methods of developing the field. Some 30 different methods were reviewed in detail during mid 1977. Considerable uncertainty existed as to the best method of exporting both the oil and the gas. An initial possibility had been to use the Norpipe line[3], from Ekofisk to Teesside. It proved politically unacceptable, however, for UK oil to be exported through a foreign facility. Another option was obviously to build a new oil pipeline, but a more economical suggestion was to load the oil offshore. As a result a modified large tanker (210,000 tons) is permanently moored to the well (by means of a single anchor leg mooring, SALM) to provide storage and allow uninterrupted

---

[2] Unitization is the arrangement under which licensees of neighbouring blocks agree the proportions they will invest and receive (in revenue) in the development of a field. As a result of the unitization agreement, Amoco, British Gas, Amerada, Texas Eastern and Mobil all took small percentage shares in the field.

[3] Norpipe is a joint venture between Statoil and Phillips Petroleum.

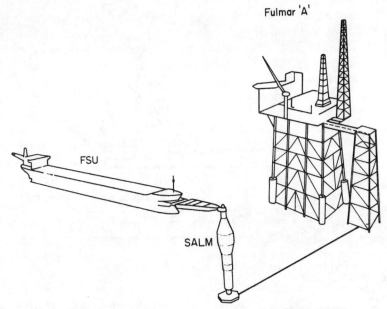

Figure 7.3 Fulmar field schematic arrangement of facilities (FSU = Floating Storage Unit; SALM = Single Anchor Leg Mooring)

production (Figure 7.3), transport to shore being provided by shuttle tankers.

The export of associated gas involved even greater uncertainty. Flaring is strictly controlled by the government and, at the time, proposals were afoot for a Central North Sea Gas-gathering System (later abandoned). Pending the resolution of these uncertainties, it was decided to inject the gas back into the reservoir as a temporary measure until a pipeline for export became available. (At the time of writing, late 1986, a gas pipeline bringing gas from Fulmar, passing near the Gannet and Kittiwake fields to land at St Fergus in north-east Scotland, was nearing completion.)

A further major design innovation concerned the method of achieving early production. For the reasons mentioned above, strong early production was highly desirable. Various early production schemes, using a semi-submersible rig (i.e. a floating structure whose buoyancy is below the wave line—see Figure 7.4), a jack-up (i.e. a structure which rests on, and is jacked-up off, the sea floor—see Figure 7.5) or the storage tanker, were investigated, but rejected for economic, weather or limitation on gas-flaring reasons [5]. Ultimately it was decided to predrill up to six wells using a jack-up, then place a well-head jacket over these wells and extend the wells up through the jacket;

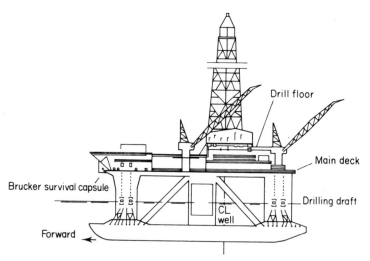

Figure 7.4 Twin-hull semi-submersible drilling rig
Source: *Whitehead [6]*

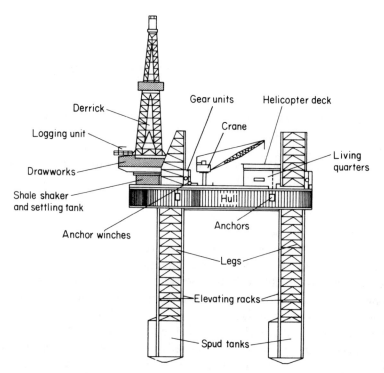

Figure 7.5 Elevation of jack-up drilling unit
Source: *Whitehead [7]*

all this going on while the oil platform jacket and topsides[4] were being fabricated and installed. Priority could then be given in hook-up[5] and commissioning to processing the oil from these wells rather than having to drill wells and extend them up the jacket simultaneously with hook-up and commissioning. This, it was hoped, might allow 'oil-out' up to five months earlier, with obvious economic advantages.

The proposed scheme—of well-head jacket, main platform, SALM, moored tanker and gas reinjection—was agreed in principle in October 1977. A management plan was agreed at the same time which defined the project objectives and the organization and procedures which were to be used to achieve them.

ORGANIZATION OF THE PROJECT

At the time the decision was taken to develop Fulmar, Shell-Expro was experiencing escalating costs and schedule overruns on its North Sea development projects, particularly on Brent, at an alarming rate. Until this time all the work on these fields had been organized on a functional basis. Because of these difficulties, however, the joint venture decided to adopt a project form of organization. The project team established in 1976 was in fact one of the first project teams to be formed in Shell-Expro.

Even then, however, not all the work was executed on a purely project basis. Both engineering and materials procurement were carried out on a largely functional basis. (Later fields have engineering and materials procurement organized as part of the project teamwork.)

ENGINEERING

Conceptual design was developed by central engineering, though detailed design was developed by a design contractor, McDermott, under Shell supervision. Unfortunately, because of uncertainty over oil

---

[4] 'Topsides' is the term which refers to all the facilities which rest on top of the platform substructure (and includes processing modules, drills, crew's quarters, helipad, etc.).

[5] 'Hook-up' is the process of installing and connecting the pre-assembled topside facilities on the platform.

and gas export options and reservoir characteristics, the field development plans were forced to retain considerable flexibility well past the date at which the schedule called for the conceptual design to be completed. Conflict was thus created, on several dimensions. Classic tensions developed between those responsible for engineering and those responsible for maintaining schedule; conceptual design was not in fact finalized until eight months after the start of the design contract so that the design consultant found that the amount of design was vastly different from what he had bid; as a result there were significant cost increases and the design was completed about 20 months late. These difficulties were exacerbated by the somewhat awkward administrative arrangements between the project team, central engineering and the design consultant. The three parties were physically separated (in the Shell Centre, Shell-Mex House and Wembley respectively); further, the design consultant had two separate contracts, for topsides and the substructure (which had been bid and won separately by McDermott), which were administered by separate teams.

During the course of the design numerous modifications were made. Some of these were required to increase efficiency, e.g. the decision to export crude oil in a 'hot' form rather than 'dead', but many were forced on the design because of unavoidable requirements. As the design developed and detailed data came in from equipment vendors, concern grew over the growth in equipment size and weight. As a result, it became apparent that the design of the deck would have to change substantially: the previously empty 'cellar' deck became filled with equipment and additional flooring and steelwork became necessary. The installation programme also had to be altered substantially.

PROCUREMENT

Virtually all the materials and equipment used in Fulmar were purchased by Shell-Expro. (The joint-venture companies prefer to retain responsibility for procurement as opposed to letting the fabricator or design consultant procure items, because they feel they can exercise better control this way.) McDermott was responsible for preparing specifications and raising requisitions. Shell's central materials purchasing function was responsible for placing orders (with McDermott) and expediting, and (with the project team) for transportation and materials control. The project team was responsible for customs.

quality and cost control, hook-up procurement and overall coordination. Procurement of steel was particularly effective; electrical cabling was another well-managed item. Transportation, warehousing and customs in general also worked well. On the other hand, because of the uncertainty and changes in design, specification preparation caused numerous problems. There were particular difficulties in the purchase of bulk materials, in great measure because this was not organized on a project-specific basis and because, in order to keep to schedule, construction of the modules began when the design was only 30–40 per cent complete. Material ordering was affected by the delay in finalizing specifications; some piping, for example, had its specification changed eight times. There was continuous updating of materials and several hundreds of small supplementary orders; material arrived late, particularly piping.

The organizational split of the materials management between engineering, project management, and central materials purchasing led to lengthening of the procurement cycle and some delays in the transmittal of vendor information to engineering, and in expediting. Coordination of materials requirements and technical and status information was further hampered by the lack of a central computerized materials control system. Few of these problems are surprising given the transition being accomplished on Fulmar from a strongly functionally orientated approach within Shell-Expro to a more purely project one.

FABRICATION

With McDermott assisting central engineering and the project team in Fulmar's design and specification preparation, and with central purchasing responsible for the ordering and expediting of materials, the stage is now set for considering the third major project activity: onshore construction. This was divided into ten major contracts, executed simultaneously at eight sites in five countries (England, France, Germany, Holland and Scotland). At peak work load, 3,500 people were involved in fabrication. Coordination of this work was the responsibility of the project team. This involved establishing contract strategy, recommending contractors and monitoring performance.

The contract strategy adopted was to let lump sum competitive bids wherever possible, using a new form of agreement developed for North Cormorant. (Previous projects had used a form developed from the Institution of Civil Engineers' Conditions of Contract, 4th Edn.) The

North Cormorant form was a version of a basic Esso contract form modified by a UK firm of quantity surveyors. As a result, it still retained reference to the independent engineer which, with hindsight, has been deemed unnecessary and has been dropped for later fields. Where the design was not sufficiently developed, bills of quantities (BOQ) contracts were used with reimbursement on a measurement basis.

An important element of the contract strategy was that the schedule had to be maintained. Accordingly, all the contracts were let between July and November 1978. Since the design was late and was not completed at this time there were numerous changes subsequently on all the contracts. Potential fabricators were sought throughout Europe and were carefully evaluated. In order to ensure that the best UK fabricators were employed, negotiations were held with two fabricators for the construction of four modules. All contracts had to pass before a tender board, which they would do at least twice: once for approval of the bid list and once for approval of contract award. Similarly, responsibilities for administration of the contracts were sometimes not as clearly defined between engineers and contracts staff as they might have been.

The main fabrication contracts were as follows:

Well-head jacket fabrication: Redpath De Groot Consortium (RGC)
Living quarters and helideck design and build: Blohm und Voss
Main jacket fabrication: Highland Fabrications
Modules M1 and M2 fabrication: Sea & Land Pipelines (SLP)
Modules M3 and M4 fabrication: William Press
Modules M5 and M6 fabrication: Ponticelli Frères
Main platform, deck and deck facilities fabrication: De Groot International
SALM fabrication: Rijn-Schelde-Verolme (RSV)
Tanker conversion and drilling packages: CNC
Drilling packages fabrication: Dan Smedvig

The RGC contract for the well-head jacket was one of the unhappiest of all the contracts. RGC had limited experience and facilities; these difficulties were exacerbated by design changes and consequent materials delivery delays. Awkward and unclear contract terms and conditions further aggravated matters. The contract was fixed price lump sum, but rates for new work were not included in the contract and there were some ambiguities in work scope. Ultimately, load-out was accomplished six weeks later than planned, primarily because of late deliveries, welding problems, poor weather and resource shortages: costs were 28 per cent higher than planned.

The Blohm und Voss work for the living quarters and helideck was let on a fixed-price, lump-sum, design and build basis. Structurally, the living quarters were built using a stressed skin system. Had the scope and performance requirements been in accordance with what Blohm und Voss thought they had contracted to undertake, the original delivery date would have been met. As it was, however, despite all attempts to freeze the design, many contract changes were created. Full compensation for changes was difficult to negotiate, in part because this was the first offshore module built by Blohm und Voss and represented design, certification and contract administration practices which were not familiar. Late drawing approval, design changes, tight specifications and the knowledge, through the North Sea 'grapevine', that the project was slipping behind schedule and that delivery was not required by the contract date, all encouraged Blohm und Voss's attitude of working at their own pace.

The fabrication of the main jacket went well, the work being completed within cost and almost on schedule. The contract was fixed price lump sum. The administration of the contract worked smoothly. There was a stoppage of the work about midway through the contract by Highland's labour force in pursuance of a wage claim.

The contract for the fabrication of Modules M1 and M2 was let when the modules design was about 35 per cent complete. It was thus difficult for SLP to assess accurately the scope of work, which in fact virtually doubled over that forecast. SLP was unable to increase its resources to the extent required to meet the original tow-out date of May 1980 and in fact tow-out occurred only in April 1981. At least nine months of this delay was primarily due to changes in design and late equipment and materials deliveries, both of which were the responsibility of Shell-Expro. Costs were approximately 106 per cent higher than originally forecast. Despite these difficulties, the working relationship between SLP and Shell-Expro was good. The form of contract was initially a measure and value contract based on bills of quantities subject to remeasurement and price fluctuation. In September 1980, shortly after most of the structural work was complete, the contract was changed to fully reimbursable. This change was made because it was claimed that heavy losses were being incurred under the bill of quantities rates and that these would be unacceptably high, possibly even threatening bankruptcy, if they were not reviewed for fit-out. SLP management not surprisingly experienced difficulty in planning for the changes required. Communication with the workforce did not always appear as good as it might. The labour force itself was very good, being industrious and having excellent site and trade supervision. The one exception was the welders who created numerous disputes, mostly over bonus.

The experience on Modules M3 and M4, fabricated by William Press, was very similar to that of M1 and M2. With contracts let when design was only 35 per cent complete, there was a substantial change in work scope. Tow-out was delayed from July 1980 to April 1981, largely as a result of design changes and equipment and materials delivery delays. Cost increases were 186 per cent, of which 60 per cent was due to escalation. The contract was changed from bill of quantities rates to enhanced daywork rates in September 1980. Press management found it difficult to plan effectively with such a high incidence of changes. Nevertheless, detailed computer networks were continually produced, although with questionable benefit. Communications between middle management and the shopfloor were not very effective as regards labour planning.

Modules M5 and M6 faired a little better. Work was completed only four and a half months later than planned and costs were only 50 per cent higher than originally forecast, due almost entirely to design changes and equipment and materials delays. The yard, which was in Bordeaux, was excellent, as was the labour force. Communication tended to be verbal rather than written. Formal planning techniques appeared to be used only to meet the requirements of Shell-Expro. Ponticelli had no experience of a bills of quantities form of contract and initially found the cost control and reporting difficult. (As, in fact, did SLP and William Press.)

De Groot International were supposed to start work on the deck fabrication contract in March 1979 but elected not to, thinking that there was plenty of time for such a relatively modest project. Installation was scheduled for June 1980. This end date could have been met had facilities design been handed over by January 1980 together with at least some 75 per cent of the materials required. In fact the lateness of design, scale of design changes and delay in materials delivery meant that there was a five-month slippage in tow-out. Costs increased by approximately 160 per cent. The contract form was measured value, based on bills of quantities. Given the extent of design changes, this was inappropriate, both as a means of assigning costs and of allocating project responsibilities. Client–contractor relationships were in consequence at times very strained. Despite these difficulties, De Groot International performed the work satisfactorily. There were no labour difficulties.

The provision of an SALM/FSU[6] was at that time unique in the North Sea. Meeting the exacting specification necessary to achieve the level of reliability demanded for the installation put substantial strain on the fabricator, Rijn-Schelde-Verolme (RSV). Further, RSV, a

---

[6] FSU is a floating storage unit, the term used for the modified tanker; the SALM is, as already noted, the single anchor leg mooring.

nationalized Dutch company, had bid low in order to win the contract. Lump sum, fixed delivery date contracts were invited from six yards in Europe. In the event only four bid: Aker (Norway), CFEM (France), Blohm und Voss (Germany) and RSV (Netherlands). Only the latter two were able to fabricate at one yard and Blohm und Voss required more time than was offered. RSV had the best facilities as well as the lowest bid and so, despite uncertainties as to the continuation of the existing corporate structure of the group, were awarded the contract in April 1979, for completion by May 1980. Problems were soon experienced, however. As a result, portions of the work were subcontracted out in an attempt to meet the delivery date, at rates well above those of the original contract. This move was opposed by the workforce, which was nervous about its future and feared that, with the worldwide decline in shipyard work and bleak outlook, this might lead to closure of the yard. Management in fact had little or no executive authority over the workforce and assembly teams. Planning and control of work was therefore weak. In general, however, the quality of work was very high. The work was ultimately completed some seven months later than originally planned. There was an increase on the tender price of some 53 per cent, RSV being understood to have suffered a substantial loss on the contract.

The conversion of a tanker to form the FSU was another unique piece of work. Several tankers (owned by different companies) were evaluated before the *Medora*, owned by Shell International Marine, was chosen. Independent valuations were obtained from three shipping brokers and the project paid $5.2 million for the ship. Shell International Marine was employed as a consultant on the conceptual design of the modification, in the selection of the conversion yard and in the supervision of the conversion. The French shipyard Chantiers Navals de la Ciotat (CNC) was chosen from amongst nine shipyards to do the conversion on the grounds of technical ability, past experience and performance, price and client suitability. The contract was awarded in September 1979 on a lump-sum basis with provision for, and anticipating, considerable changes in scope. Completion was scheduled for July 1980. Two companies, GEC and Bluewater, were invited to design the offtake system for a fee. Ashlow Steel offered to complete a design at no cost; this was agreed even though they were not considered potential designers at the time. In fact, Ashlow's design proved the preferable and a contract for detailed design, fabrication and on-site erection and commissioning was signed in July 1979, again on a lump-sum basis with provision for modifications. The tanker conversion was completed about ten months later than originally planned; the final contract price, which was the subject of substantial negotiation, was 95 per cent higher than the original sum, primarily because of design changes, unexpected work, certification requirements, escalation and finance costs. Work on the offtake structure began in the summer of 1979. In September, Ashlow ran into financial difficulties, largely caused by the UK national steel strike. Ashlow's parent company took responsibility for the contract but much of the steel fabrication had to be subcontracted, labour relations deteriorated and progress suffered. Ultimately, CNC were required to complete the offtake connection and commissioning on site in France, at Shell-Expro/Ashlow's expense.

Contractual arrangements for the final major system, the drilling packages, were complex and not particularly satisfactory. Under PRT, there are advantages in co-ventures leasing drilling packages rather than owning them. Agreement was accordingly reached with the Royal Bank of Scotland to finance and own the modules, on a project finance basis, with Shell-Expro acting initially as the engineer (to manage the design and fabrication) and as the lessor. The major contracts were thus placed in the name of Royal Bank Leasing Ltd as the principal, with Shell-Expro as a nominating party. Preliminary design was subcontracted to Dentag (Germany). Dan Smedvig (Holland) obtained the fabrication contract, with Mercon (Holland) as subcontractor, and also the hook-up, commissioning and drilling contract. The contracts were fixed price lump sum, nominated in five currencies. To strengthen its management capability, Dan Smedvig formed a joint venture with Marcom (Holland).[7] Lloyds provided certification and there were half a dozen or so subcontractors. In addition, Mather & Platt designed the fire-fighting facilities. Problems arose in poor change control, resulting in several serious omissions, and in QA, resulting in an absence of requisite documentation. Unfortunately, both these problems only surfaced at the commissioning stage. In March 1980, Shell-Expro was forced to put in a management team of its own and effectively take control of the contract. By June 1980, some commissioning was ready to begin. The contractors were totally unprepared for commissioning and this too had to be taken over by Shell-Expro. Load-out of the pump module and sub-base/substructure was achieved on 15 September. During sea fastening and 100 per cent documentation, and completion of these modules, certain QA documentation was found to be missing. This ultimately necessitated re-inspection during which three weld cracks were found, four days before the barge was due to float downriver. Correction of these took three weeks, final sail-out being on 30 November 1980. Having learnt the hard way, more systematic checks were now made on the remaining engine module, which

---

[7] Marcom is not the same company as Mercon.

amounted almost to a new project; as a result, float-out occurred four months later, on 20 March 1981. The contract was completed almost nine months late; the final contract price was some 42 per cent higher than the original forecast cost.

INSTALLATION, HOOK-UP AND COMMISSIONING

Float-out and installation involved transporting and positioning the 13,000-tonne jacket, the 5,000-tonne deck (in three sections), the six modules (weighing 9,000 tonnes in total) and the 3,000-tonne living quarters and helideck. This was originally scheduled for the summer of 1980, but because of the problems described above it was delayed until

Figure 7.6 Lift-in of the Fulmar A living quarters and helideck
Source: *Shell UK Exploration and Production*

the winter of 1980/1. (Installation was completed in April 1981 with the lift of the living quarters.) As a result, bad weather severely disrupted the programme. For example, the deck was to have been loaded as a single unit. This was in fact attempted five times, each attempt being aborted because of excessive movement of the transporter barge caused by bad weather, before being towed out in three sections. Stormy weather led to a critical situation in the hire of barges and was responsible for some damage to the structures and modules during installation.

All the installation work was carried out by Hereema on a lump-sum basis at a cost of around £35 million. Fulmar was the first platform to use the huge semi-submersibles the *Balder* and the *Hermod*, each of which is fitted with one 3,000-tonne and one 2,000-tonne fully revolving crane. The barges were commissioned on a purely speculative basis by Pieter Hereema in order to provide a year-round heavy lifting capability, something previously unobtainable, and were constructed in Japanese yards. Shell-Expro negotiated the hire of the barges while they were still being built.[8] The vessels could accommodate a workforce of about 200 although the workforce was in fact housed on a 'flotel'. The flotel accommodated at peak during hook-up and commissioning almost 700 persons (of whom almost 400 would be management, supervision, operations and services). This workforce changed on a staggered basis every two weeks, all trips to and from the platform being by helicopter.

Hook-up involves the marrying of the pre-assembled facilities. The awkwardness of hook-up is, in simple English, the lack of space to store anything. On an offshore oil platform, the topside facilities are very tightly packed. Hence, all material must be brought out in barges daily. The logistics operation is thus highly demanding. Hook-up began in December 1980 with the installation of the module support frame to the jacket and the installation of modules M5 and M6. Hook-up lasted about eighteen months, the bulk of it being completed within twelve months. The work was accomplished on time and within budgeted cost. Man-hours (1.4 million) were about 40 per cent higher than foreseen by detailed planning but within management expectation. The success of the hook-up was due in very great measure to the commitment and enthusiasm of the offshore team backed up by the efficiency and dedication of the support staff at Montrose and Wembley. (The project

[8] It is not an exaggeration to say that these huge semi-submersibles, and those which have succeeded them, have almost revolutionized North Sea work. The weather window is no longer the threat that it was and the heavy lifts they are capable of allow increased onshore work and reduced hook-up, which is highly desirable since hook-up is awkward, complex and expensive.

team had moved from London to Scotland as fabrication got under way.) Probably, an even more important cause of the success of hook-up was management's concern to achieve full completion and pre-commissioning onshore, even where this might mean delays offshore. This policy was adopted in consequence of bitter experiences on earlier fields where substantial and expensive delays had been experienced, even when work was apparently 90 per cent complete.

Planning of hook-up had been particularly good. Detailed procedures were ready and there was extensive computer back-up in Montrose. Communications between offshore and onshore were excellent. There were, however, extensive difficulties with the availability of materials. Design changes continued to appear throughout hook-up and there were problems with one or two items of equipment, particularly the gas compressor module which unexpectedly required real gas testing onshore (with all the problems of installing a complete recirculating and flare system in an urban environment) because of potential synchronous vibration problems. Materials problems were caused primarily by the delays in procurement caused by the earlier changes in specification and by understaffing of the onshore base materials group (where staffing levels were deliberately kept down following the feeling that on Brent this function had become too large).

At peak time, 130 people were involved offshore during commissioning, which progressed smoothly.

Oil-out was achieved in February 1982, some ten months later than planned. The final cost of the project was £417 million, about £53 million less than the 1976 forecast of £470 million. The work on the installation proved to be of high quality and has met fully the requirements of Shell-Expro operations.

OVERALL SUMMARY

Fulmar is a successful project. The question at issue is only whether it could have been managed more successfully. This is a question which applies to many if not most North Sea projects because of the tremendous uncertainties and the learning process which the development of the North Sea has represented.

The development of North Sea oil and gas is an astonishing story of industrial endeavour. Major engineering achievements have been accomplished rapidly in conditions of physical uncertainty and hostility. Fortunately, market conditions have been favourable and the government has taken an enlightened fiscal and regulatory stance which has

*Figure 7.7 Fulmar A production platform. The Shell/Esso Fulmar field in the
North Sea started production in February 1982*
Source: *Shell UK Exploration and Production*

permitted these projects to prosper. Recently, however, market
conditions have been becoming more demanding, and government
controls have gradually tightened. All this has meant that there has
been increasing pressure to manage North Sea projects better and
better.

The essential conundrum on Fulmar was whether to wait and resolve
certain outstanding technical issues or whether to push ahead and maintain schedule. Project management chose the latter course. As a result,
the unresolved technical uncertainties trickled all the way through the

project causing enormous problems of changes, extra costs and delay so that the project ended 10 months late. With hindsight, it can be questioned whether fabrication should have proceeded with such an incomplete state of design. Greater realism in appraising the capabilities of the fabricators and the impact of the technical uncertainties on their capacity to perform to schedule might have led to a different decision. Yet, dealing with such uncertainty is the essence of project management: it is inevitable that there will be second thoughts in an industry as young and evolving as North Sea oil and gas was in the late 1970s. Certainly the overall record of Fulmar was far superior to that of earlier North Sea projects.

REFERENCES

1. Thomas, W. A., 1984.
2. Ibid.
3. Whitehead, H., 1983.
4. Lavers, B. A., 1985.
5. Innes, G., 1979.
6. Whitehead, H., 1983.
7. Ibid.

Chapter Eight

The Computerization of PAYE

Computerizing the tax process has long been seen as an undertaking of potential benefit. There are over 27 million taxpayers, 24 million of whom have active records; there are 1.1 million employers. Vast quantities of data need to be processed in a systematic manner. To the extent that computerization would enable data to be processed more quickly, perhaps more accurately, using fewer staff, this would clearly be in the nation's interest.

The Pay-As-You-Earn (PAYE) system of taxation was introduced in 1944. The Department of the Inland Revenue first started looking at the possibility of computerizing PAYE early in the 1960s. A study was commissioned within the department late in 1962. The state of computer technology at the time dictated that processing be done in batch. To reduce data inputting, PAYE work and staff would have to be brought from local offices into nine large clerical centres, each supported by its own computer. The recommendations of the study were costed and approved in mid-1963. A project team was formed and the first system installed, using an ICL 1904, at East Kilbride. Operation began in 1968 and has continued to handle the PAYE of some 2 million persons based in Scotland since then.

The plan was to evaluate the system after a couple of years and then expand it to the other centres as appropriate. The second region was to have been the North West, from Liverpool to Scotland. In fact a building was built in Merseyside, a computer installed and staff were being recruited when there was a change of government in 1970. The Chancellor of the new Heath Government, Ian MacLeod, announced shortly after taking office the suspension of the project while the government investigated the feasibility of a totally new taxation scheme: PAYE was to be abolished and taxation and social security payments were to be merged into one comprehensive tax credit scheme. Upon MacLeod's death in 1970, the new Chancellor, Anthony Barber, continued to work on the scheme. These proposals generated considerable public debate and controversy. Legislation was to be introduced in 1974 to come fully into effect in 1978. The tax credit scheme was to have been computerized. With the change of government in 1974, these proposals were dropped and the computerization of PAYE revived.

Technology had now progressed to the point of permitting on-line data entry using terminals on Revenue staff's desks; this would facilitate data entry and in fact allow decentralized operation. The Inland Revenue accordingly recommended that computerization of PAYE thus proceed along these line. The Treasury and the government Central Computing Agency, however, were not convinced that such a scheme would be practicable, partly, no doubt, because of the difficulties being experienced in computerizing driving licence records at the Driver and Vehicle Licensing Centre (DVLC) at Swansea.[1] Fears were expressed, for example, as to whether staff could perform reliably if working in an on-line, decentralized operation. The Inland Revenue therefore proposed that an experimental pilot project be conducted. The pilot project was approved and a small on-line system (known as PLANET) was accordingly implemented at six tax offices in the West Midlands district in 1977 (Burton, Stafford, Cannock and Shrewsbury). The system was run over lines to a Honeywell computer in Liverpool. There were only sufficient funds sometimes to permit one Visual Display Unit (VDU) between two persons. Nevertheless, the project appeared a significant success when evaluated in 1978. Evaluation was carried out by a group drawn both from the Treasury, the Inland Revenue Department, the Central Computer Agency and 'Trade Union Side' representatives. The evaluation concluded that computerization in this manner posed no problems and that not only could staff adapt to, but in fact many preferred working with, VDUs compared with manual methods.

In 1977, work began on a prefeasibility study for the computerization of PAYE at the national level. This study, which reported favourably in 1977, was led by Steve Matheson who had been secretary to the Chancellor of the Exchequer in 1976 and who was subsequently to play a key role in the project. Early in 1978, a full feasibility study was begun of the project, which was now termed COP—Computerization of PAYE—again under Matheson's leadership. The feasibility study took over 450 person-months of effort and took over two and a half years to complete. Partly this was because the proper study of a complex computerization project should necessarily be rigorous—computerization projects are difficult at the best of times; the risk in this case of

---

[1] The DVLC continued to be plagued by problems for a number of years, most of these being centred on the manual data handling procedures rather than the hardware. Management of that programme has been severely criticized.

failure, and the colossal exposure such failure would receive, meant that more than ordinary care in scrutiny and preparation was required. Partly, the length of feasibility study reflected the typical case of government projects drawing on the public purse. Partly, however, it reflected the defensive climate within Whitehall at the time where there was enormous sensitivity to suggestions, reflecting the DVLC trauma, but made no better by the overruns then being experienced in the construction industries, that such projects would 'inevitably' overrun.

Justification for the project centred on staff savings which computerization would achieve (originally estimated at 6,800 units). The full list of COP's objectives was:

—to increase the efficiency of PAYE, in particular through a reduction in staff costs;
—to improve the service to the public through greater accuracy, reliability and speed of response to communications;
—to provide up-to-date facilities for staff and offer greater job satisfaction;
—to create a system offering greater flexibility for the implementation of future change, either within the present tax structure or in more far-reaching reforms of personal taxation.

COP now represented the largest civil computer project yet undertaken in Europe. With the DVLC troubles still rumbling on, a proposal for another, very large government computer project sent tremors through many quarters of government and industry. The thought of a massive confusion of the public's tax records was sufficient to cause many in Whitehall to pause and think. But also, a government computer contract of this size was creating enormous interest amongst the hardware manufacturers. Under the existing EEC and GATT rules, the government would have been within its rights to award the contract on a sole source basis to ICL, the United Kingdom's only manufacturer of very large computers. Indeed not to have done so might well be seen as a vote of no confidence in British technology. US manufacturers, seeing the contract as the first of several in the important European government market, and having been encouraged by an inquiry from the Treasury early in 1979 outlining user specifications and seeking expressions of interest, were further encouraged in that these EEC and GATT rules were soon due to change. From 1 January 1981 government support contracts, of the kind ICL had previously been receiving from the government (particularly in the development of its 2900 range of computers), would not automatically go to ICL on a single tender basis.

Recognizing the management challenge of the project, several innovative proposals were incorporated into the feasibility recommendations, some quite radical within the context of government projects. First, outside consultants were to be employed in areas where the department felt it was lacking either the technical experience or the commercial bite that this project was felt to require. Crucially, these consultants were to be employed in a line capacity, taking responsibility for their management decisions, directing the work of civil servants working for them, and contributing as full members to the COP team. Second, COP was to have a steering committee overseeing it, comprised of the highest levels of management within the government and project contractors. (It was chaired, for example, by the Permanent Secretary of the Inland Revenue.) Third, a special 'project office' was to be created, under the direction of a single 'project manager' (Matheson, at Assistant Secretary level), to be located in a new town, Telford. This was a bold move since over 120 staff would have to be found right at the outset of the project and relocated to Telford (where they would have little to do except work). Several other extremely sound 'project management' decisions were proposed, which will be described shortly. It would be a mistake, though, to suppose that everything was plain sailing at the 'feasibility' stage.

Sensitivity towards the project remained at a high level within both the industry and Whitehall throughout 1980. Senior civil servants considered the project to be a very high risk one and forecast that it would take two years longer than scheduled, particularly in the initial design, code and test stage up to end 1983. There was also some resistance to certain of the key suggestions such as the use of consultants and the move to Telford. There was particular difficulty over selecting the mainframe (computer) manufacturer. The Treasury, haunted by the DVLC experience, wanted to minimize any project risks as much as possible. Of particular concern was the system software, especially that part concerned with data handling between computer centres ('networking'). The Treasury thus favoured using proven technology. Computer projects of this size had been running in the United States of America for some years and several US firms had adequate technology; ICL, on the other hand, did not. Foreign firms had been lobbying hard to be allowed to bid for the project. By mid 1980, the political pressure was becoming intense. Three Commons motions were tabled urging that the contract be given to ICL. The Cabinet postponed a decision on the contract (16 July) and Callaghan told Thatcher to 'stop dithering'. Then in August, a compromise was suggested in Cabinet that the systems specification should be scaled down so that the overall risk of project failure would be reduced and the specifications be more in line with ICL's existing capability. With the Prime Minister now persuaded of the merits of 'enlightened public purchasing', discussions were held with ICL to see to what extent the project specifications could be satisfactorily met.

The new project specification was that,

—the project be phased,
—there should be four or five networks per region instead of one,
—the programme should be extended to, say, 1987–90 in order to provide the national communications and training facilities and a multi-processing architecture, and
—on-line data transmission between processing centres should only be attempted later in the programme (around 1987–90).

All these adjustments were towards ICL's existing capabilities, although many within the industry were still sceptical over the ability of ICL's software to meet the system's requirements and of the Inland Revenue's ability to see the project through successfully.

On 10 November, the Chancellor, Geoffrey Howe, announced that the project would proceed along these lines with the contract being awarded to ICL. In the same week, ICL publicly announced two new machines, the 2966 and 2955 (large and medium sized processors respectively). The 2966 was, of course, the computer to be used for PAYE and had incurred within the industry the sobriquet, 'the PAYE machine'. Negotiations over the contract were concluded within six weeks and a contract was signed on the 23 December 1980, just seven days after a sharp drop in profits was announced by ICL. On 1 January 1981, the new EEC/GATT rules precluding the award of sole source contracts came into effect. The 'sharp drop in profits' was the harbinger of the near collapse of ICL. By March 1981, the government had to bail out ICL with a £200 million loan guarantee.[2] By May, there was a complete change in ICL top management—a change which, with the announcement by the new managing director, Robb Wilmot, in October 1981 of a collaborative agreement with Fujitsu, has had an important consequence on ICL's ability to develop equipment to meet COP's requirements, as will be described shortly.

As noted, the feasibility study included several 'sound project management' proposals which later proved important to COP's success. Detailed definition of the 'user requirement', careful documentation of system design and resisting the temptation to begin writing the computer programs before fully ready ('rush to code'), were critical

---

[2] There were many and good reasons for supporting ICL but one of the more piquant, in view of the foregoing, was the fact offered by the Minister of Industry, Sir Keith Joseph, that 'There are a lot of ICL computers in Whitehall' [1].

computer project decisions, recognized as 'good practice' for software projects in general [2]. The COP design, it was decided, should reflect fairly closely the existing PAYE working methods in the local tax offices so as to limit the total amount of change for local office staff and thus reduce the risk of possible loss of output upon transferring to computers. Most of the Inland Revenue staff who were to work on the project were intimately familiar with PAYE—some had also worked on the PLANET pilot scheme—and thus brought to the project substantial 'user knowledge'. It was also decided to secure recognition of the need for restraint in making far-reaching changes to the personal tax system during system design and implementation in tax offices. Thus while there have been two major changes dictated by government policy—beginning the taxation of unemployment benefit in 1982 and the introduction of mortgage tax relief at source, also in 1982—fundamental change while computerization is in process has wherever possible been avoided. (Though, this said, there were in addition to the two major legislative changes over 7,000 smaller changes to the specification during the project.)

The project schedule called for the design, development, programming (coding) and testing of the system to be completed in 30 months at a cost, in 1980 prices, of £180 million, including hardware and buildings as well as software. The system was to be installed on a pilot basis in the West Midlands by the end of 1983—1 July 1983 was the target date for system completion/handover for user acceptance trials and 1 October 1983 for going live. The team which had worked on the feasibility study, which included the two firms of Computer Sciences Corporation (CSC) and PACTEL, who had both been retained in a consulting capacity, provided the nucleus of the project management team. Additional staff had to be mustered from within the Inland Revenue Department. It was recognized that consistency of personnel would be an important element of project success. Unusually for a civil service project, therefore, there has been next to no staff turnover (moving to other assignments) except, and this is another unusual aspect, where performance has been inadequate (there has been a tough management policy of 'shape up or ship out'). Even more unusually, there has been promotion 'on the job'. The team, 120 or so, had to begin work in Telford in mid 1981. (The building which had been identified for the Inland Revenue was not ready until mid 1982 so Telford Development Corporation gave temporary accommodation to the department rent free until the building was ready.) The hardest staffing job was finding experienced programmers. In fact, many of the initial team were inexperienced in computer projects. This inexperience of the programmers may have been a blessing in disguise since it forced senior management in the early stages of the project to go to extreme lengths to ensure design requirements were clearly specified and to develop clear coding rules, and it generally helped resist the temptation to rush to code. In fact, almost no one on the project had had experience of a computer project the size of COP.

The project was to be executed by a number of different entities. The Inland Revenue was responsible for the computer systems design, development, coding and testing. Most of this work was managed by CSC staff who were retained as technical management and support consultants. CSC used as their primary management tool their Digital System Development Methodology—a methodology which incorporates in a rigorous way state-of-the-art computer system management processes. Inland Revenue staff have great respect for CSC's methodology, which is discussed further below. PACTEL was responsible for providing an independent project planning and control function, a function which, as shall be seen, provided an essential 'glue' for the project. The Artemis project management computer system was used by PACTEL for this function. ICL provided the mainframes. ICL also won (competitively) the contract for the supply and installation of the VDUs and for the cabling between the VDUs and the processing centre's (computer) controller. (Figure 8.1 illustrates the basic network layout.) Plessey provided a data communications management system. British Telecom provided the long distance data transmission system. Buildings were refurbished by the Property Services Agency (PSA), a government department.

The project organization is shown in Figure 8.2. The principal parties were managed by a single project manager (Matheson), with the exception, that is, of PSA.

The exception of PSA is in some ways curious. As a branch of government, PSA did not feel it appropriate either to assign staff directly to the project under the Inland Revenue's management or to enter into formal (contractual) project commitments. Instead, project staff discussed with PSA staff the need for detailed work planning, the necessity of commitments to work schedules and the importance of tight monitoring. These discussions were given increased weight due to difficulties experienced on the PLANET pilot project. The PSA does not manage building work like that required for COP on a project basis. As the *de facto* landlord of the government's civil estate, the PSA is functionally organized into Regional PSAs, Area PSAs and District Works, great weight being put on the value of local knowledge, (COP is organized by region/processing centre, as shown in Figure 8.3; the COP regions are not the same as the PSA regions.) On PLANET, PSA District Works managers placed orders for jobs to be done but did not

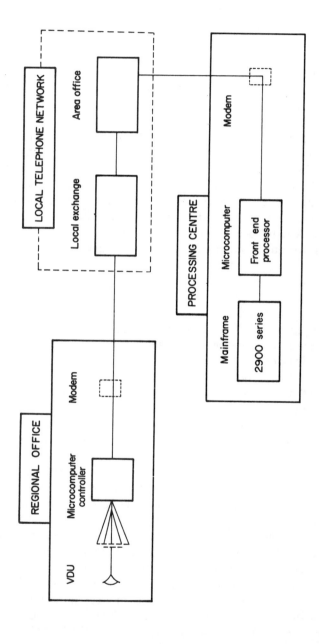

Figure 8.1 Structure of COP network

Source: *Inland Revenue*

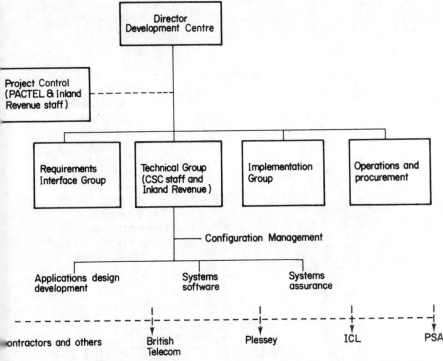

Figure 8.2 Organization of COP

Source: *Inland Revenue*

always follow up the preparation of work. As a result, delays in the building work were frequent. On COP, therefore, the project team were able to talk from a strong position. With their highly detailed project planning and control information, the team were often able to provide PSA with as much or more information on the status of work than PSA staff themselves had. The COP team was thus able to exert real leverage over PSA and control its work as an effective part of the project. The result is that in a project having over 600 offices to rewire and 11 centres to build, at the time of writing, not one deadline has been missed. Should anything go wrong, however, the only sanction COP would have over PSA is ultimately that of the steering committee.

Given the political nature of many of the relationships on COP, e.g. those between the Inland Revenue and ICL, and with PSA, the steering committee was of the utmost importance. As a powerful ultimate sanction, it was a real 'stick'; as a symbol, and a vehicle, of communication and trust between project parties, it was a real 'carrot'. Representation was at the highest level. Its membership was:

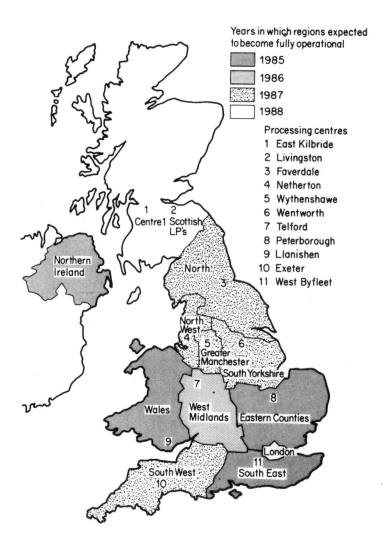

Figure 8.3 COP regions and processing centres
Source: *Inland Revenue*

NOTES
LONDON REGION
1. London Region will have no processing centre of its own. It will be served by the processing centre at Peterborough

SCOTLAND AND NORTHERN IRELAND
2. The Livingston processing centre (operational in 1986) will serve Northern Ireland and London Provincial districts (i.e. tax offices dealing with the PAYE affairs of London-based employers) located in Scotland. Employers based in Scotland will be handled by the Centre 1 processing centre which will be fully operational in 1988.

Permanent Secretary and Chairman of
  Department of Inland Revenue (Chairman)
Deputy Secretary (Policy)
Director General (Technical)   Inland Revenue
Director General (Management)
Director Data Processing
Director Operations
Director Central Computer and Telecommunications Agency
  Under Secretary, Property Services Agency
Managing Director, CSC Ltd
Managing Director, Plessey
Deputy Director, British Telecom
Secretary to the steering committee

In the early phases of the project, the steering committee also included a Deputy Secretary from the Treasury who remained a member effectively until the Treasury was assured that the staffing savings claimed for the project would be achieved. In the view of several of COP's senior management, the steering committee was the single most important reason for the success of the project.

The first task of the consultants upon joining the project was to review the feasibility plan. This contained an implementation plan of unusual detail. Their conclusion was that the plan was 'tight but achievable'. PACTEL's early work centred on reviewing detailed schedules and plans and studying particularly the interfacing aspects and resource requirements. In the event, this proved a difficult task though rather more from a management side than a technical one. Early planning work had a tendency to be dictatorial. Naturally enough, technical experts resented being told by planners what they could, should or should not do. They felt threatened. An uncomfortable climate of over-planning began to emerge which after some months required very careful defusing—as one senior manger put it, 'traumatic accommodation'. PACTEL staff worked hard to correct their approach, adopting instead the highly successful emphasis on integrating the plans of others into a coherent project 'whole' and providing people with the information they want—a manner of working which became the hallmark of COP project management. Early planning of multi-team project work is always difficult; as can be seen in COP, this is not only because of the technical skills required but because of the human ones at a time when relationships are just developing and people are often feeling sensitive and uncertain.

CSC's early tasks centred on establishing the technical capabilities of ICL's hardware and software and the Inland Revenue staff's systems design and coding skills. As noted, there was scepticism as to whether the hardware could in fact meet COP's practical requirements: nominally it could, at least on the phased basis as then defined, but in practice it proved extremely difficult to ascertain whether the hardware was capable, for example, of supporting the volume of transactions COP required—ICL did not appear to have a system of comparable size and type. Further, ICL's software gave considerable cause for concern. The loading on ICL's software would be substantially greater than anything it had previously experienced. Some of the software proposed was on general release but much was pre-release, particularly in the areas of security, recovery and communications. In order to identify those system requirements which could not be met by the ICL proposal, shortly after the contract with ICL was signed, COP decided to require ICL to respond formally to an OR (operations requirement). Some 40 items were subsequently identified as failing to meet COP requirements. COP consequently spent most of 1981 in rigorous verification of the ICL system performance and functionality. Demonstrations of software capability lasted almost one year, at which time there were still deficiencies in the communications software, IPA (Information Processing Architecture). To help protect itself from possible breakdown, COP wrote a huge volume of its own software to interface with ICL's software—so-called 'middleware'. From a technical aspect, the risks posed by this systems environment undoubtedly posed a big threat to the project. There is still in fact a view amongst some senior COP managers that it would have been beneficial if more time could have been spent increasing the security of COP's program environment. That more time was not spent was due partly to the demands made on staff to plan the project at an appropriate level of detail, partly to the need to train new project staff, and partly to the schedule pressure of the project.

Not one person on the project had worked on an on-line database system the size of COP (with the possible exception of the senior CSC consultant, and his experience only approached systems of this size: none had been as big). In fact, as already noted, some of the project team had next to no knowledge of systems design or programming at all. There was thus a very obvious requirement both to train staff and to manage their work in as simple and controlled a manner as possible. Thus in addition to early technical training, the COP Technical Group developed a 'program support environment' which provided a methodology of programming (code writing) which was both extremely clear and had extensive built-in controls. CSC's Digital System Development Methodology (DSDM) had been developed in the mid 1970s to tackle some of the special difficulties faced by computer system development projects.[3] The methodology emphasizes systems definition, multi-faceted emphasis on quality and product assurance, the quantitative measurement of performance (using earned value), and structured system development and configuration management [3]. Care over system definition, in-built quality controls and structured programming permeates the methodology. On COP, this meant that there was great emphasis on the full validation and checking of user requirements to produce a stable, agreed system baseline; a clearly articulated, modularized system architecture and data dictionary; strict control of all changes proposed to the system base (configuration management), all changes being tested on an automated basis; and a rigorous process of system validation. DSDM is a more formal, disciplined version of the way the Department of the Inland Revenue had been controlling systems projects before. DSDM added overhead and in the early stages the value of this extra cost was sometimes questioned. The methodology was soon accepted, however, as invaluable. It turned information technology from, in the words of one manager, 'a black art into a manageable process'. Using DSDM, COP's Technical Group thus created a systems development environment which became standardized to a degree which is both unusual and healthy among systems projects. (For programmers have a natural but dangerous tendency to 'do their own thing' which makes more difficult the management tasks of control and investigation, for instance when searching for an error, coding in the original programmer's absence or determining interface requirements with other programs.) Having inexperienced staff thus proved in many ways an advantage.

COP's first eight to twelve months were, therefore, to some extent frustrating. Less experienced and able management might have been strongly tempted to panic at this time and to have begun 'work' (i.e. coding) before being fully ready. Management resisted this temptation and instead used the early phase of the project for extensive project planning, staff training and the preparation of a secure software environment.

Two other aspects of the project's management, in addition to this very great emphasis on careful documentation of the system requirements and change control, must be mentioned as keys to COP's success. First, there was an overwhelming commitment to success at senior management level. The thought that the schedule might slip was not permitted. (As Brooks has said of systems development, 'you slip a year one day at a time' [4].) If slippage seemed likely, and no other

---

[3] Such as the measurement of progress, control of design quality and high costs of use and maintenance.

way could be found round the problem, more resources were requested. Second, there was no attitude of 'it cannot be done'. If external forces requested modification, COP's response was, 'Yes . . . but here is what it will cost.' Both these points can be subsumed under the heading of good leadership.

The method of project control developed by PACTEL was essentially the classic one of an 'independent project planning and control group'. As Archibald describes it [5], this involves pulling together the plans of others to ensure project objectives will be met and monitoring performance to permit the project team to control progress towards those objectives. The PACTEL project control function is totally independent of the rest of the project team—it acts as an independent 'auditing' group—reporting both to the COP team, the project manager and the steering committee. Outline schedules are developed on Artemis using durations and resources suggested by the functional groups. There may then be four or five resource scheduling iterations before PACTEL asks the functional manager if he will sign off on the final version. Scheduled milestones then become immutable, although the manager is free to reschedule work between the milestones. There are weekly meetings with COP staff and regular meetings with contractors and PSA. Detailed meeting minutes are kept. Artemis has proved essential to COP's project control success. As a sophisticated data-based project control system, COP has been able to tailor Artemis to supply specially designed reports to the many different groups with which PACTEL works. Artemis reports are issued to line managers every Thursday with a request to return them with any changes in activity status duly noted. In this way, the Artemis 'turn-around' document becomes a record of each manager's own statement of his progress. The project control function is not intended as a threat to managers but merely to provide information. Managers thus have the possibility of reviewing matters and if necessary initiating corrective action before discussing progress with senior management.

COP's project plan required the system to go 'live' by 1 October 1983. That day was a Saturday and the system actually went live on Monday, 3 October: an achievement of which COP staff are very proud. The remainder of 1983 was spent keying in data on the 650,000 taxpayers in the West Midlands region so that the system was fully live in the region by 1 January 1984. The system then entered a period of extensive use and overall evaluation lasting until June 1984.

The project budget approved in 1980 for installing the COP system and running the computer centres as they came on stream was (at 1980 prices) £180 million, as previously noted. Updated to 1985–6 prices, using the Retail Price Index, this figure becomes £266 million. The actual cost is currently estimated as £240 million (Table 8.1).

Table 8.1   Comparative costs of PAYE

	1980 £m	1985[1] £m
Hardware and software	98	97
Staff including consultancy support	38	81
Accommodation (computer centres, conversion of local offices)	41	56
Other (travel, removals, establishment and other CCTA charges)	3	6
Total	180	240

[1] 1985–6 prices.
Source: Treasury and Civil Service Committee [6].

In July 1984 the decision was taken to extend the system to the rest of the country. Figure 8.3 shows the eleven regions to be computerized. As of the time of writing, September 1985, work in all regions is on schedule. The balance of the West Midland's system was installed by June 1985 and was on-line in December; Eastern Counties region installation was completed by August 1985 (on-line in March 1986); Wales began testing COP on 9 September 1985 (installation October, on-line March 1986). The system as a whole should be on-line in March 1988.

There is every reason, therefore, to judge this major project to have been a real and considerable success—at least from a systems development viewpoint. Is there another viewpoint?

The users are certainly happy. All user tests have been successful; broad based evaluations by the Treasury, unions, the department and others have been quite satisfactory. In fact, so impressed have been the department that in July 1984 the decision was taken to begin the computerization of the last remaining area of substantial manual operations in the department, Schedule D (the 'self-employed' tax—the so-called CODA (Computerization of Schedule D Assessment) project). The contractors and consultants must also judge the project a success: none has lost money and for some, ICL for example, the project has been of the greatest importance.

Yet the challenges faced by COP are not totally over. One way to describe the situation might be to say that though the project was a success, the programme is not yet over. There are still questions outstanding: whether ICL's new hardware will be ready on schedule, whether its software will meet the system's final performance requirements, and whether COP staff can continue to work under such extreme pressures. The story is not yet over.

When the contract was placed with ICL in December 1980, the 2966 was ICL's largest computer. Unfortunately, a single 2966 is not large enough to meet the needs of a single processing centre; it was therefore decided that there would be two or more 2966s at each centre. This was still basically undesirable—it increased the risk of error and thus potentially raised the maintenance load. In October 1981, ICL announced its cooperative agreement with Fujitsu (Fujitsu provide the memory software 'cubes' for ICL). As a result of the agreement, a larger mainframe, the S39 Estriel, was developed.[4] Since 1981, enhanced versions of the 2966 have been developed—the 2966 is a single processor machine: the 2988 is a dual processor 2966 and there is now a four processor 'super dual' 2988—so that instead of 4 x 11 x 2966s it is now planned that there should be 32 x 2988s for COP. Nevertheless, ultimate data handling requirements at certain of the centres, particularly at East Kilbride,[5] will be very stretched with 2988s. Further, the 32 x 2988 arrangement is additionally unsatisfactory in that each processor requires its own software (VME, IDMS, TPMS and IPA),[6] thus again increasing the operating risks. Two or more Estriels, on the other hand, may be combined and operated by the same software, thus reducing operating risk.

With the advent of the Estriel programme, it was also perceived that it was no longer necessary to wait until 1987 to develop the integrated network between the eleven processing centres. The 2988s with IPA could be used as a fall-back, but why not develop new networking software to go with the Estriels? BT, ICL and Plessey were therefore asked to develop a new, purpose-built, packet-switching networking system, which they did. In addition, Estriel is sufficiently large that it has the capacity to accommodate CODA as well as COP. The decision to begin CODA thus assumes that Estriel will be successfully developed by ICL.

By 1985, COP's staff were working closely with ICL to assist develop Estriel. COP staff are working on ICL premises, assisting ICL with system validation (using a specially developed validation program known as Heineken—the program which reaches where other programs do not!) under an arrangement whereby the Inland Revenue will ulti-

---

[4] The Estriel is 3.5 Mips (million instructions per second) capacity; the 2966 is 1 Mips. The largest IBM machines are about 25 Mips.

[5] Where, for historical reasons stretching back to the earlier 1968 system, taxpayer records are addressed by National Insurance Number rather than employer address, as in COP, so that COP records will at East Kilbride have on COP to be kept on both bases, thus substantially increasing the computer sizing requirements.

[6] VME (Virtual Machine Environment), IDMS (Integrated Data Management System), TPMS (Transaction Processing Management System) and IPA (Information Processing Architecture).

mately purchase the Estriel at list price less a discount, subject, that is, to a maximum price limitation. In effect the programme has developed into an extensive joint collaboration between ICL and the Inland Revenue wherein the Revenue is assisting validate the most advanced Japanese-based products. There is now considerably greater confidence in ICL's performance than there was in 1980.

At the time of writing, people have been working on COP for four or five years. The project has proved an exciting one on which to work but the pace has been tough ('benevolent dictatorship, with the benevolence optional'). With CODA, both the work load and the organization have grown. Telford now represents more a functional organization—actually a weak matrix [7]—than the pure project organization it was from 1981 to 1984. People have to be getting tired. As the first centres come on-line, the operational support load will increase. System faults will inevitably surface—one or two have already—particularly with the capacity of the system as originally configured being stretched to the extent that it is. The unions are beginning to demand a greater say in the running of the project and to object to the presence of the outside consultants in line positions. All of which is to say no more than that the Inland Revenue now faces a new phase in its programme—an organizational one. COP is in many ways a heroic story. How do you maintain heroism over six, seven, ten years on large, complex government computer projects?

OVERALL SUMMARY

At the time of its feasibility study, 1979–80, the prognosis for any large government computerisation project was very poor. Despite several changes, imposed largely for political reasons, the system was developed on time, in budget, to specification; implementation is similarly on course. This is a notable success; that it has been so successful is, in large part, due to the leadership of its senior management. Management has been of a very high standard, both strategically (in the use of a steering committee; extensive prefeasibility and feasibility study periods; the use of outside consultants in line positions) and technically (the DSDM approach), and in terms of leadership and commitment. That the programme may still face one or two threats (Estriel, IPA, motivation) is due partly to its success (the addition of CODA) and partly to its political dimension.

In 1980, COP was the largest civil computerization project in Europe.

It offered an enormous opportunity to ICL, the only UK owned manufacturer of large computers, as well as to foreign computer companies. The issue of whether to award the contract to ICL or to a US company was a crucial one, made harder by the fact that ICL did not have the requisite products. For political and managerial (risk minimization) reasons, the government awarded a rescoped contract to ICL. ICL nearly went bankrupt and then, under new leadership, introduced new technology. COP, which had been protecting itself from the potential unreliability of ICL's software, now actively moved to incorporate this new technology, Estriel, into its programme. It also persuaded Plessey to develop a new private packet-switching network so that the fully integrated system could be implemented sooner than originally planned. With the new capacity of the system, the decision was taken to begin Schedule D compterization, CODA.

In short, COP has displayed a thrusting, prudent management strategy which has not only ensured the development of the system on schedule, but has actively sought ways to enhance the programme to the benefit of the Inland Revenue, the taxpayer and the British computer industry.

REFERENCES

1. Elliott, J., 1981.
2. Bunyard, J. M., 1982; De Marco. T., 1982; Metzger, P. W., 1981.
3. *Digital System Development Methodology*, 1985.
4. Brooks, F. P., 1982.
5. Archibald, R. D., 1976.
6. Treasury and Civil Service Committee, 1985.
7. Morris P. W. G., 1982b.

Chapter Nine

Project Giotto[1]

Project Giotto involved the launching of a spacecraft (Giotto) into a geostationary transfer orbit and its subsequent injection into an interplanetary space path to intercept Halley's Comet on 13 March 1986 approximately 100 million miles away from the Earth. The spacecraft carried ten scientific experiments to image the nucleus and to make detailed measurements of the physical characteristics of the comet. The craft's encounter with the comet threatened its destruction.

The European Space Agency, ESA, was formed to replace the former European Launcher Development Organization, ELDO, and the European Space Research Organization, ESRO. The new organization covers the complete range of civilian space activities in Europe; the convention covering it was signed on 30 May 1975 and ratified 30 October 1980. The member states are Austria, Belgium, Denmark, France, Germany, Ireland, Italy, Netherlands, Norway, Spain, Sweden, Switzerland and the United Kingdom with the 'close cooperation' of Canada.

The aims of ESA are:

—to provide for and promote, for exclusively peaceful purposes, cooperation between European states in the fields of:

  space research
  space technology
  space applications;

—to elaborate and implement a long term European space policy;
—to elaborate and implement a European space programme;
—to progressively Europeanize national space programmes;
—to elaborate and implement an industrial policy.

[1] For background information on Giotto see ESA, 1985, and Jenkins and Link, 1984 [1].

The ESA programmes are divided into two categories, mandatory and optional. All states contribute to the mandatory programmes on the basis of a percentage of gross national product and these programmes cover the basic activities of ESA like general studies, information retrieval service and scientific satellites. The optional programmes cover telecommunications, meteorology, remote sensing, climatology, etc., space transportation systems like Ariane and Spacelab, and micro-gravity research programmes. The total ESA budget for 1985 was 1,134 MAU[2] and the scientific programmes used 12.5 per cent of this, i.e. 142 MAU. (The UK contribution to the 1985 budget was 10.8 per cent = 122.9 MAU.)

The general aim of the programme directorate in ESA is to ensure that each state recovers contracts proportional to its contribution to the project. This means that bids made by a prime contractor on behalf of its international consortium have to be arranged to have a compliant geographical distribution of work and costs.

The first successful ESRO satellite, ESRO II, was launched on 17 May 1968, since which time approximately twelve more scientific satellites have been launched. These include Geos I, on 20 April 1977, the objective of which was to investigate particle fluxes, electric and magnetic fields in the outer magnetosphere in a geostationary orbit. Geos I failed to reach the planned geostationary orbit due to the malfunctioning of the launcher but by using the apogee boost motor the satellite was put into a 12-hour orbit and made useful measurements for about a year before it was switched off. A replacement, Geos II, was successfully launched on 14 July 1978 and reached synchronous orbit two days later. The satellite functioned correctly for three years and from 1983 to the present has been operating at a reduced level of data acquisition.

The normal procedures developed by ESA to select a project for funding from the mandatory budget are shown in Figure 9.1 which carries a note to the effect that normally they take a period of two years. In the case of Giotto this was not possible since the urgent scientific requirements to measure the physical characteristics of Halley's Comet did not materialize until the launching window forced a curtailment of normal procedures.

At the celebration lunch given for Geos II, the British Aircraft Corporation (BAC), who were the prime contractors for Geos, floated the idea that a third satellite could be put together very cheaply using the Geos spares. The suggestion was that Geos III should be launched into a neutral gravity zone where it would make scientific measurements

[2] 1 Accounting Unit (AU) = £0.59249 in 1985 (1 MAU = £592,490).

ESA issues a request to the European and scientific community for ideas.

Ideas received are examined by the Solar System Working Group (SSWG) and the Astronomical Working Group (AWG).

The selected ideas are submitted to the Solar System Advisory Committee (SSAC) who carry out a further selection process.

The ideas selected by the SSAC are then recommended to, and then further screened by, the Director of Science (of ESA).

ESA then carries out an in-house assessment study and reports the conclusions to the working groups and SSAC. Following a selection phase and with the agreement of the Scientific Programme Committee (SPC) a Phase A study for these projects is let to industry. Under ESA direction a first system level study based upon very preliminary design requirements and a model payload is made.

The results of these Phase A studies are fed back into the previous loop and progress again through the SSWG and AWG.

After further in-house refinement and review of the requirements and completion of estimates, the Director General of ESA makes a proposal to the SPC to proceed with the selected project.

The SPC, which has a delegate from each member state, formally approves that the project should proceed and a budget is allocated to cover the costs to completiton.

The normal time-cycle to complete the above process is approximately two years.

Composition of the committees:

SSWG/AWG/SSAC Eminent scientists from all over Europe.
SPC   One government delegate from each member country, each having one vote.

Figure 9.1 Stages of project development and approval

similar to those of Geos II. Having occupied this position for sometime it would then swing round the moon and into space to make measurements of comets. The proposal was declined by ESA because of insufficient scientific support. Following exploratory discussions with ESA and the scientific community, BAC made an unsolicited bid to ESA to build a spacecraft to accommodate a payload that would perform measurements of Halley's Comet's physical characteristics. ESA had performed joint studies with NASA to have a cometary mission with NASA and ESA probes jointly launched on the Shuttle. This US proposal was not approved by the US government so that a curtailed selection procedure, referred to above, was finally used. The BAC[3] bid then went through a fast approval procedure ending up with the Space Policy Committee approval. Then ESA formally requested a tender from BAC for a spacecraft they named Giotto after the Italian painter who in 1301 saw and painted Halley's Comet, whose physical characteristics the project was set up to measure.

The recent appearance of Halley's Comet was the fourth predicted

---

[3] BAC was nationalized on 1 April 1977 and became part of British Aerospace Dynamics (BAeD) on that date.

apparition, and it was the first occasion on which it was possible to send spacecraft to intercept it. Although comets are common, and at the same time spectacular objects in the sky, very little is known about them. The comet's nucleus consists of a mixture of ices and solid material in the form of dust and grains which when heated by the sun realease vast quantities of gas and particles. The nucleus may be only a few kilometres in diameter but the coma (tail) can be more than 100,000 kilometres in length. The neutral gas is ionized and swept by the solar wind to form a long straight ion tail, similarly the dust particles form a tail by virtue of the radiation pressure, and both tails are in an anti-solar direction. It is reflected sunlight and fluorescence from the tail that makes the comet visible to the human eye. The Giotto space-craft, then, was envisaged as the carrier of scientific instruments to provide scientists with the first reall information on:

—the nucleus of the comet,
—the chemistry of the coma,
—plasma analysis,
—dust particle size, distribution and numbers.

The total cost of the Giotto project in the ESA budget was a little over 160 MAU (£94.8 million).

Similar procedures as are used to select ESA projects were used to select the payloads for the Giotto project. First, there was an Announcement of Opportunity by ESA. The first screening of the proposals was done by ESA technical experts who examined them for technical compliance and then added comments on their feasibility and the strength of the financial resources to support them. The various proposals then went through the Solar System Working Group and SSAC to the Director of Science and Director General of ESA who made a proposal to the Science Policy Committee for their formal approval (see Figure 9.1).

During evaluation the following criteria were used:

—scientific value ot the cometary mission,
—adequacy of the proposed technique,
—competence of the team to produce space-worthy equipment.

Table 9.1 lists the experiments chosen and the university or institute concerned.

The scientific payloads or experiments were funded through part of the university, college or institute's normal research funding, and neither this figure nor the cost of the analysis of the results, is included in the Giotto cost figure given previously. As a broad indication, it may

Table 9.1   Giotto scientific payload

Experiment	Principal investigator	Institute	Measurement
Camera (HMC)	Dr H. U. Keller	Max-Planck-Institut für Aeronomie (Lindau, West Germany)	Colour imaging of cometary nucleus and inner coma
Neutral mass spectrometer (NMS)	Dr D. Krankowsky	Max-Planck-Institut für Kernphysik (Heidelberg, West Germany)	Energy and mass of ions
Ion Mass Spectrometer (IMS)	Dr H. Balsiger	University of Bern (Bern, Switzerland)	Energy and mass of ions
Dust mass spectrometer (PIA)	Dr J. Kissel	Max-Planck-Institut für Kernphysik (Heidelberg, West Germany)	Mass and compostion (1–110amu) of individual dust particles
Dust impact detector system (DID)	Prof. J. A. M. McDonnell	University of Kent (Canterbury, England)	Determination of the mass spectrum of dust particles from three different detectors
Plasma analysers (JPA)	Dr A. Johnstone	MSSL, University College London (Holmbury St Mary, England)	Solar wind ions, cometary ions in the outer coma
Plasma analysers (RPA)	Prof. H. Rème	Centre d'Etudes Spatiales des Rayonnements (Toulouse, France)	Solar wind electrons, cometary ions in the inner coma
Energetic particles (EPA)	Dr S. McKenna-Lawlor	St Patrick's College (Maynooth, Ireland)	3-D measurement of protons, electrons and alphas
Magnetometer (MAG)	Prof. E. M. Neubauer	University of Cologne (Cologne, West Germany)	Interplanetary and cometary magnetic field
Optical probe experiment (OPE)	Prof. A. C. Levasseur-Regourd	Service d'Aéronomie du CNRS (Verrières le Buisson, France)	Coma brightness in four continuous (dust) bands and at discrete wavelengths (gaseous emissions of OH, CN, CO^+, C_2)
Radio Science (GRE)[1]	Prof. P. Edenhofer	University of Bochum (West Germany)	Cometary electron content. Cometary mass (coma dust and gas) fluence

[1] This experiment does not comprise any on-board hardware but makes use of the Doppler measurements made on the telemetry downlink.

be assumed that the cost of the experiments was approximately equal to the cost of the spacecraft.

Each payload equipment accepted was defined in detail, weight, shape, size, window requirements, thermal and electrical characteristics, and data transmission requirements. The ESA spacecraft project manager then included these interface data in the spacecraft design specification and was responsible for the interface throughout the development. Typically there were contingencies included to ensure that adequate design tolerances were built into the requirements and supervision by ESA ensured that the design task did not escalate by adding contingency on contingency. For example, the total payload weight estimates came to 48.1 killograms and a single contingency was added to take it up to 56 kilograms.

The BAe Dynamics' (BAeD) response to the ESA formal request for proposal against the detailed Giotto specification was submitted on 9 March 1981. A formal evaluation by ESA followed and resulted in the decision that the proposal was unacceptable. This was reported in an ESA Industrial Policy Committee paper dated 15 May 1981 which recommended an alternative procedure whereby the system definition phase (B.1) of the spacecraft design would be carried out by the ESA executive. Subsequently subsystem requirements would be derived from the system design and subsystem specifications generated. Subsystem contractors would then be selected by ESA on a competitive basis. It was also proposed to hold a competition to select the system contractor for the subsequent phases of the programme. This new management proposal was in turn rejected by the delegates and the programme director was instructed to negotiate with BAeD, who would be the prime contractor for the spacecraft, to explore what could be achieved conjointly. ESA had overall project management responsibility (launchers, operations, spacecraft data acquisition and funding) whilst BAeD had responsibility for procurement of a spacecraft against ESA design requirements.

ESA divided the programme into the following phases:

B.0	6 weeks	System concept. ESA and BAeD working together.
B.1	4 months	Subsystem definition and bids (autumn 1981). ESA and BAeD working together.
B.2		Project definition and prime contractor's formal bid on a February 1982 standard for delivery of the spacecraft on 31 January 1985 and launch 2 July 1985. BAeD and ESA working together.
C/D		Construction, assembly, test and delivery of spacecraft to meet the above dates. BAeD prime contractor.

The ESA project manager and BAeD teams, in spite of an unpleasant period preceding the delegates' instructions, worked together to achieve very good progress on all aspects. The ESA project director and the BAeD project manager agreed that if any member of either team referred to the differences or difficulties which existed during evaluation of BAC's rejected proposal they would be removed from the team. An efficient, mixed ESA/industry team was the result, and phases B.0 and B.1 were conducted as a joint operation with ESA's initial dominance diminishing until BAeD established a dominant prime contractor's position in B.2. The total industrial team deployed on the spacecraft was as shown in Table 9.2.

Table 9.2 Giotto contractor team

Contractor	Country	Responsibility
AEG Telefunken	West Germany	Solar array
Alcatel-Thomson Espace	France	Telemetry tracking and command systems
British Aerospace	United Kingdom	Coordinate manufacture, assemble, integrate and test supply and fit cable harness
BTM	Belgium	Pryotechnic electronic unit
Dornier System GmbH	West Germany	Structure, antenna attitude and orbit control system
Electronikcentralen	Denmark	Thermal control unit
ETCA	Belgium	Electrical ground support equipment
FIAR	Italy	Power supply
Fokker	Netherlands	Thermal control system
Laben	Italy	On-board data handling
ORS	Austria	Mechanical groud support equipment
SEP (Bordeaux)	France	Transfer propulsion system
SEP (Vernon)	France	De-spin mechanism and de-spin control electronics
Subcontractors		
Contraves	Switzerland	Spacecraft structure
DFVLR	West Germany	Plume impingement studies
Ericsson	Sweden	Antenna system
Fokker	Netherlands	Nutation dampers, overall check-out equipment
Galileo	Italy	Earth and sun sensors
Laben	Italy	Power distribution equipment for altitude and orbit control systems
MB β-ERNO	West Germany	Reaction control electronics
TPD	Netherlands	Star mapper

Sources: ESA/Arianspace, CNES/British Aerospace.

At the end of Phase A the project was approved by SPC (see Figure 9.1) in July 1980. The approved cost to completion (CtC) included an estimate of 54.9 MAU for the spacecraft contract which covered phase B, phase C/D and launch support. The cost for which the baseline contracts were placed amounted to 57.2 MAU, which represents an increase of 4 per cent. On this basis, the SPC approved in June 1982 an increased CtC which included an allocation of 57.6 MAU for the spacecraft contract. The difference of 0.4 MAU is accounted for by final changes in subcontractors' phase C/D costs, after completion of phase B for which ESA bore responsibility under the phase B management scheme.

The final cost of 63.3 MAU shows an excess of 5.7 MAU with respect to the approved CtC at the end of phase B which represents an overrun of about 10 per cent. This overrun is almost solely due to contractor induced changes (phase B modifications) and overruns in cost reimbursement contracts (5.4 MAU in total).[4]

Each work package was defined in detail and programmed in the B.1 and B.2 phases so that a comprehensive management plan existed at the beginning of the C/D phase. All programmes were computerized, and throughout the project ESA had direct access to a read-out facility in the BAeD computer at Bristol. Contract changes proposed by BAeD to cover modifications required in the design standard were dealt with promptly and it was ESA's policy neither to allow the number outstanding to exceed three of four nor to allow any to stand for a decision for more than three or four weeks. This clean client/contractor management relationship is considered to have been of considerable importance in preserving good working relations—an essential ingredient to success. The BAeD project manager and the ESA spacecraft project manager met regularly at approximately ten-day intervals throughout the period and ESA had full visibility of BAeD's management of its task.

As recorded previously, ESA was responsible for the interface control between the experiments and the spacecraft and also for the programming and delivery of the experiments to BAeD. The mission-worthiness of the experiments was ESA's responsibility and BAeD was responsible for their integration into the spacecraft. It was no mean task to ensure that the hardware and software for all the experiments would be available on time. It was probably achieved by constant supervision of the institutes and universities and the threat that if the equipment was not ready on time it would be left out of the spacecraft.

Within the C/D phase three spacecraft models were fabricated:

The structure model	This was tested exhaustively to ensure the mechanical integrity of the design.
The electrical model	This was used to test the electrical functional aspects of the design to ensure that it was clean in all respects.
Qualification and flight models	For flight qualifications and launch. (In order to abbreviate the programme the qualification and flight models were on the same assembly.)

---

[4] All costs in these paragraphs have been established at mid 1981 price levels using 1982 AU exchange rates (1 AU = £0.53928).

Additionally, spares were provided for each spacecraft subsystem and also for all experiments, the only exception being the camera (which was by far the most expensive experiment carried on the spacecraft). The Giotto spacecraft trajectory was calculated precisely in order to make the interception with the comet at the optimum position in space. This interception, on 13 March 1986, could only be achieved if the launch on Ariane was made on 2 July 1985. Hence the meeting of the programme schedule and a successful launch had the utmost significance since a failure in either of these would have meant a catastrophic failure of the project. It was considered by both BAeD and ESA that more effective schedule control data dissemination would be achieved by providing ESA with direct access to the PERT network and so, as stated above, direct entry into the programme was arranged.

The BAeD project team in collaboroation with the ESA team ran regular progress meetings with the spacecraft contractors and subcontractors. The system design philosophy was aimed at minimizing risks by using, wherever possible, equipment which was already space proven, incorporating design margins, and exercising the good basic management principles of clearly defining interfaces and ensuring that the right level of resources were deployed so that where problems existed they were recognized and solved rapidly. The technical and design standards were controlled through a comprehensive system summary document which defined all systems and subsystems in complete detail.

The major design requirements which dictated the mechanical configuration of the spacecraft were:

—the dual shield dust protection system at the base of the spacecraft;
—the detailed viewing requirements of the individual payloads;
—the orbit transfer propulsion motor;
—a high gain antenna system with a de-spun RF (radio frequency) beam.

The configuration was dual spin arrangement with the main spacecraft carrying subsystems and the payloads being the rotor and the stator comprising the high gain antenna. At interception with the comet, the craft was rotating at 15 r.p.m. The following are some of the design parameters:

Size
  Diameter 1.867 metres
  Height 2.848 metres
Mass
  Launch mass 960 kilograms
Payload data rate in thousand b.p.s.,
  switchable 39,393, 19,696 and 4,653

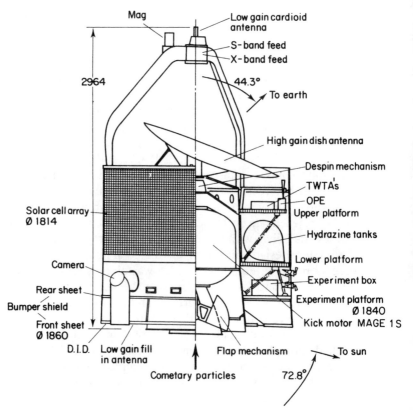

Figure 9.2 Diagram of Giotto

Source: *ESA*

Tracking, telemetry and command
  Uplink data rate 15–625 b.p.s.
  Downlink data rate 360 b.p.s.
Scientific and housekeeping downlink data rate,
  switchable 46,080, 23,040 and 5,760 thousand b.p.s. options
Power source
  Cylindrical solar array giving 152 watts minimum

The programme was maintained and the spacecraft, which had almost completed assembly, was moved out of BAeD Filton laboratories to Toulouse for its final assembly tests just two days before union action closed the Filton Works. (The strike went on for eight weeks.) During the early months of 1985 the system-level testing was completed in the Interspace facility in Toulouse as planned and all the payloads were successfully integrated. The spacecraft was accepted by ESA from BAeD on 22 April 1985 and subsequently shipped to the launch site in

Figure 9.3 Thermal vacuum test in Toulouse
Source: *British Aerospace*

Guiana on 29 April 1985. The flight model of one of the payloads was not available at that time and was subsequently installed at the launch site. Upon arrival at Kourou (Guiana) the spacecraft was installed in the clean room facilities and integrated with the electrical check-out equipment to be used during the launch countdown procedure.

The preparation of Ariane[5] (V14) for the launch started on 28 May 1985 with the inspection of the first stage of the launcher. It proceeded through inspection and erection of the three stage launcher and culminated in the mating of Ariane and Giotto on 27 June 1985. The count-down sequence started on 30 June (at 0900 hours) and proceeded

---

[5] The Ariane hardware is produced in France, Germany, Belgium, Denmark, Spain, Italy, Holland, Sweden, Switzerland and the United Kingdom.

without any problems to lift-off on 2 July at 0813 am. After 72 seconds the vehicle was transonic and after 852.2 seconds the injection velocity was achieved and the third stage shut down. Giotto was successfully separated at 899.2 seconds and the kick motor was successfully operated at the fourth Perigree passage.

On 14 and 16 October 1985, the spacecraft, when on course to make its interception, had a simulated encounter with Halley's Comet. All the spacecraft systems, the different payloads, the associated ground stations and their data recording systems were activated in a realistic rehearsal. This rehearsal confirmed that all systems were working satisfactorily and proved an excellent training exercise, which was repeated four times more before the actual interception on 13 March 1986.

THE COMETARY ARMADA

In addition to the Giotto project, the USSR, the United States of America and Japan all had spacecraft programmes to intercept Halley's Comet. Table 9.3 gives the key data.

Table 9.3   Other spacecraft programmes to intercept Halley's Comet

Agency	Project	Launch date	Fly past date	Fly past distance
ESA	Giotto	2 July 1985	13 March 1986	500 km
Intercosmos	Veg I	15 December 1984	6 March 1986	10,000 km
	Veg II	21 December 1984	9 March 1986	10,000 km
ISAS	Sakigiki	8 January 1985	11 March 1986	7 million km
	Plant A	14 August 1985	8 March 1986	200,000 km
NASA	ICE[1]	20 December 1983	28 March 1986	32 million km

[1] International Cometary Observatory.

The different missions are complementary and an Inter-Agency Consultation Group was set up to coordinate informally all matters related to the encounters in space. The first meeting took place in Italy in September 1981 when details of the various spacecraft and their payloads were exchanged and the principles of collaboration established. After that first meeting others were held in Hungary, Japan, the USSR and the United States and the cooperation was 100 per cent. It was planned that data from the first passes would be examined rapidly and fed to the project controllers of spacecraft yet to make the pass so that any corrections which might improve the pass conditions could be made. As a result of this international collaboration making available the earlier spacecraft intercept data, it was possible to plan the Giotto interception to occur at a distance of 500 ± 70 kilometres. Without this final correction, the pass would have to have been planned to be at twice the distance, thereby reducing all images and some data accuracy by a factor of about two. All the scientific data achieved will be made available to all countries so that the chances of there being a universal success have been maximized.

OVERALL SUMMARY

The Giotto programme proper started with a discordant background, an exacting performance specification and a demanding, inflexible completion date. The senior managers appointed in ESA and industry to run the project rapidly overcame the background problems and, by using good management principles, modern management tools and in particular a well organized communications system, completely succeeded in achieving their objectives. This multinational project is an excellent example of the use of modern management methods and management technology. The complex project produced the spectacular interception of Halley's Comet which was witnessed by the many who watched the BBC television programme of the event.

REFERENCE

1. Esa, 1985a, 1985b; Jenkins, R. H. and Link, D. C. R., 1984.

PART THREE

The Anatomy of Major Projects

Chapter Ten

The Question of Success and Failure

In Chapter 1, the case was made that the failure rate for projects is high, and for major projects unacceptably so. Although we have not yet defined the terms 'success' and 'failure', in the summaries of the eight major projects which we have just reviewed the reasons for considering the projects successes or failures were given in relatively specific terms. If we wish to be more precise in understanding the sources of success or failure we must be more precise in defining what we mean by these terms.

It is readily apparent from the case studies that there are several different perspectives which must be employed when assessing whether or not a project was successful. At least three measures of project success can be identified:

(1) *Project functionality*   Does the project perform financially, technically or otherwise in the way expected by the project's sponsors? (This is primarily an owner measure although financiers, regulators, citizens, governments, evironmentalists and others having a secondary or indirect relationship with the project could have their own 'performance requirements' which could create quite distinct definitions of success and which, if jeopardized, could seriously threaten the implementation of the projects.)
(2) *Project management*   Was the project implemented to budget, on schedule, to technical specification?
(3) *Contractors' commercial performance*   Did those who provided a service for the project benefit commercially (in either the short or long term)?

There could also be a fourth measure: in the event that a project needed to be cancelled, was the cancellation made on a reasonable basis and terminated efficiently [1]? For it has been argued by some that the process of termination is sometimes of great importance but is often poorly managed [2]. Too many projects go ahead which, if evaluated properly, would have been terminated; on the other hand, many projects are terminated on ill-conceived grounds when really they should be allowed to proceed. (This of course was the case with the Channel Tunnel which was terminated in 1975 essentially because it lacked effective championship, and in particular, government will.)

There are therefore many levels of measurement for evaluating project success.[1] These vary from the contractor and project manager to the owner, his financier, the government and the community. In the same way, the evaluation of project success varies through time. A contractor may not know whether his project is a success or not until he has had his claims finally adjudicated. A project's principal success criteria often vary as the project unfolds. As DeWit has described, for example, during an oil development project there are at least three different measures of success (Figure 10.1): discover oil, develop the oil field, and commercially exploit the field [4]. Over the longer term, too, the evaluation of the success or failure of a project will vary. The success of most projects from an owner's point of view would be unknown until at least the payback period has been achieved but often not until the internal rate of return has been shown to be satisfactory. In many major projects. e.g. in the aircraft industry, this may take many years. Indeed some projects may go for a very long time before there is any test of their success or failure: the Maginot Line, for example. Thus, not only is the future difficult to predict, so too is the evaluation of those predictions.

The definition of whether a project is a success or a failure, then, is

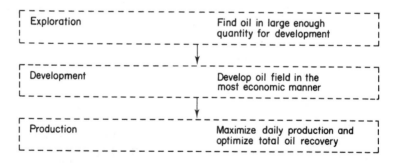

Figure 10.1 Measures of success on an oil field project

---

[1] Morgan and Soden, for example, in discussing information systems failures have, as measures, operational failure, economic failure, technical failure, development failure and priority failure; DeCotiis and Dyer define five measures of R & D project performance—manufacturability and business performance, technical performance, efficiency, personal growth experience, and technological innovativeness [3].

not always an easy one. Let us look at how the eight case studies compare along the three (or four) dimensions of project success and failure that we have identified—project functionality, project management, and contractors' commercial performance (and project termination)—beginning with project functionality.

PROJECT FUNCTIONALITY—THE SPONSOR'S PERSPECTIVE

The Channel Tunnel, 1960–75

In so far as the Channel Tunnel project of 1960–75 was never built, it is almost impossible to talk of its success or failure to those promoting or paying for it—its owners. It had every likelihood of proving to be successful from the owners' point of view. All the cost–benefit studies (such as Coopers & Lybrand's and Cairncross's [5]) showed the project to be economic.

The project failed for political and organizational reasons, not because of engineering, project management or financial difficulties. These factors might have been mitigated and even forestalled had the project had a real owner. In fact, no real client existed. The project had no effective champion. There was no one fighting for the project *per se*.

Concorde

Like the Channel Tunnel, Concorde was also a political project, although unlike the tunnel it was able to retain its political support. It was able to do so at least in its early days because of its International Treaty which made the costs of cancellation unacceptably high. Later the impact of cancellation on employment ensured the political support of the Labour Government.

Concorde was embarked upon by four partners: the UK and French Governments and the two aircraft industries in the two countries. The two governments had a common aim which was to develop a supersonic commercial aircraft. From the beginning officials in both countries had little or no hope that the project would be commercially viable.

Additionally, each government had its own political or national aims. The French Government wished to establish its aircraft industry and to build up the necessary support facilities. The British Government wished to demonstrate its willingness to be a European partner to further the chances of its entry into the European Economic Community (EEC).

The French aircraft industry benefited enormously from the project and acquired modern facilities (such as wind tunnels, environmental test houses) and is now one of the leading aircraft industries in Europe. No reliable figures for the supplementary French costs in the project have been uncovered but under the treaty agreement the intention was to share the costs equally. There is no doubt, then, that in France, as in the United Kingdom, there was a vast spending overrun; the general view is that this was accepted by the French Government and its officials as a reasonable cost for modernizing the industry. In respect of the primary aims of the French Government the project must, therefore, be considered a success.

The United Kingdom is now a member of the EEC. The significance of the role that the Concorde project played in convincing the original seven that the United Kingdom would be a fully participating, responsible member of the community is impossible to assess. But on the basis that the political objective was achieved during the lifetime of the project, then it must be assumed that it was literally used by the politicians as an example of the willingness of the United Kingdom to collaborate and that its contribution was at least positive and, possibly, significant.

Recognizing the vast overrun, it is a matter of some speculation whether the cost of Concorde was a reasonable one and whether that amount of money ought to have been spent in the aircraft industry at that time. It is clear that the Labour Government would have cancelled the P1154, the HS681 and the TSR2 irrespective of whether they had succeeded in their attempt to cancel Concorde [6]. In view of the ineffective and indecisive way in which the UK Government approached the French Government to cancel the project in 1964, it is tempting to believe that there was no real determination to cancel and that the proceedings were postures to satisfy the many Concorde critics both at home and overseas. However, discussion with politicians associated with the attempt to cancel the project has confirmed that it was primarily the French threat to take the dispute to the International Court that ended the cancellation threat [7]. Had Concorde been cancelled, this, coupled with the other three aircraft cancellations, would have placed the British aircraft industry in a parlous position. Its recovery would have been lengthy and extremely expensive.

Concorde eventually reached commercial service and is now being operated profitably by British Airways, and somewhat less so by Air France, so that technically there is no doubt that the project was a success.

The many and varied groups both in Europe and the United States who opposed the development of Concorde, especially on environmental grounds, can claim that their persistence achieved a quieter aircraft whose noise characteristics have become acceptable on both sides of the Atlantic. The sonic boom is restricted to flight over the high seas and Concorde now, having been in commercial operation for some nine years, has been accepted as part of the modern transport systems of the world.

The Advanced Passenger Train (APT)

The aim of the Advanced Passenger Train was to design and produce new rolling equipment to decrease journey times for both passengers and goods on existing tracks. This aim was promoted strongly by the Research Centre but the Railways Board was less committed. The engineering concept was basically achieved but the development into a practical reality was not, partly due to small engineering problems but largely due to lack of top management will. Since the project never reached commercial functionality it must necessarily be considered a failure from the sponsor's point of view.

The Thames Barrier

The Thames Barrier works and, in that it has and will save London from flooding, is undoubtedly worth its cost. The clients—the GLC and the government—are well content with the structure.[2] The barrier's use should increase as we move into the next century and tides rise. Whether the barrier's owners were happy to pay as much for the project as they did is unlikely, though it should be borne in mind that only 15 per cent of the overrun—admittedly over £36 million—was due to lower than anticipated productivity, and indeed a good portion of this was due to labour problems that everyone knew, at heart, were inevitable. The truth is that a very great portion of the overrun, say 75–80 per

[2] The present tense is used even though the GLC was disbanded in April 1986.

cent (£248–64 million), is due to inflation and poor labour relations, consequences of the actions of the barrier's owners themselves— government.

Heysham 2

Strictly speaking, it is too early yet to comment on the project functionality success of Heysham 2 since, at the time of writing, the project has only just entered its commissioning phase. Being so carefully based on the Hinkley Point B technical design, however, there is every reason to believe the station would perform as predicted. Commissioning tests carried out in the summer of 1986 were generally satisfactory but close examination of certain reactor components revealed some unexpected damage. At the time of writing (November 1986) the problem was still being assessed. Initial indications are that some in-line delay to commissioning is unavoidable. A small change from Hinkley Point B, regarded at the time as insignificant—the reversal of the control rod and fuel rod nozzles in the gas baffle—appears to have caused vibration of the control rods. If this is so, it is a very painful lesson about the need for total replication of a proven satisfactory design. The cost of the station is within 5 per cent of the original scheme sanction and despite this recent difficulty there is every likelihood that the station will be commercially successful.

Fulmar

Fulmar has proved a highly profitable field due primarily to its excellent geological characteristics but also to the absence of adverse fiscal or legislative policies. Some in the oil industry would count the 10 months' schedule delay as a failure from an owner's viewpoint but the overall feeling must be that, from a functionality viewpoint, the project was undoubtedly a major success.

The Computerization of PAYE

Although the computer system was developed to specification, at the time of writing the full system is not yet completely implemented. It is thus too early to say whether the system works to the final satisfaction of the Treasury, Whitehall and the public. This said, despite the one or two challenges currently facing the project, there is every reason to expect that the system will be implemented to specification, on time, in budget, and will perform satisfactorily. Two indicators on the current satisfactory performance of the system are that (1) staff savings from COP outweigh its cost, and (2) arrears in the treatment of tax mail are decreasing in those areas which have been automated though they are increasing in other areas.

Giotto

The ultimate success of Giotto became known on 13–14 March 1986 when the planned intercept of the spacecraft with Halley's Comet took place. At the time of writing, the mass of scientific data acquired in the interception is being analysed and the project appears to have been highly successful. The project's success lies in the achievement of the accuracy of interception, and in the fact that the experiments functioned and provided the data which they had been designed to achieve.

These brief descriptions of the success or failure of the projects from a functionality viewpoint immediately suggest one important point: it is easier to describe a project's functional success when its objectives are clear. Concorde's objectives were complex and its analysis was hence lengthy; Heysham 2, on the other hand, had relatively straightforward objectives, allowing a simpler immediate evaluation.
Let us now consider the 'project management' measure.

PROJECT MANAGEMENT

Was the project completed to budget, on schedule, to technical specification?

The Channel Tunnel, 1960–75

The project appeared to be progressing well when it was cancelled. Although the budget was escalating, this was primarily due to inflation and the costs of the high-speed rail link. With the proper managerial will, British Rail's budget could probably have been trimmed. In fact, British Rail, a key party to the project (and indeed a member of the British Channel Tunnel Company), was insufficiently committed to the project; it should have been integrated much more into the project team. (This would really only have been effective if British Rail's senior management had been committed to the project.)

The project would probably have benefited from a simpler organization structure and one overall head, though in practice it is difficult to see how this might have been arranged given the *moitié-moitié* principle and the impossibility of either the British or the French admitting to a supremo of the opposite nationality.

Concorde

The costs of the project were far in excess of those originally envisaged when the treaty was signed in November 1962. In the United Kingdom additional monies were authorized almost annually by Parliament until the end of the project, by which time the total had reached a factor of about seven over the original estimates. There were, of course, several items in the final figures which were not included in the original estimate (such as production tooling). Additionally, the project was carried out during years of high inflation so that changes in money values and exchange rates accounted for over 50 per cent of the increased costs. In spite of these mitigating factors, which it can be argued should have been recognized in the original estimates, there can be no doubt that, from the limited aspect of cost overrun, the project was a failure.

The attempts to monitor and predict costs and to evaluate the merits of the programme in the development phase were bound to be difficult due to the inherent technical uncertainties, the institutional arrangements which typified arrangements between and amongst government and manufacturers, and the organizational and contractual forms which described relationships between the various participants.

The 1962 programme schedule had a Certificate of Airworthiness date of end 1969; in 1969 the project's date to enter service was 1973; the actual date for the Certificate of Airworthiness was December 1975 and the first commercial service was 24 May 1976. In general, a slip of some seven years had occurred. There is no evidence to suggest that this was in any way embarrassing to the clients except that indirectly it contributed significantly to the cost overrun. However, on a literal analysis the project clearly failed to run to schedule.

The broadest technical specification existed at the start of the programme and the detailed performance specifications of the various systems that comprised the aircraft were evolved as development advanced. Many of these specifications were interrelated and the evolution of a satisfactory design was an iterative process resulting in a number of attempts having to be made to achieve the objectives. Ultimately a design was achieved which was totally successful but with hindsight it is obvious that time and money could have been saved during the programme by reducing the number of design steps and eliminating one or more of the prototype aircraft built and by eliminating one of the final assembly lines.

The treaty defined the initial management structure which set the pattern for the project. It suffered from many problems, e.g. the lack of a clearly identified client, the absence of a single manager in overall charge or a central project management unit, contract responsibilities inadequately defined, lack of proper budgetary control and problems with schedule reporting. The project succeeded technically in spite of the management structure. The management lessons, however, were applied in the subsequent European collaborative aircraft projects and as a result successful organizations have been set up which have achieved success and continue to be successful.

Finally the aircraft went into airline service and is flown with the same sort of tolerances as any other commercial airliner. The pilots who fly it have the same affection for it as other pilots have for other good aeroplanes and its reliability is above average. Out of what may be considered as a difficult design environment emerged a technically brilliant success which was both late and vastly overspent.

The Advanced Passenger Train

In spite of the intrusive action by unions, progress on the experimental train was, at the end of the five-year programme, sufficiently well advanced to allow the Railways Board to authorize the second phase of the programme, the prototype APT(P), on schedule. The APT(P) programme was always behind schedule: seven years elapsed before the prototype train carried farepaying passengers, at which stage the project has been variously estimated as being between fourteen and thirty months late. Despite this schedule failure, the budgets allocated were not exceeded. Significantly, however, the rolling stock reliability and passenger comfort requirements were not attained and it was these failures that ostensibly caused the train to be withdrawn. The project failed basically on this technical count. Part of the problem was the handover from the Research Centre to the Engineering department. Engineering, as part of the Railways Board, thus became simultaneously both the project's client and its contractor. This is generally an unhealthy and inefficient arrangement. There was little evidence of any project management leadership of the quality required.

The Thames Barrier

By the traditional measures of cost and schedule overrun the Thames Barrier must be classed a project management failure: final costs were some four times the original budget (although the impact of inflation must be noted) and the project took almost twice as long to construct as was planned—seven and a half years for construction work (after six months' mobilization by CTH) as opposed to the four years which had been planned. Technically the project turned out well.

The project management of the Thames Barrier suffered not just the usual difficulties of the traditional UK civil engineering approach to projects. In addition, the public accountability requirements of local government prohibited the GLC from appointing a project manager with significant executive authority, especially as regards approval of expenditure. Thus, the client's role became predominantly a monitoring and final approval one. Day-to-day administration of the contracts was in the hands of the design consultant whose role, as formalized in the Institution of Civil Engineers' Conditions of Contract, is, at least in matters of production management, basically reactive: production is left to the contractor(s).[3] CTH did not appear to gear-up for the real scale of the management challenge facing the project until the change of project manager in 1976. There was considerable attention given by CTH to planning and control systems but insufficient to leadership and man-management. Quite why that should have been so is difficult to say. Partly it was simply that the wrong man was picked to manage CTH's work. Possibly, CTH's approach would have been different if it had been brought in earlier, perhaps on different terms. It must be said, however, that it would have been highly unusual had this happened. The GLC had suffered substantially with a cost reimbursable contract on Thamesmead just prior to the Thames Barrier work beginning and the new concepts of management contracting and project

---

[3] This is as true of the current fifth edition of the ICE Conditions of Contract as it was of the fourth edition used on the barrier project.

management—to be discussed further in Chapter 11—were only just emerging in the construction industry around the early 1970s [8]. The unfortunate result was that the level of management was pushed down by this contracting policy and lack of leadership so that technical and industrial relations problems became harder to manage.

The Thames Barrier would thus appear to raise broader questions for the management of large civil engineering work:

(1) For large, complex civil engineering projects, should the form of contract allow a more proactive, energetic form of management by the owner's project manager, or his agent?
(2) For larger, more risky projects, should the contractor be brought in earlier in the project?
(3) Should the patchwork system of shift and bonus payments be rationalized? (The project ended with a site-wide, comprehensive, three 8-hour shift system—it should surely have begun in like manner.)
(4) Should estimates for inflation be included (as a special line item) in the initial budget? Drawing down from this account would give project management a chance of guiding final expenditure to within initial budget. Also, preparing that estimate should require a full financial risk analysis of the project. Since financial risk is in large part a reflection of other risk, having to estimate for inflation ought to have the important benefit of stimulating a much fuller risk analysis.

Heysham 2

Until very recently, the project was within schedule and budget. In late 1986, the estimated final cost increased by 5 per cent and an unexpected but significant technical problem—the rubbing and fretting of the control rods—was identified which appears likely to delay commissioning of the first unit by some months. The second unit remains on schedule. When this study was carried out, this problem had not surfaced and there was great confidence amongst those involved in the project that it was a success. This assurance has been somewhat dented by recent events although there is no doubt that the construction phase, which was only one month behind the target programme, has been more successful than for any previous AGR. This is a considerable achievement particularly given the complexity of the project and the history of delays and overruns on other nuclear and fossil power stations. This success was due to careful planning and strict design control, disciplined site-wide industrial relations, positive leadership and a clear contracting policy.

Fulmar

Fulmar was developed over a six-year period within budget and to specification. The schedule slipped, however, by about 10 months from 59 to 69 months (counting from when the project team was formed), i.e. about 17 per cent, even though schedule had very high priority on the project. The principal reason for the schedule slippage was, paradoxically, the desire in the early stages to maintain progress. Detailed design was begun despite uncertainties over reservoir characteristics and oil and gas export options; these uncertainties caused numerous later changes so that the detailed design was completed 20 months late. An additional factor contributing to this early slippage was a certain organizational awkwardness. In spite of this schedule slippage, fabrication was still begun per the initial schedule, even though detailed design was in some cases only 30–40 per cent complete. Fabricators' plans were not realistically assessed and with fabrication being seriously disrupted by design changes, inevitably fabrication soon became late with several contracts requiring substantial modification. As a result of this slippage, installation had to be conducted in the winter which, though now much easier with the new Hereema barges, still meant that bad weather added further delay to the programme.

The Computerization of PAYE

The basic computer system was developed on time, in budget, to technical specification. System implementation is likewise on schedule, to specification, in budget. That COP's project management has been so successful has been due to many factors, not least top management commitment, consistent senior management leadership, careful planning, strict design control, effective contract management and good project control. (It might, with some justification, be noted that the Retail Price Index is not the appropriate index to use to adjust the 1980 budget to current prices; the point is a little niggardly, though, given the broader achievement of COP and is anyway part of the wider problem of the budgeting and cost control of government projects, namely that the Treasury rules are that no estimation should be made of possible price escalation when preparing capital expenditure budgets.)

Giotto

The project was implemented within the total ESA budget, and was launched and made the interception on schedule. All experiments were on board and functioned during the interception. This project management success was due to strong leadership, the presence of an absolute schedule deadline, effective contracts, careful application of technology and the tackling of technical uncertainty on a priority basis, and excellent communications.

From a project management perspective, then, several different kinds of factors can be seen as contributing to the projects' success or failure. Most appear several times.

Channel Tunnel:	Organizational and political problems and lack of overall championing.
Concorde:	Poor organization, ineffective budgeting (including no allowance for escalation), weak contracting arrangements, ineffective controls, design control difficulties.
APT:	Design and quality management problems, lack of top management commitment, inappropriate organizational arrangements, industrial relations pressures.
Thames Barrier:	Industrial relations difficulties, budgeting which did not account for escalation, sub-optimal integration of production expertise early in the project, quality of management dipping rather than rising—many or most of these factors being exacerbated severely by the traditional UK form of civil engineering contract which fails to provide proper management input early in a project.
Heysham 2:	Strong design management, careful contracting policy, site-wide integration of industrial relations, strong leadership; technical problems.
Fulmar:	Technical uncertainties, schedule pressure, some early organizational awkwardness, contracting difficulties, effective leadership.
COP:	Top management support, consistent leadership, detailed planning, good controls, effective contracting.
Giotto:	Strong leadership, an absolute schedule deadline, effective contracts, careful technology management, excellent communications.

We shall be examining what is known of the relationships between these characteristics and their impact on project success in the next chapter. Meanwhile, what does an analysis from the contractors' perspective show?

CONTRACTORS' COMMERCIAL PERFOMANCE

Did those who provided a service for the project benefit commercially?

The Channel Tunnel, 1960–75

Because the project was cancelled before work really began, the question of contractors' commercial performance does not arise. None of the parties working on the project suffered financially.

Concorde

The principal airframe companies, BAC and Sud, and their engine suppliers, Bristol Siddeley and SNECMA, were all operating basically on a cost plus basis; hence their financial gains were limited to the prevalent government formulae. This was also true of a number of subcontractors supplying major systems. There was at least one exception, however, where a major system was developed on a fixed price basis. Because of the restricted production run, there was no opportunity to recover the investment made on the R & D programme. In such cases, subcontractors showed a significant loss on the project. In the longer term, however, the investment made on the R & D necessary to meet the advanced technical requirements of Concorde resulted in the investors moving ahead of their competition and being well placed to win a greater proportion of contracts on later aircraft. Thus, even the subcontractors who nominally lost money on the Concorde project benefited over a longer time-frame from the Concorde exercise.

The Advanced Passenger Train

Although this was a British Rail in-house project there were many subcontractors involved in the programme. Some subcontractors supplied specialist services at a minimum profit and, as is normally the case, invested their design effort in the project on the basis of earning profits in the subsequent production programme. Because of the failure of the project there were investments in the project which ended up as losses although none was large enough to affect significantly the financial stability of the firm concerned.

The Thames Barrier

At the time of writing, claims on several of the Thames Barrier's contracts are still outstanding, thus it is not possible to obtain hard data on participant profitability. Nevertheless most contractors seem to have avoided incurring losses on this large, prestigious and really very risky project and indeed have ended up making good profits and enhancing their reputation.

Heysham 2

With all the contracts on Heysham 2 still open it is not possible to be precise about the outcome of the contractors' profitability. Despite one or two large claims which are being contested, however, the contractors appear generally not to be dissatisfied with the project and it is probable that in general the contractors have found the project to have been a commercially successful one.

Fulmar

A few contractors found Fulmar a commercial success, many probably did not. Hereema negotiated a good contract in the sellers' market. Ponticelli and Highland Fabricators ought to have been commercially successful. McDermott worked on a cost reimbursable basis. CNC and De Groot International probably concluded profitably. There was some feeling that SLP and William Press had negotiated very favourable terms; in so far as both ultimately ended working on a reimbursable/dayworks basis, they are likely to have finished profitably but there is no doubt that the number of changes and the late supply of materials caused many problems. Most of the other major contractors probably lost money, however, or were close to the break-even mark, in part for the above reasons but also in large measure because of their own managerial problems.

The Computerization of PAYE

No contractor appears to have suffered commercially on COP. Some have had to respond energetically to requests for fundamental changes, Plessey for example with the development of the private packet-switching network. For ICL the project has been a lifeline, several times over. Not only is COP a major order, it was a major source of government support at a time when the company could have collapsed; and in so far as COP assisted ICL in the development of Estriel, real substantial assistance is being provided for the development of new, much needed products. This is project support of the most valuable kind.

In 1980, UKITO (the United Kingdom Information Technology Organization) urged government support for the British owned computer industry through (1) the identification of potential projects and (2) the placing of research development and engineering contracts [9]. COP has proved an outstanding example of this policy, at times no doubt to the frustration of COP's technical staff, certainly stretching the ultimate performance capability of the system, but to the benefit of the nation's computer industry in the long term.

Giotto

All the contractors made a small profit with the exception of the contractor who was responsible for the development of the thermal model. By and large, the participants' commercial performance was satisfactory.

Central to the whole question of the contractors' commercial performance is the nature of the contract upon which they were engaged. Where contract policies did not allow the necessary management input to be obtained early enough, like the Thames Barrier, or proved unduly onerous, like some on Fulmar, the project suffered, often quite severely. There are several examples of onerous contracts which required renegotiation. Many involved changes and the negotiation of claims. Cost reimbursable contracts clearly were beneficial to the contractors but were often unsatisfactory to the owner (as the CEGB felt in formulating its contract policy for Heysham 2), although not necessarily always. (The case of Giotto is interesting: ESA originally proposed competitive subsystem bidding with ESA as the system manager though this was ultimately not accepted politically and the more traditional management contractor-cost reimbursable contract was used.) The form and method of contracting is clearly, therefore, an issue to which we must return in the next chapter.

Several projects raise the issue of the long term commercial health of the contractor. Projects which are part of potential long term programmes, like Concorde and APT, may involve an initial significant investment to be amortized over the programme duration. This of course did not happen on these two projects and the contractors suffered accordingly.

On COP, and indeed in the nuclear and North Sea oil (and other) industries, the issue of preferential support for national contractors arises, leading to issues of trade-offs between project optimization and longer term national issues.

PROJECT TERMINATION

Finally, what is there to say as regards project termination?

Channel Tunnel 1960–75

Ascertaining the reasonableness of the cancellation of the Channel Tunnel involves judging several differing viewpoints. The government did not wish the project to be cancelled outright, only that the decision on its treaty ratification be postponed by a year or so; the project's sponsors recognized the financial wisdom of not proceeding further given the financial returns for an essentially no-risk decision—cancellation—should the project not proceed at that time. The financiers essentially had a unique window of opportunity, which it would have been foolish to ignore from their particular, limited viewpoint. To the sponsors, cancellation was obviously a reasonable decision and the terms of the cancellation were 'efficient', but on balance it must be thought that overall the tunnel's cancellation was neither very reasonable nor very efficient.

Advanced Passenger Train

The APT programme as such was terminated by the Railways Board in effect shunting the programme into a hold position. Although the decision was timely, it appears to have been taken under pressure from the media, the unions and the government. Some of the more advanced concepts have been further developed in the research laboratories for application in future systems.

SUMMARY

It has become clear in this chapter that the reasons for the success or failure of the eight different projects arise from many different quarters. It is therefore evident that it would be useful—indeed is necessary—to look more deeply at these factors in order to understand better their importance to the successful accomplishment of projects.

REFERENCES

1. Balachandra R. and Raelin, J. A., 1984; Bedell, R. J., 1983; DeCotiis, T. A. and Dyer, L., 1979; Morgan, H. and Soden, J., 1973.
2. Hall, P., 1980; Sykes, A., 1982, 1986.
3. Morgan, H. and Soden, J., 1973; DeCotiis, T. A. and Dyer, L., 1979.
4. DeWit, A., 1985.
5. Coopers & Lybrand, 1973; *Report of the Channel Tunnel Advisory Group*, 1975.
6. Wilson, A., 1973; Wood, D., 1975.
7. The Rt Hon. Roy Jenkins interviewed by the authors.
8. Franks, J., 1984; Hayes, R. W. *et al.*, 1983; Morris, P. W. G., 1973, 1974; Vicklund, C. A. and Craft, W. S., 1981; Walker, A., 1984.
9. Owen, K., 1980.

Chapter Eleven

The Dimensions of Project Success

In Chapter 10 a wide range of factors having a bearing on the potential success or failure of a project were identified. In this chapter we shall explore in a more systematic way the relevance of these factors to success and failure in the light of both the eight case studies' experience and what other research has to say about such factors. While the analysis is orientated towards the special challenges of major projects, it will be seen that most of the findings are also relevant to the management of projects in general.

PROJECT OBJECTIVES AND THEIR VIABILITY

There is very great agreement in the literature on the importance of a comprehensively investigated project definition which is clearly communicated and agreed [1]. Yet the large size, complexity and technical uncertainty typical of major projects can make harder the task of identifying goals and objectives clearly.

The effect of technical uncertainty is often subtle. The management challenges of technical innovation and uncertainty may be apparent [2] but the effect on project objectives may be less evident. For example, some projects are launched with clear objectives but with considerable uncertainty as to whether, or how, they will be technically achievable; as the technical 'means' develop, 'ends' may be forced to change, often substantially. Sometimes technical change is necessary because objectives change during the project—a situation particularly common in defence projects as the 'threat analysis' changes.

The definition of what a project really involves affects fundamentally the way the management of the project is defined and executed. Broadening the perception of the project has led in certain cases to the concept of 'systems management'.[1] Both the Channel Tunnel, the Thames Barrier and Concorde demonstrate the need to attend to the broader social, community, political and other 'systems' aspects affected by and affecting these projects. All three projects were significantly affected by interaction with local (and not so local) communities. As was noted in the previous chapter, Concorde's management was concerned primarily with technical issues and was insufficiently concerned with the broader issues of sonic boom and airworthiness certification; the Channel Tunnel's project managers were not in control of the rail aspect of the tunnel; and in the Thames Barrier, the local docklands community was a running sore in the effective management of the project.

The importance of evaluating fully the separate dimensions of the project and relating these to the different ones of the project participants has already been noted. In certain situations it is inherently hard to describe precisely or to achieve consensus on project goals, as in many social programmes for example [7]. The worst situation, perhaps, is where the objectives of the project change imprecisely during the project without proper recognition of the new situation. Unrecognized change is a classic cause of catastrophic failure, as the works of Turner and of Bignell and Fortune have demonstrated [8]. Because of their long duration and size, major projects are particularly susceptible to changes in the socio-economic environment affecting fundamentally the appropriateness of the project's original definition.

The case studies provide clear evidence of the importance of objectives. Giotto had carefully formulated objectives which were defined in considerable detail. COP's objectives were clearly stated and exhaustively researched (although they later became compromised by the ICL and CODA decisions). Heysham 2 had very clear objectives and indeed a very tight project specification. Fulmar had clear objectives although

---

[1] The usage of the term 'systems management' varies from industry to industry and organization to organization. The US Commission on Government Procurement defined a (major Federal Government) system as 'a collection of interrelated parts that combine together to perform a specific function to meet a [national] need' [3]. The origins of the concept derive from systems engineering and systems theory, central to which are the notions of interrelatedness, boundaries and control [4]. Admiral Sir Lindsay Bryson put it simply when reviewing the somewhat sorry story of British torpedo projects from 1945 to 1985: 'Why had we got ourselves into such a situation? Firstly, there was no one at an appropriate management level responsible for the *total* weapon system' [5] (emphasis added). The Channel Tunnel, the Thames Barrier and Concorde illustrate the notion of extended systems: 'The concept of extended systems must include significant others in the environment who have control over resources required by the systems, and who consume its outputs. Not only is there dependency and consequent significant interface with labor unions, but the extended systems must also include suppliers of materials, financial institutions, government, consumer pressure groups, educational institutions and customers' (Flippo and Musinger [6]).

not all the uncertainties could be resolved. Both APT and Concorde had objectives which were ostensibly very clear but which in fact concealed some uncertainty and conflict.

In APT the primary problem was the point of origin of the objectives. The objectives came from the newly formed Research Centre, with the support of the Minister of Transport. But they were not fully supported by the British Railways Board—the lack of top management commitment to these objectives was a fundamental weakness. Concorde's objective was merely (sic) the development of a supersonic commercial jet airliner. There was no objective of profitability or even project cost or schedule. This lack of detail in the project's definition later allowed critics of Concorde to question, quite rightly, the enormous cost growth of the programme.

Concorde was of great symbolic importance (politically symbolic of Britain's attitude to the European Community and technologically symbolic to the French Government, seeking as it was to strengthen substantially France's aircraft industry). The way in which this symbolism was articulated and the extent to which later recognition was made that the programme had met these primary objectives is worth considering, particularly in comparison to the Apollo Programme.[2] Apollo, too, was primarily symbolic. It, too, had broad objectives. Indeed, because of these projects' very imprecision it would have been wrong to define their objectives more precisely. Yet the Apollo Programme did have a defined budget which was established at its outset. And the American nation felt proud of Apollo's achievement. The fact that the Apollo Programme included an almost 60 per cent contingency rarely seems to have worried the American public or government. The fact that Concorde overspent its baseline budget by 100 per cent, including inflation, has worried the United Kingdom (and possibly France) enormously. Concorde fared worse than Apollo because its primary objective was not comprehensively investigated prior to commitment, because of several conflicting secondary objectives and because of the inability (and often unwillingness) of government to mobilize support for the project's primary objective.

The Channel Tunnel, too, illustrates the importance of secondary objectives. Like Concorde, the primary objective of the Channel Tunnel was clear but it was the inconsistencies and conflicts amongst the secondary objectives of financiers, British Rail, project managers

---

[2] Indeed, closer analysis of Concorde and Apollo suggests that the current academic interest in organizational symbolism [9], the language of which tends at times towards the esoteric and complex, has in fact much of relevance to the management of projects, particularly major ones.

and different British governments, which were at the heart of the project's difficulties.

We have indicated on several occasions our conviction that projects need to be evaluated in a systematic and objective fashion. Indeed, the Major Projects Association has concluded on several occasions that too many projects proceed that should not have done and that too many proceed only after unnecessarily large sums of money have been spent ascertaining whether or not the project has the preconditions necessary for future success. Since a large number of different parties are generally involved in projects, their different interests need to be recognized: not doing so, e.g. through weak legal agreements or inappropriate contract policies, can lead to project failure. We might therefore believe that a project's viability should be evaluated on an objective basis in the light of the different participants' objectives, strategies and resources.

The COP project certainly demonstrated the merit of careful and systematic evaluation by all parties. The Inland Revenue staff spent considerable time evaluating the project before Cabinet permission was eventually obtained. After the Cabinet decision that ICL should be a major supplier the redefinition of the project that was consequently required involved further careful project evaluation. As the project changed later, e.g. with the ICL agreement with Fujitsu leading to the development of the Estriel programme, the changes in project strategy which were adopted were again carefully evaluated.

Heysham 2 also illustrates the benefit of careful project evaluation. The CEGB had had the opportunity to learn extensively from previous experience (principally the difficulties of the first AGR programme and the industrial relations problems on large sites in the 1970s). The long period in the 1970s when there was no immediate prospect of a further nuclear power station being built allowed the CEGB the time to reflect in depth on how future nuclear power stations should be managed. Further, the initial intention of having the National Nuclear Corporation tender for the construction of the nuclear island on a fixed price basis led to an extremely hard-headed evaluation of the risks involved in that portion of Heysham 2; this allowed a particularly realistic budget to be prepared. The fact that all the major system supply contracts on Heysham 2 were fixed price has similarly encouraged objective evaluation (in this second phase of the AGR programme at least). Importantly, both the NNC and the system suppliers were given adequate time to appraise the project. The use by the CEGB of design contracts with manufacturers prior to the letting of their hardware contracts allowed the manufacturers a year or two of working on the project prior to the submission of their final fixed-price supply and installation bids. All this ensured that the CEGB and its contractors approached the project in a realistic way, with risk appropriately evaluated and objectives jointly shared. The late discovery of the control rod problem in no way invalidates this management approach, but rather makes a different point about the need for enormous care in the technology management of such technically complex projects.

The Thames Barrier, in contrast, demonstrates the tendency in certain projects, particularly those in the civil construction industry, for the management aspects to be evaluated neither early enough in the project nor in sufficient detail. The Thames Barrier was indeed evaluated in great detail from a technical viewpoint but it was assumed that the implementation of the barrier works would be the responsibility of the contractor and that the contractor could adequately do this when employed under the traditional form of civil engineering contract. This, briefly, is that tenders are invited once the design has been prepared and that these tenders are submitted and selected on a competitive basis. Responsibility for the planning and implementation of the construction work then rests with the contractor, working under the 'independent' authority of the consulting engineer. The consulting engineer acts to ensure that the work is performed adequately to the specification and under the terms of the contract. It is assumed that the contractor will, as part of his commercial responsibilities, ensure that the work is adequately planned and managed. There is no suggestion that the implementation skills—in this case the contractor's—need be brought in early in the planning and design phase. This, at any rate, has and continues to be the traditional approach to civil engineering work, although there have been moves during the 1970s and 1980s to introduce more management earlier in the project, e.g. through the development of the management contractor role, to deal with the project more as an integrated 'whole' [10]. It is, however, questionable whether such management input is broad enough or whether a wider 'systems' management approach might not be beneficial on large, complex construction jobs, particularly those which interact with their local environment significantly. Fulmar too seems to have demonstrated problems of contractors properly evaluating the risks posed by the project. The very considerable overruns experienced by most of the contractors on Fulmar show that the evaluation of the difficulties posed by the project was inadequate.

The Channel Tunnel was assessed objectively by all parties but, crucially, there was no one person 'objectively' representing the project's interests who had the aim, need and charter to discuss and interact with these parties. Had there been an effecive project champion it may well have been that the various parties 'objective evaluations' would have produced different conclusions. Partly this gets back to the philosophical issue of whether knowledge—that is, knowledge of the evaluation of the project—can truly be objective or whether it must not inevitably involve a degree of subjectivism. Knowledge which is of a people-type reality must involve some subjectivism [11]. Where those people have very strong personalities it is inevitable that objective knowledge becomes harder to obtain. Leaders change values. They force commitment. Leaders influence people's evaluation through both their charisma and their ability to change the terms of a discussion— both reality and its perception change as terms are negotiated.

Hence, this analysis of the case studies shows that previous research into the importance of objectives to project success has not gone far enough. It is not merely the identification and investigation of project objectives and the communication of these which is important. Motivations for these objectives, and the secondary objectives which the project inevitably has, can cause fundamental problems. What seemed on the face of it to be a plausible suggestion, that the evaluation of project viability should be objective and realistic from the participants' individual viewpoints, is shown, particularly by the Channel Tunnel case, to mask some deeper uncertainties, though the thesis remains none the less important. Certainly, projects must be evaluated objectively by their individual participants but effective leadership can, indeed must, provide both the will and the practical terms and conditions necessary for a project to go ahead. In the absence of such leadership, an overly objective evaluation of the high risks invariably posed by major projects can too easily lead to the decision not to proceed. Lastly, the broader definition of what accomplishing the project really involves—the so-called systems approach to the project— is of fundamental importance in establishing if the project will be a success.

TECHNICAL UNCERTAINTY AND INNOVATION

Many studies, in particular by the Rand Corporation, have indicated the important effect of technical uncertainty on the likelihood of projects suffering overruns [12]. The amount of technical innovation in a project can pose enormous challenges to budget and schedule estimating and ultimately compromise the very attainment of the desired technical performance [13]. Of the case studies we have examined, those having high technical uncertainty, like Concorde and the AGR programme, clearly have the largest overruns.

Great caution is required where there is overlapping of design and production, particularly if there are resource shortages as well as innovation [14]. This is the situation known technically as concurrency [15], an issue which we shall examine in detail below (pp.228–9).[3] Suffice it to say for the moment that both Concorde, the early AGR programme and Fulmar exhibited overlapping and interrelated design and production. In the case of the first AGR station, Dungeness B, the problems of substantial technical uncertainties being resolved during construction were compounded by the inexperience of the consortium building the plant. Similarly on the Thames Barrier, the technical problems experienced in piling and the coffer dam work, for example, might have been reduced by a more experienced management.

On APT the degree of innovation was high, from a British Rail viewpoint at least, perhaps unnecessarily and dangerously so. Indeed, some of the early projects which have been examined, such as Concorde and the AGRs, exhibit almost a technological bravura—a lack of caution in the face of high innovation which does not fit well with today's knowledge of managing projects. Giotto, for example, minimized technical uncertainty by using established technology and resolving outstanding uncertainties on a priority basis. If this strategy had not been adopted there is little doubt that the spacecraft could not have made the interception with Halley's Comet. On COP, too, there were always fall-back positions ready to cover the several high level technical risks, e.g. those posed by the decision to adopt ICL hardware and software, and particularly the decision to develop the Estriel machine. The extent to which design and development were accomplished before the commitment to production was made was clearly important on Concorde. Being a political project, commitment was given very early in the project—at 5 per cent of project completion—long before the technical risks had been fully appraised. In most aerospace projects today, commitment would not normally be given until around the 20 per cent mark. On the early AGR programme too, commitment was given with design in only an outline form. When committed to in such a state of technological uncertainty, opportunities for unforeseen development problems to occur are potentially enormous. In the first phase of the AGR programme not only was the technology not known, the 36-pin design had only just been conceived. On Heysham 2, on the other hand, full commitment was given only after groundwork had begun and the basic design work was complete. On COP, commitment was given only after a very considerable period

---

[3] *Concurrency* is the practice of initiating some production activities prior to the completion of full-scale development. It has also been invested by some with the broader meaning of simultaneous and interrelated development to a tight schedule.

of prefeasibility/feasibility studies and after the supplier options had been investigated thoroughly together with an analysis of the implications to the programme of contracting with ICL.

As we saw with APC and Dungeness B, the assessment of the key parties' technological and managerial abilities, and their needs, comes out as an important aspect of the case studies' histories. COP would have been a different story if the Inland Revenue had not had to procure from ICL and could have used more powerful equipment with developed software from, say, IBM. The abilities of the fabricators on Fulmar could have been more accurately appraised. Had British Rail been managed as an indispensable element of the success of the 1960–75 Channel Tunnel, then that project might have turned out very differently.

Design philosophies should be flexible; unnecessarily burdensome specifications should be avoided [16]. Once agreed, design should be 'frozen' and changes made only in the most controlled of circumstances [17]. Fulmar is a classic example of a project where design management difficulties caused substantial problems. The question will always remain for Fulmar as to whether or not management should have resolved the outstanding technical issues before letting the fabrication contracts. The answer is of course unknowable. Shell-Expro, however, are convinced of the rightness of their decision to go ahead. First, they argue, it was not appreciated at the time that design was in fact only 35 per cent or so complete; second, even if it had been, the pressure to move ahead was such at the time that it was unlikely that a different course of action would have been chosen; and third, even in retrospect it is not clear that delaying the letting of contracts until the design was further developed would necessarily have led to a shorter overall project duration. The first reason demonstrates one of the major difficulties of design management—knowing when design will be complete, i.e. what is 100 per cent; and hence what is 35 per cent or any other degree of completion. On Heysham 2, design was managed as rigorously as was absolutely possible while on COP great efforts were made to create a standardized design environment. Concorde, on the other hand, experienced great difficulties in design management, not just because of the truly enormous technical challenges, nor because of the relative crudeness of our design management tools in the 1960s, but because of the complex management structure predicated by the international treaty.

The situation of innovative design should be distinguished as tougher than that of mere technical uncertainty. The basic rule applies in both situations, however, that novelty should be kept to the point such that, beyond key 'terminal points', tasks can be allocated and carried out without unforeseen repercussions [18]. This philosophy (part of what is sometimes known as 'interface management') was extremely important and successfully managed on Giotto, COP and Heysham 2. On Concorde, on the other hand, doing this was difficult and was not effectively performed, for the reasons just described.

Use of established designs, as we saw in Giotto and the AGR programme, can, where appropriate, lead to substantial cost and schedule efficiencies. In the North Sea, second and third generation projects are using technologies and designs developed in earlier phases.

The fretting and rubbing of the control rods on Heysham 2, discovered during commissioning tests in October 1986, makes a bitter addendum to these observations. The design change which lies behind this problem (the reversal of the control rod and fuel rod nozzles on the gas baffle with the consequent change in gas turbulence around the rods at these nozzles) was considered so minor at the time it was made that, despite the great sensitivity on the part of the CEGB to the potential dangers of technology changes, they were not thought large enough to warrant full rig tests. The lesson can only be, with hindsight, that in technically complex and sensitive designs such as nuclear reactor pressure vessels, all design changes have to be fully investigated. The possible costs of future changes are just too great for this not to be the case.

Introducing new technology can produce quality control and assurance problems which may seriously affect the ability to achieve budgets and schedules. This was seen in Concorde in the length of time required to obtain the Certificate of Airworthiness. Quality Assurance has similarly had a major effect on nuclear power projects, especially in the 1970s in the licensing of the US plants and in the discussion of the choice of new reactor type for the United Kingdom. As has just been noted in the case of Heysham 2, such attention to quality assurance is necessary not simply to satisfy the public. Complex technology, particularly where failure would have severe or catastrophic consequences, as in aerospace and nuclear power, is unforgiving in its unremitting demand for sustained attention to quality, by all involved in the project, in design, manufacture and assembly.[4]

The special difficulty of projects, of course, is their temporal nature. Once the decision to commit is made, things are in many ways easier. But prior to the decision to commit the question of timing can have a crucial effect on the degree of technical difficulty. Had the Thames Barrier been built before the decline of the Port of London, its technology and design, and its impact on the community, might have been

---

[4] The case of the NASA Space Shuttle's 'O' rings is a tragic case in point.

much larger, more complex and awkward. The selection of nuclear power technology (AGR, SGHWR, PWR) was done under schedule pressure and often without formal or frank appraisal of the managerial issues posed by the new technology. The tendency to force the pace of early project decisions is notable in several of the cases (AGR, Fulmar, Concorde, Giotto) nearly always because of the belief that the opportunity had not to be lost. Grabbing the moment because the time is politically or commercially ripe is often essential; but there should be careful analysis of the market's need for technological innovation. And it must be remembered that if grabbing the moment involves decisions being inadequately investigated, work must be done later to rectify the deficiencies in the understanding of the project which will inevitably exist. Concorde and the AGR programme were technology dominated (by a technological elite who had poor technology management skills). Marketing was given little detailed attention. It was assumed that sales would emerge once the technological advantages could be demonstrated. Nowadays organizations involved in major projects having technological uncertainty where possible reduce this uncertainty to almost predictable dimensions, through prefeasibility, feasibility and design studies before final commitment is given, the project then being carefully reviewed at each stage. They also, hopefully, give more detailed attention to overall reliability. (This applies equally to contractors and owners.) Where this careful precommitment appraisal is not possible, the project budget must be recognized as uncertain (it then being better perhaps to represent estimates as a range rather than as a single figure): sponsors should recognize the likelihood of initial budget overruns; contractors should secure reimbursable contracts on the best possible terms, and manage their claims process professionally.

POLITICS

The influence of politics on projects has received surprisingly little study, despite its evident significance. Politics has an impact on projects through funding, sponsorship and legislation over fiscal, safety, employment and other matters. This influence can be direct, as for example in Concorde or the North Sea, or indirect [19]. Political considerations invariably dominate decision making in Third World development projects and in developed world projects in or affecting the public domain, particularly in infrastructure and high technology [20]. Indeed, political sponsorship is viewed by many as one of the single most critical 'success' factors for such projects. Though political over-dominance generally reduces managerial efficiency, government commitment to a project can be an essential precondition of project success. As Paul found in his study of six large Third World projects, government must provide clear objectives, allow flexibility of management approach, monitor progress, and provide stability, commitment and continuity [21]. To say this, is not to argue for government interference, however. Government's role is an enabling one. Management must be left to manage, while government must provide the conditions necessary for project success.

Government played an enormous role in almost all the cases studied. It initiated the Channel Tunnel, the Thames Barrier (sic), COP and Concorde and it played an important role in North Sea oil and the AGR and APT projects. And, of course, the change in government in 1974 fundamentally weakened the Channel Tunnel's chances of success. Government is inescapably a major player in major projects, as sponsor, regulator, champion or owner.[5]

Government as Sponsor

Until the Thatcher administration, it was common practice for governments in the United Kingdom, as elsewhere, to act as the principal sponsor of major projects. Government involved itself willingly in the selection of the UK's commercial nuclear reactor type in 1962 with the establishment of the Powell Committee[6], though much less willingly in the PWR/AGR debate of the late 1970s. Concorde, as has been noted on several occasions, was pre-eminently a political project enthusiastically sponsored by the Conservative Government of Harold Macmillan.

Such direct sponsorship stems from an era when it was considered quite natural for government to shoulder the financial risk of large, technology driven, technologically innovative projects. Large vested interests of technical experts, such as the UKAEA and Royal Aircraft Establishment, exerted great power on the centralized, governmental

---

[5] In the case of overseas export projects, a class or projects not studied or reported on in this work, government also provides a crucial role in the provision of financial guarantees, aid and other assistance.

[6] Sir Christopher Hinton, Chairman of the CEGB, began to advocate in 1961 that the Canadian CANDU heavy water reactor was the best replacement for the board's existing magnox reactor. The government rebuked him for his candour and, being persuaded by the UKAEA and others of the merits of the AGR reactor, established the Powell Committee in 1962 to choose the successor to the magnox, with the results described in Chapter 6 [22].

sponsorship of major projects. In the end this often became exceedingly frustrating, as for example when 'electricity experts' like the Electricity Council, CEGB, SSEB and UKAEA disagreed fundamentally on whether to opt for the PWR or the AGR [23] or when communities objected strenuously to the siting of motorways like the M3, the M40 and the London motorway box, or the third London airport [24]. Politicians were then left exposed and were often forced, as in the PWR/AGR case, to take technological decisions for which they were not technically qualified.

In such circumstances it is little wonder that government becomes secretive, for there is much at stake while the decision-making criteria are foggy and the data themselves soft. Public accountability then becomes a central issue, as it has been in the nuclear and aerospace industries now for several years [25]. A further unfortunate conse-quence is that clear project monitoring and evaluation is often frus-trated. There is no evidence, for example, of anyone in government having attempted a full cost–benefit analysis of the investment put into Concorde.

The current political climate of market based economics must surely, therefore, have merit. Yet it would be wrong to suppose that govern-ment can simply absent itself from the sponsorship of major projects altogether. Even in a healthy market driven environment, government has a *de facto* sponsoring role as regulator, champion or owner.

Government as Regulator

Government provides the regulatory framework within which projects operate. Most obviously such regulation pertains to health and safety: the role of governmental agencies in setting safety standards in the nuclear power industry and the effects of changing standards on project costs (regulatory ratchetting: Chapter 6), for example, are well known. It is often also an economic and administrative regulator, as in the development of North Sea oil, in ways which are generally less well appreciated.

The North Sea oil business hardly existed at the beginning of the 1970s and market conditions were such then that neither the British nor the Norwegian Governments were in a strong position. They had essentially to induce the multinationals to enter the province. Neither government understood the oil industry well enough and had difficulty in formulating effective strategies. Both governments consequently adopted innovative economic and administrative approaches for the control of North Sea exploration and development. First, data was collected on the industry in a systematic manner in order to understand it better. Second, a policy of administrative allocation of licences for oil field development was implemented with the aim not just of actively promoting exploration and production but of encouraging the involvement of domestic industry as opposed to the multinationals. The British Government was even prepared to have the Offshore Supplies Office (OSO) take an active 'venture management' role in suggesting opportunities for UK firms [26]. Following the quadrupling of oil prices in 1973, the government was able, third, to tighten up the tax system without the same fear of depressing the rate of exploration and production activity. Petroleum Revenue Tax, which was introduced in 1979, constitutes an important innovation in UK taxation policy. Prior to PRT the oil companies had been operating with fiscal policies that were undoubtedly very generous. PRT, while still far from ungenerous and admittedly having some administrative drawbacks, through its application at individual field level is operated as a targetted, effective tool of fiscal regulation, balancing income distribution and companies' rate of return on capital employed, combining fiscal responsibility with industrial initiative.

Government as Champion

Through their economic and industrial policies the British and Norwegian Governments were acting as *de facto* champions of North Sea oil projects. Without these encouraging frameworks these projects would not have been initiated. Major projects constitute such large risks that governmental encouragement is generally essential in order to provide the stimulus necessary to those contemplating them. Such encouragement is often, perhaps generally, direct, as in the case of the fiscal treatment of North Sea oil projects. But when government ostensibly forbears direct involvement, an indirect champion is necessary. In the current Channel Link venture, for example, governmental championing in the form of guarantees against government cancellation and the tabling of the Hybrid Bill enabling legislation has been crucial to the project. And of course withdrawal of the government's championship was a direct cause of the failure of the previous Channel project.

The role of government is particularly important where major projects do not have an obvious owner. Such projects are most commonly found in the public sector, particularly in infrastructure (the

Channel Link being an obvious example). While private companies contemplating major projects can typically do so within a framework of relatively robust corporate strategies, profitability criteria and decision-making processes, projects which do not have an obvious owner can fail to have any of these. The champions of such projects have to put together frameworks to provide them. Doing so involves, at the very least, considerable integration with the regulatory authorities; it more generally requires political support and possibly direct championship on the part of government, for instance in obtaining planning approvals, fiscal support and other legislation.

Aerospace is another sector requiring governmental championship, often in an obvious and direct form. Concorde illustrated clearly the limitations of private financing. Three or four hundred Concordes would have had to have been sold in order to provide the payback on the plane's research, development and production costs. This posed too great a marketing risk for industry, particularly given the technological and other uncertainties. Aircraft projects still pose huge risks; companies thus look for strong indications of sales before committing to production and where possible for government assistance either through launch aid—that requested for the Airbus medium and long haul A-330 and A-340 being a current example—or more indirectly through sales assistance or, particularly in the United States, by offset-ting costs on government defence and space work. These matters are a particular concern in the up-coming generation of space projects. Creating an infrastructure in near-space, through projects such as Hotol and the space station, will be enormously expensive: since industry will benefit, how should private funding be obtained for these programmes? To what extent will government not have to take a championship role (as it has consistently in the United States since the 1960s, with Presi-dent Kennedy championing Apollo, Nixon initiating the Shuttle, and Reagan the space station and the US spaceplane)?

Government as Owner

Finally, government often has an important role as the direct owner of a major project. This is true of all defence projects, for example. Large systems implementation projects, like COP and the DHSS computeriz-ation, represent another class. Local authority projects, like the Thames Barrier and possibly the proposed Mersey and Severn barrages, represent another.

Defence projects currently constitute the largest single sector of major projects in both the United Kingdom and the majority of the developed world. This study has not examined a defence project in detail, however, and thus will not comment upon this important sector except to note that virtually all the issues raised in this analysis—whether of finance or leadership, the pre-eminence of research organizations or the absence of a systems management perspective, contracting policy or technical uncertainty—apply equally to defence (as the recent report of the Auditor General illustrates [27]). And the attitudes and practices of government and its agencies on defence projects affect the firms it employs in various ways, whether through the value of the work it places, the tools and techniques it uses, or the attitudes it adopts, e.g. in contracting.

We see in COP the subtler issue of government support for industry. Should government be criticized for wanting the ICL industry-support contract? Is it not right after all for government to wish to protect and develop the nation's industrial base; and did not good management, in the Inland Revenue and ICL, in fact ultimately prove the decision to have been a good one?

The apparent legal obstacles which prevent elected local authority officials from delegating full project management authority to their employees, coupled with the perhaps inevitable inexperience on major projects of local authorities, calls into question the very possibility of whether a local authority will ever be able to manage such projects effectively. Where there clearly is a 'skills gap' of this nature it would seem highly desirable for outside assistance to be brought in, either from central government or from the private sector in the form of management contractors or consultants.

Perhaps the biggest single impact of government on major projects, and the cause of greatest regrets, has been the making of commitments without a proper investigation of the consequences. Concorde's treaty was signed with virtually no investigations. The experimental phase of the Advanced Passenger Train, APT(E), went ahead without detailed review and against the wishes of the British Railways Board but because of the persistence of the research director and the championing of the minister. Similarly, the Humber Bridge was built primarily in fulfilment of an electoral promise made by Barbara Castle [28]. The Lear fan jet was initiated by the Northern Ireland office without proper financial or technical risk assessment because it seemed a good way of creating employment [29]. Likewise, projects have been cancelled without serious study of the losses which will be suffered and the opportunities forgone. Government cannot always be expected to act with a rationality that appeals to every businessman. Yet in so far as major projects contribute to our industrial, social and economic well being, there is a case for greater consistency and more careful systematic analysis of decisions on the nation's major projects by our politicians and their agents. Where there is not this consistency, the consequences can be very costly.

Government has to provide the conditions for long term implementation success. It is not merely that governments of different hue may impose changes in industrial policy, taxation and economic management and thereby cause substantial problems to major projects (and indeed to business generally [30]). Government must provide the requisite regulatory support and political will over a sustained period, taking cognizance of the market and technology risk posed by such projects and the management structures and resources available. When Concorde was begun, France had an inadequate aerospace industry. Largely through Concorde, it has developed a first rate one (with Europe as a whole benefiting, as for example in the development of Airbus Industries). With the same kind of government support France has similarly revolutionized the state of its telecommunications and power industries. In Britain, government support has ensured the massive exploitation of North Sea Oil.

COMMUNITY INVOLVEMENT

It is clear that public attitudes towards major projects are becoming increasingly important—at least in the United Kingdom: in the United States they have been extremely important for over a decade, as the US SST, the whole nuclear programme and TAPS illustrated [31]. The Channel Link has experienced frustration in its initiation as a result of the very large number of planning objections lodged against it; the CEGB's nuclear power building programme has suffered considerable uncertainty as a result of Chernobyl and communities' consequent nervousness of nuclear power. Yet in the case studies, community opposition was not truly a significant item, except with Concorde.

The Channel Tunnel began to suffer from community opposition, generated in large part by the ferries (Keith Wickenden emerged as a lobbyist), and it is probable that this opposition would have got worse had the project continued. Heysham 2 suffered no adverse community reaction, partly because of the very positive efforts made by the CEGB towards the local community, partly because of the depressed employment situation of Morecambe and North Lancashire. Apart from

Concorde, the other case studies hardly affected the population in any sizeable way. Concorde, however, affected a great many people very severely. Opposition against the project was formidably led [32]. Being truly international, political opposition, for instance in approvals for over-flying and landing rights, was very important; for the same reasons, political support was crucial.

The number of people affected by a project would thus seem a matter of first importance. Their political clout is clearly another factor, as the opposition to the various London airport schemes makes clear [33]. The role of the media is obviously also important. APT, though not suffering from community opposition, clearly suffered from the media sensing a kill. Dealing with the media is a skill in itself. Perhaps managers of major projects should be trained in this art. They should certainly give more attention to the management of the project's public relations.

SCHEDULE DURATION AND URGENCY

Major projects' success can be jeopardized by their long schedule duration. The success of lengthy projects is hostage to changes in output prices, demand, regulation, technical developments and changes in government, corporate organization, staffing, personnel or policy— almost everything, in fact [34]. These changes can alter the entire basis on which the project was undertaken. We saw this dramatically in the case of the Channel Tunnel with the change in government in 1974. The threat of possible changes in governmental legislation was also important with Fulmar. Of all the cases, however, Concorde most vividly illustrates the dangers of long duration. Its budget, which included no allowance for cost escalation, was soon out of date as inflation increased sharply in the mid-to-late 1960s and 1970s and as the sterling–franc exchange rate deteriorated; the economics of air travel changed totally with the 700 per cent increase in oil price between the early 1960s and mid 1970s (and in so far as Concorde is a long range supersonic aircraft, it is very sensitive to the fuel:payload relationship); community activism increased sharply.

The special problem of the Channel Tunnel was that its schedule was at its most vulnerable when the crucial political changes occurred in 1974 (the possibility of a general election representing a similar threat to Eurotunnel in 1987.) This experience of the Channel Tunnel on two distinct occasions suggests that there is a real problem for those major

The Anatomy of Major Projects

projects which are dependent upon political support. It is often only after a government has been in power for some time that the decision is taken to commence such a project; by the time the necessary preparatory work has been done the project is at its most vulnerable, with finance having to be raised and planning objections met, only by then the government is likely to be facing a re-election. Indeed it is a feature of major projects that their implementation may span the duration of two or three elected governments. One obvious way of coping with this problem is to undertake major projects where possible in stages, phased to the internal development of the project and to external events outside the project [35][7].

COP's schedule was explicitly designed to minimize the risk of failure. There were strategic review points in the schedule, e.g. there was a major evaluation period in 1983 upon completion of the initial system. There were several strategic reviews on Fulmar in 1977 and early 1978 on how to develop the field. Up to 30 different schemes were investigated before the final scheme was selected. Once engineering got under way, however, the high net present value of the oil, created in part by the fiscal environment and the threat of changed governmental legislation but typical of the industry in general, created considerable urgency. In fact, this urgency became overriding, and while it can be argued that for sensible control reasons it would have been prudent to have had a major review of the project at the completion of design prior to letting the fabrication contracts, at which time the wisdom of proceeding with design only 30–40 per cent complete might have been questioned, in practice it was considered best to keep to the original schedule.[8] The result unfortunately was the situation known as concurrency.

Concurrency, as we have already noted, is the practice of initiating some production activities prior to the completion of full scale development. Concurrency has also come to take on the broader meaning of simultaneous and interrelated development of design and production to a tight schedule. Research has shown that on high technology projects concurrency invariably leads to project overruns [37]. Concurrency has been common practice on defence projects since at least the 1950s, although there has been serious debate about its benefits and for a

---

[7] This strategy may be used in a more ambitious way in high technology programmes where technological development may be 'terraced' so that immediate objectives may be specified with reasonable assurance of success, the next terraced step being specified later as more information becomes available, the overall programme goal being specified not on the basis of project-specific R & D but on generic technical development [36].

[8] This said, however, it is worth recalling that each individual contract was reviewed twice, first at the preparation of the tender list, and second, prior to the award of the contract to the eventual winner.

while it was officially banned on US defence projects [38]. Hence, for example, the case of the US General Accounting Office which, in a 1985 study of production problems in defence projects, was specifically asked by the Department of Defense to 'highlight the benefit of concurrent development and production in some of the cases GAO studied since it provided more opportunity to attend to produceability matters early in development'. The GAO did report that concurrency 'enables more informed production decisions to be made' but would not endorse starting production of units before they are sufficiently designed and tested [39]. Research on process plant projects has similarly shown concurrency to be associated with overruns [40]. The CEGB has now firmly come down against the beginning of site work before design has been sufficiently tested—a practice which, of course, caused enormous problems in the development of the AGR reactors.

The essential problem of urgency is to know when haste becomes counterproductive. In the Thames Barrier case, the known urgency of the project provided a weapon for militant operatives to slow the project down in order to strengthen their bargaining position. In the case of Fulmar there is the conundrum of whether proceeding with the fabrication contracts in the autumn of 1978 with the design relatively incomplete ultimately caused so many problems that it negated and even worked against the project schedule. On the other hand, there is no doubt that the presence of a finite deadline on the Giotto project was of enormous benefit. In fact, many managers of projects, major and otherwise, have commented on the value—indeed the necessity—of maintaining schedule pressure, and there is no better way of doing this than through an immutable end date! Concorde is the exception which proves the rule. Once the US SST was cancelled in 1971 the urgency to complete Concorde was removed and the project was allowed to be completed in its own time.

FINANCIAL, LEGAL AND CONTRACTUAL MATTERS

One might expect the biggest single challenge on major projects to be that of assembling the required finance. Certainly the Channel Tunnel exhibited the difficulties of raising funds on the private market. Although these difficulties had not proved great at the time of its cancellation there were fears that they would be much greater in Phase 3. The same difficulties applied on the current Channel Link project.

Yet on most of the other projects, difficulties of raising the required finance were much less in evidence than might at first be supposed. Certainly Concorde came under considerable pressure from Parliament and the government because of its cost growth; in spite of the attempts to cancel the project the money was forthcoming. On the Thames Barrier too there was generally little difficulty in obtaining the required funds (70 per cent coming from the Ministry of Agriculture, Fisheries and Food, the rest from the GLC) despite the substantial cost growth, although of course as the project cost grew there were some (generally rather feeble) attempts made to improve the management of the project. The absence of funding difficulties in the other case studies can be explained partly because the private sector projects did not exceed their approved budgets or because public sector funding continued to be made available despite cost growth, where this occurred. Clearly, then, the manner of project finance influences its chances of success.

The practice in government projects of not having to estimate actual out-turn costs, as is the case in private projects, has to be questionable. The discipline of having to define what the actual final cost will be, including an allowance for cost escalation and contingencies, forces the project sponsors to undertake a most rigorous and comprehensive risk analysis of the project. For in effect financial risk analysis is an analysis of all the risks of the project—technical, organizational, managerial, political—as well as the specific financial factors such as exchange rate risks, bad debts and so on. Surely the attitude typified by a senior manager at the Thames Barrier, that money was not a useful measure of project performance but that projects should be controlled rather through physical resources such as man-hours, is an extremely unhealthy one [41].

Cost escalation and exchange rate fluctuations had a near catastrophic effect on the ability of certain of the case studies to meet their project budgets. The effect of exchange rate variations on increasing the project out-turn cost was seen clearly on the Channel Tunnel. As noted, 57 per cent of Concorde's cost overrun was due to exchange rate variations and cost escalation. (That these factors did not seem to be a particular problem on the Fulmar project was largely because of the short duration of the multinational fabrication contracts.) Modern techniques of handling exchange rate fluctuations have reduced significantly many of these currency risks, but the disruption both these factors may cause to this measure of project success remains potent [42].

In general, the legal agreements between parties in the various case studies worked well. Legal agreements should be clear and equitable. They should reflect properly the parties' key objectives, financial provisions, problems of sovereignty, taxation, rights and responsibilities and the respective assessment of risks. The joint ventures in the case studies—such as Fulmar (Shell-Expro), the Thames Barrier (CTH) and COP (ICL–Fujitsu)—in general respected these principles and worked well. On the Channel Tunnel it is said that almost more attention was given to negotiating the break clauses in the legal agreements than was spent on relating to how the parties would work together. In fact, when all is said and done, commitment to making the contract work and the project a success is many times more important than the terms and conditions of the contract. This is seen time and again in the case studies, most notably in COP, Giotto and Fulmar.

The form of contract used for engaging services, particularly of the main contractor, has a direct influence on the financial and organizational basis upon which the project is undertaken. As such it clearly influences the likelihood of project success or failure. Yet there are relatively few studies of the extent to which this is the case [43].

The contracting strategy adopted will depend considerably upon the experience, resources and preferences of the owner. The case studies represent an interesting array of different roles adopted by owners on projects, some of which reflect primarily the characteristics of the owner firms but many of which are typical of their industries (Table 11.1).

Channel Tunnel 1960–75 (Civil/Mechanical)—No Owner

The owner was represented by the project management groups but in effect did not exist as a long term operator, broadly based decision maker and champion.

Concord (Aerospace)—A Weak to Almost Non-existent Owner

The government's involvement as owner was very weak. Two aircraft campanies designed, developed, built and tested the plane. Many commercial questions, e.g. landing rights, received very little attention until late in the programme.

Table 11.1   Owner–contractor relationships

Industry	Typical owner–contractor relationship
CIVIL CONSTRUCTION (e.g. Channel Tunnel, Thames Barrier)	The civil construction industry, reflecting its situation of numerous, often inexperienced owners, relies on the consulting engineer to prepare the design and administer the contract. The problem with this arrangement is that the consulting engineer may have a primary concern with 'the design' as opposed to subtler aspects of the project such as the trade-off between schedule and cost, let alone the owner's longer term or broader operating and community interests.
POWER (e.g. Heysham 2)	The power industry is dominated by the CEGB and the SSEB and has a limited number of suppliers; the nuclear stations represent such complex technical issues that the CEGB would prefer to put as much managerial responsibility on the contractors as possible and to concentrate on managing technical and interface matters. Both boards rely heavily on the technical expertise of the NNC for the design and administration of work on the nuclear island.
NORTH SEA OIL (e.g. Fulmar)	In the North Sea oil and gas industry, the owner generally has a strong involvement in the direct management of the project, usually because he believes he may have a better knowledge, or wants more control, of the interplay of 'high stake' factors involved than any contractor.
PRODUCT DEVELOPMENT (e.g. APT)	Product development is typically an in-house function; care should be taken, however, to ensure there is some form of formal ('contracting') or project arrangement.
COMPUTERIZATION (e.g. COP)	Computerization projects involve: software development, which may be done in-house or contracted out; equipment supply (and possibly development); and in-house organization development. Management approaches to this work vary but owners often take an active involvement.
AEROSPACE (e.g. Concorde, Giotto)	In aerospace, requirements or specifications are usually developed by the owner (e.g. government, ESA), in broad terms at least; contractors then develop and build the project, usually under the direction of a lead management contractor. Note that on Giotto ESA officials attempted to exert a much more direct control of the project by developing the system specification themselves and contracting out subsystem manufacture competitively. This process was rejected on political grounds, however. (See Chapter 9.)

APT (In-company Product Development)—A Muddled Owner

The owner designed and built the product himself using the same department as both client and contractor with a limited amount of subcontracting.

The Thames Barrier (Civil Construction)—A Weak Owner

The owner took a relatively passive role, delegating the design and the administration of the contract(or)s to the consulting engineer. The owner's role was largely reactive: the design and contracting decisions were substantially the responsibility of the consulting engineer. The contractor procured, fabricated and installed within the relatively tight limits of the contract drawings, specifications and priced bills of quantities (which were ultimately put on a reimbursable basis).

Heysham 2 (Power Station)—A Learning Owner

The owner prepared the basic design; contractors assisted, working as design consultants. Contractors then negotiated fixed-price contracts for the detailed design, fabrication, installation and testing of material and equipment. The owner administered and coordinated these contracts and their technical interfacing.

Fulmar (North Sea oil and gas)—A Strong but Still Learning Owner

The owner prepared the conceptual design but had a design consultant to assist with detailed design. The owner procured materials and equipment. Contractors fabricated and installed on a fixed-price basis as far as possible (but also using bills of quantities). The owner administered and coordinated contracts and on at least one occasion had to take direct charge of the contracted work.

COP (Computerization)—A Strong Owner

The owner engaged consultants to assist in preparing specifications and a development plan. Equipment suppliers were contracted (fixed/target price) to supply/develop equipment. The owner (and consultants) developed software and planned, coordinated and controlled the overall project work.

Giotto (Aerospace)—A Strong Participatory Owner

The owner responded to a proposal from the contractor and ultimately they together developed a design specification. A European aerospace contractor conducted detailed design and development, and built and tested the spacecraft, essentially on a cost-plus basis.

These different industry practices create different expectations as to what constitutes an appropriate contracting policy. In fact, the case studies illustrate at times quite conflicting contracting policies.

First, there is the issue of what roles owners require of themselves and their contractors. In the heavy engineering industries (power generation and oil, gas and petrochemicals) where owners are experienced they typically take a strong involvement in the management of their projects and engage contractors generally on a well defined (e.g. fixed-price) basis. Where they are not experienced, project management expertise may be contracted-in, basically through a project services contractor (PSC) or a management contractor (Figure 11.1).

(Definitions of these terms are notoriously vague. The PSC concept (used, for example, by Alyeska on the Trans-Alaskan Pipeline [44]) is fairly constant: an intermingling of the contractor's project staff with the owner's to work jointly as the owner's project management (in Alyeska's jargon, on a salt-and-pepper basis). The terms 'management contractor' and 'project manager' differ between construction and aerospace in whether or not a management contractor accepts responsibility for project performance. In construction he generally would not whereas a project management contractor would (Figure 11.1) [45]; in aerospace this distinction is not often made.)

Second, the different industries have different traditions of fixed-price versus cost-sharing forms of contract (and in a similar way, of using turnkey versus component contracting [46]). Aerospace, being a high risk industry, has traditionally used cost-plus contracting— Concorde was largely cost reimbursable as was Giotto (at least within its target budget)—albeit this is currently changing as the Ministry of Defence introduces more competitive procurement practices. The power industry, however, has a history of fixed-price contracting, even in conditions of high technical uncertainty and risk, as in the early AGRs. The CEGB regretted severely its decision to implement the 1970 NEDO recommendation that it place its major contracts on a

I. OWNER MANAGED

Single contractor

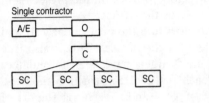

Multiple contractors

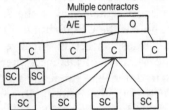

Owner has direct contract with one or more contractors; contractors may have subcontractors. Owner may have a separate contract with consultants such as an Architect/Engineer.

II. MANAGEMENT CONTRACTOR

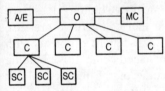

Owner engages Management Contractor to assist in planning and supervising work. Management Contractor may direct Contractors but contracts are generally between contractors and Owner.

III. PROJECT MANAGER

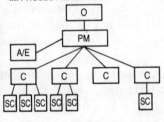

Owner engages Project Manager who coordinates and supervises the work of all project participants, often taking (some) contractual responsibility for project performance. Contracts are generally between Project Manager and Contractors.

IV. PROJECT SERVICES CONTRACTOR

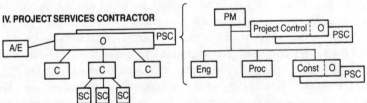

Project Services Contractor joins Owner's project management organization. Staff from the two groups work jointly in a salt-and-pepper fashion. Contractors contract directly with the owner.

Figure 11.1 Owner/consultant/contractor roles

reimbursable basis [47] since it felt this took the pressure off contractors to manage their labour effectively and to contain their costs.

The process of selecting the contractors to work on the project is of the utmost significance to the success of the project. As has already been noted, the CEGB bring contractors into the project early so that both parties can get an effective feel for the project. This is also true of the Ministry of Defence when staff targets have been formulated. This tradition has yet really to reach the civil construction industry. Though both the Banwell Report of 1964 and the Harris Report of 1968 noted the merit of having contractors join the project early [48] this was essentially to get the contractors' production expertise fed into the design rather than to allow contractors sufficient time to appraise properly the risks posed by the projects.

Most owners favour some form of competitive selection of their contractors. While this is doubtless wise, competitive bidding does have its dangers. There is considerable evidence that competitive pressure can lead to contractors underbidding with consequent problems with claims and cost overruns [49]. Inexpertly managed competitive bidding can severely prejudice the successful outcome of the project. Major projects are typically complex: expecting contractors to have to bid relatively quickly, only on the basis of a large quantity of document-ation, is hardly an effective way of getting the best input from the contractors' expertise. The cheapest bid may well not be the best one: accepting it simply because it is the cheapest may well be a serious mistake.

An essential aspect of contracting is to ensure the motivation of contractors. On fixed-price contracts the motivation is clearly the significant profit potential: with a fixed scope, good management should be able to maximize profits. Where the scope is not known, the alternative is some form of reimbursement contracting. The problem then is how to put an incentive in the contract. Target reimbursable or incentive contracts are forms of contract used to provide increased profit the nearer final costs are to the contract targets, or the lower the final cost or the shorter the duration of the project ultimately prove to be. Despite considerable study, however, the benefits of incentive contracts are still not totally clear [50]. While they are generally considered to assist in reducing cost growth, they require a reasonable degree of specification and not too high a level of technical uncertainty. Where this is not the case their benefit can be questionable. Following the shift by the US Department of Defense in 1962 from cost reimbursable to incentive contracting, for example, several studies of subsequent contract experi-ence showed that, during the course of their use, the incentive contracts were modified so that they followed rather than influenced project costs [51].

In fact, the same problem applies to the general question of forms of contract. An exhaustive review by De Mong on the various forms of contract was unable to conclude definitively whether or not cost-plus contracts were cost effective, largely perhaps because, as a Rand study put it, contract type is, quite properly, chosen with a 'prior expectation of uncertainty' [52].

Another form of motivation is that of providing financial incentives for the attainment of key milestones [53]. The obverse of this, penalties for the failure to reach these milestones, was of course used by the CEGB on Heysham 2. As was noted in Chapter 6, however, an important part of the key date procedure is not simply the withholding of payment but the fact that contractors' senior managers are required to meet the CEGB at approximately six-monthly intervals to review progress. In this way, senior management involvement in the project is guaranteed.

Since forms of contract are essentially ways of allocating and limiting risk, it might be interesting to study the fundamental risks posed by the case studies and the forms of contract which were in fact employed (Table 11.2).

What principles of contracting can be seen from the case studies? First, fixed-price contracting is inappropriate in high risk situations: (Heysham 2 was not considered a very high risk situation, so that firm price bids were used.) Second, where the risk is high, provision for cost recovery must be allowed. There is a scale of recovery methods ranging from unit rates through incentives to full reimbursement (Figure 11.2). Third, the risk should be put on to the contractor only to the extent that he is able to assess it logically and bear it financially. Fourth, the contracting policy should be clearly established early in the project and should be firm but once established it need not be immutable: contract type might have to be changed during the project as the perception of risk changes. (The method known as 'convertible contracts' [55].) This is in fact the method generally used now on aerospace projects where the early, prototype phase is often contracted on a reimbursable basis but the later detailed development and production phases are done on some form of firm-price contract.[9] Fifth, reimbursable forms of con-

---

[9] A practice which is favoured in the United States of America is that of commissioning prototype development on a reimbursable basis and then selecting a prototype in competition. In Europe there is rarely either the market or the resources for prototype competition (although this may change with greater use of consortia and pooled national purchasing contracts). Prototype competition might be considered for other kinds of projects, e.g. computers (it was used in this way on the rehosting of the FAA's guidance and tracking systems).

Table 11.2   Areas of risk and contract forms used in the case studies

Project	Risk	Contract	Remarks
Thames Barrier	Labour unrest	Fixed price with release on excessive labour disputes; changed to cost reimbursable	Cost reimbursable/Green Book allowed new bonus scheme which solved labour issues
Heysham 2	Technical, delivery, labour	Fixed price	Worked well for all parties, except where contractors failed to perform
Fulmar	Design changes (also weather, labour)	Fixed price except where design incomplete, then BOQ or even fully reimbursable	Largely unsatisfactory; contractors had large claims problems
COP	Technical performance	Incentive	Worked well largely because of significant leverage and managerial involvement of Inland Revenue
Concorde	Technical performance, design changes	Cost reimbursable	Large overruns (weak owner control)
Giotto	Schedule and technical performance	Cost reimbursable, incentive and fixed price	Adjustments to contract type were made during the course of the project

tract inevitably involve greater management effort on the part of the owner (e.g. CEGB) or his agent (e.g. Rendel, Palmer & Tritton). On Heysham 2, fixed-price contracts definitely assisted the CEGB by allowing them to concentrate on design and interface management. Research in the United States has recently verified most of this 'conventional wisdom' [56].

PROJECT IMPLEMENTATION

What have previous research and the case studies to say about the actual process of implementing projects?

Beginning with the organization of the project, two issues stand out: the arrangement of the parties to be involved in the project and the form of authority given to project management. The project organization should be appropriate to the project, clear and comprehensible [57]. Essentially, three forms of organization are commonly found in projects—functional, project and matrix (as described in Figure 11.3)—

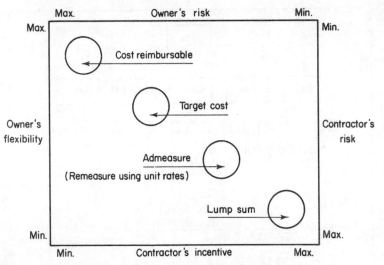

Figure 11.2 Allocation of risks and incentives between owners and contractors for different contract types [54]

although deciding definitively which is the appropriate form for any given project is not always easy since the best form depends significantly both on the characteristics of the project (particularly its size, complexity and urgency [65]) and on the companies building the project, both owner and contractor(s). Nor indeed is it easy to determine what is an 'efficient' organizational level of effort, either in total or on the individual part of the owner, consultants, contractors or subcontractors [66].

There is strong agreement among both researchers and practitioners that there should be one person or group in overall charge of a project, having strong overall authority, although the extent to which this is possible may be constrained by the form of contract employed and the 'culture' of the parent organization [67]. The extent of the project manager's authority might grow as a project develops. Often this is done on a planned basis (Figure 11.4). The Shell-Expro corporate culture at the time of Fulmar was changing away from that of a functional organization to that of a more project one. Fulmar was consequently caught in certain of the strains which any such move is liable to create, namely those of (the engineering and procurement) functions surrendering authority while project management acquired it [68]; and more importantly, of not having a 'fully project orientated' background of experience to fall back on, e.g. in contract administration, control systems, and design management. In truth, Fulmar's organization did not 'fit' the project to the extent that it probably could have. The change to a

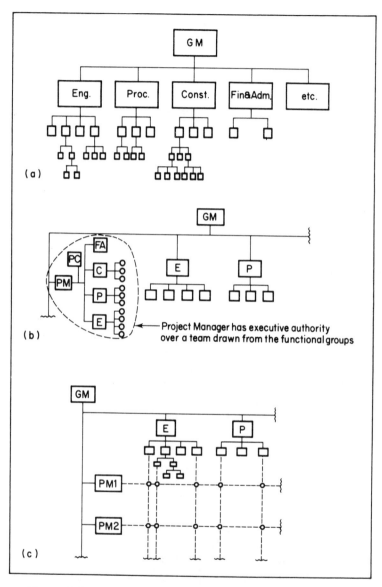

Figure 11.3 Functional, project and matrix forms of organization
(a) Functional—all work is planned, directed and controlled by functional groups
(b) Project
(c) Individuals are allocated from the functional groups to work on a project team (not necessarily on a full-time basis). Authority over these persons is shared between their functional and their project 'bosses'

fuller project orientation in Shell-Expro's later fields bears witness to this. In both the Channel Tunnel and Concorde there were fundamental problems in the structure of the project, through the effective exclusion of British Rail in the former case and due to the bureaucratic, unwieldly form of organization dictated by the treaty in the latter. Additionally, neither organization had one person in overall charge. Both Heysham 2 and COP used strongly project orientated forms of organization although both also exhibited some difficulties in integrating their project organization with the different forms of organization employed by other major parties working on the projects, e.g. the matrix organization of NNC and the functional organization of PSA. The case studies thus suggest firmly that the chances of project success are increased the stronger the project orientation of the organization.

The question of leadership has already been touched upon several times in this chapter. All projects challenge qualities of leadership; major projects do so severely [69]. People with the talent and capacity to manage undertakings of the kind major projects pose are rare. All the case studies demonstrate in one way or another the importance of leadership. Research on the topic, however, is somewhat scanty. Myers and Devey found leadership to be a significant factor in their study of process plants [70]. Other research has found a correlation between project success and experienced leadership when that leadership is coupled with strong top management support [71]. Ruskin and Lerner found some correlation between individual project administrators and cost overruns [72] and several authors have noted the importance of local leadership in Third World development programmes [73]. These formal studies on leadership in projects are complemented by several accounts of projects in which the significance of the individual is stressed, such as those on Polaris, the US Supersonic Transport plane and Caro's study of Robert Moses [74]. Generally, however, the academic work on describing the attributes and importance of leadership seems to be slight, at least in comparison with its practical importance and recognition. Without its strong leadership, the early difficulties on Giotto might have wrecked the project. The outstanding top management commitment and the presence of a manager with sustained commitment and drive on COP was fundamental to the project's success. Leadership was extremely important on both the Thames Barrier and Heysham 2. The arrival of a new project manager on the barrier in 1976 brought about fundamental changes in the pattern of work, in the attitude towards labour relations, and not least in the attitudes between the major parties – the clients, the consulting engineer and the joint venture. On Heysham 2, strong leadership was required in both the CEGB and the NNC, particularly in making the

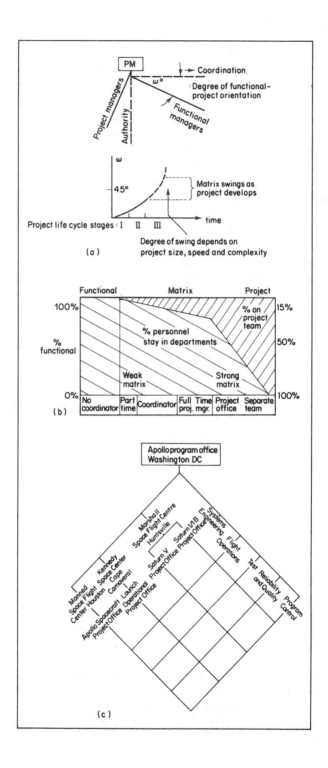

PM

→ Coordination

Degree of functional-
project orientation

ω°

Project managers
Authority
Functional managers

ω

45°

Matrix swings as
project develops

Project life cycle stages : I   II   III

time

Degree of swing depends on
project size, speed and complexity

(a)

Functional   Matrix   Project

100%   % on   15%
                                        project
                                        team
%   % personnel
functional stay in departments   50%

Weak   Strong
matrix   matrix

0%   No   Part Coordinator Full Time Project Separate 100%
     coordinator time   proj. mgr. office   team

(b)

Apollo program office
Washington DC

Manned Space Flight Space Center Center Houston Cope Canaveral
Kennedy Space Center
Apollo Spacecraft Launch Operational Project Office Project Office
Saturn V Project Office
Marshall Space Flight Centre Huntsville
Saturn I/IB Project Office
Systems Engineering Flight Operations
Test Reliability and Quality Program Control

(c)

new relationship between the two work effectively in 1980. On APT the leadership changed at the prototype stage and there was no project management leadership of the requisite quality evident during prototype development or thereafter.

Closely associated with the issue of leadership is that of teamwork. Projects are inherently flat organizations with considerable peer group working. In other words, teamwork is particularly important. Murphy, Baker and Fisher found an adequately sized team, organized appropriately, with the project manager having maximum authority, to be principal factors associated with success in their survey of 646 US projects [75]. Researchers in project management have put considerable emphasis on the importance of participative styles of decision making and conflict resolution in project teams [76]. All the cases demonstrated the importance of effective teamworking to the success of the project. Both the Channel Tunnel and Concorde experienced difficulties in joint Anglo-French working for a while but the problems were eventually substantially reduced. The importance of teamworking on the CTH joint venture and in the NNC–CEGB relationship have already been mentioned. Unfortunately, the difficult relations between the 'new' researchers and the 'old' engineers on the APT were sufficient virtually to cause the failure of this project.

Teams develop concepts, tools and ways of working, yet at the end of a project they often break up. How can one retain their expertise? Because major projects typically take so long to accomplish, and because teams do break up so that experience tends to become lost, the concept of the Project Directorate has been advocated. The Project

---

Figure 11.4 Variations in the degree of functional–project orientation in project organizations

(a) The degree of project management–functional management power and authority in a matrix can vary. Based on experience in a Brazilian steel mill, Morris and Reis de Carvalho suggested the matrix might move from a functional to a project orientation as the project moves into implementation [58]. Wearne suggested ω° (project management orientation) increases as the frequency, variety and uncertainty of the decisions increase [59]; Davis and Lawrence, and Whitmore, suggested it was a function of time [60]; Morris found that increased project size, speed and complexity increase the need for a project orientation [61]

(b) Youker [62] has illustrated the range of coordinating mechanisms potentially available. A fully functional organization has no direct lateral coordination. A matrix can have a little lateral coordination (project coordinator) or a lot (project manager) as ω° increases. A team organized on a fully project basis clearly has the strongest lateral coordination.

(c) The three forms—project, matrix, functional—are not, of course, mutually exclusive. Apollo was organized as a matrix under a program manger, and had a functional organization within parts of the matrix [63]. Similarly, matrices may be found within matrices [64].

Directorate is a high level group of persons, experienced in the kind of project being undertaken, who work directly for the owner. As far as possible, members' compensation is structured in a way that is not tied to whether or not the project goes ahead. In this manner the objectivity of the team is maintained as far as possible [77].

Labour relations can completely disrupt project implementation, as they did for a while on the Thames Barrier and on many large sites in the United Kingdom in the 1970s. Labour problems at BAeD could have jeopardized the Giotto project had industrial relations not been closely monitored and action taken to remove the spacecraft from Bristol before union action closed down the plant. The union blacking of the Advanced Passenger Train and the later strike action contributed substantially to the abandonment of APT. Heysham 2 demonstrated the importance of starting off properly in industrial relations: Taylor Woodrow was very firm in resisting two or three 'trial of strength' strikes. CTH on the Thames Barrier was less firm. On the other hand, double day shift was not introduced at the outset of Whessoe's contract on Heysham 2 and the change to a difficult and unpopular regime caused resentment and lack of productivity. It would be difficult to say that current labour management practices have necessarily resolved the difficulties of the 1970s, for the economic situations of the two decades are so totally different. There is now a generally reduced level of industrial unrest throughout the country during a period of very high unemployment. Nevertheless, the move towards site agreements which were formalized under NAECI have to be significant. Site agreements are common practice on major US projects, such as TAPS, River Bend and the Great Plains Coal Gas classification projects [78]. A site agreement and tougher management in the early stages of the Thames Barrier might well have improved the performance of the barrier project. Certainly the CEGB have found the NAECI agreements and the Management Group to have been of great benefit on Heysham 2.

Communication has been cited by many as an essential part of good industrial relations. On the Advanced Passenger Train there was an over-emphasis on 'standard British Rail practice' which created communication problems on the project. Perversely, on the Thames Barrier communications were almost too good, at least between the owner and the operatives. The operatives often knew of GLC decisions regarding spending and other project finance matters before management itself did. In other words, communication is not just about the flow of information but about the quality and pattern of information flow. On Fulmar the geographical distribution, contract arrangements and organizational conflicts amongst the groups undertaking engineering design and procurement impeded communication. This had a material impact on the delays experienced by the project at this time. The steering committee of COP was an important vehicle for assuring efficient communications between the major contractors, as indeed is the key date procedure used by the CEGB. Having COP developed at Telford, a new town with comparatively spartan social attractions, was an effective way of ensuring good team and management–union communications. People talked together at work partly because their work relations were of importance in their social life. Giotto maximized effective communication, particularly between the client and the contractor but also with the universities. Without efficient communications, the spacecraft would almost certainly not have met its schedule deadlines.

An important part of project communications is obtaining accurate control information on the state of the project. Giotto's contract terms ensured good communication. ESA had on-line access to BAeD data. COP had a detailed, regular, extensive control system which contributed significantly to the project's success. Fulmar, on the other hand, experienced a number of difficulties in measuring progress on several parts of the project. Concorde had terrible difficulties in getting accurate information on the status of progress: the size of the programme, the number of technical unknowns and the transnational management problems created severe control and monitoring problems on Concorde (PERT being formally abandoned in 1972 as unreliable and unworkable). In view of these problems it is not surprising that the government found difficulty in obtaining accurate information on the status of the project [79]. It should, however, be observed that since the desire to communicate is a prerequisite to effective communication, it is not necessarily surprising that communication was not always efficient between the parties on Concorde or between the various arms of government.

An interesting paper by Thamhain and Wilemon published in 1986 highlights the importance of these organizational factors. Whereas senior managers consider the causes of missed schedule and budget targets to be often due to inadequate project definition, planning and control, the 'real' reasons, these researchers found, are in the 'social' areas, specifically: problems with organizing the project team; weak leadership; communications problems; conflict and confusion; and insufficient upper management involvement [80].

In the final analysis, projects are implemented by people. People are human and humans sometimes err. One does not have to look very far in any of the case studies before one encounters examples of error. These have only seriously impacted the projects, however, in one or two cases. The reasons for such difficulties are of course various and often occur all too easily. On Fulmar, for example, problems of misunderstanding between Shell-Expro and the fabricators and suppliers were perhaps the biggest source of error. On the APT the trivial design faults and unreliability problems finally provided the opportunity, at the time of the national rail strike, for the British Rail Board to kill the project. Since projects are built by people, not one of whom is perfect, management should make allowance for errors and plan, supervise and control with this expectation.

SUMMARY

In reciting these many factors which can cause projects to go wrong there is a danger of an overwhelming negative sense developing. If incompetence is so common, if the challenges are so great, is one not necessarily imprudent to embark upon any project, but particularly a major project? Certainly the overall record of major projects' success is not encouraging, but in part surely this is because, as the major project and macro-engineering societies take as their credo, we are only just beginning to understand the dynamics of their management. In reality, there are outstanding major project success – D-Day, the Berlin Airlift, Apollo, COP, the French nuclear programme, Giotto, the Los Angeles Olympics. Guided by organizational structures and controls of considerable sophistication, with their strong goal orientation, multi-organizational framework and emphasis on teamwork, projects are accomplished through personal and collective enthusiasms often only liberated by the very challenge of undertaking a truly exceptional task. Since the very first monuments of history, major projects have represented, both physically and spiritually, the highest aspirations of society. Our task is to increase the success rate – to do better – not to give up.

REFERENCES

1. Baker, B. N., Murphy, D. C. and Fisher, D., 1982; Baum, W. C. and Tolbert, S. M., 1985; Feldman, E. J. and Milch, J., 1982; Gott, H. H., 1969; Hayfield, F., 1985; Herbert, E., 1983; Myers, C. W. and Devey, M. R., 1984; National Economic Development Office, 1982; Ruskin, A. M.,

1982; Sykes, A., 1979; Vicklund, C. A. and Craft, W. S., 1981; Wearne, S. H., 1973.

2. Baker, B. N., Murphy, D. C. and Fisher, D., 1982; Bryson, L., 1982; Department of Energy, 1976; Hayfield, F., 1985; Marquis, D. G. and Straight, D. M., 1965; Merrow, E., Chapel, S. W. and Worthing, C. A., 1979; Might, R. J. and Fischer, W. A., 1985; Murphy, D. C., Baker, B. N. and Fisher, D., 1974; Pugh, P. G., 1985.

3. *Report of the Commission on Government Procurement*, 1972.

4. Checkland, P., 1981; Davies, C., Demb, A. and Espejo, R., 1979; Morris, P. W. G., 1982b.

5. Bryson, L., 1986.

6. Flippo, E. B. and Munsinger, G. M., 1976; Kerzner, H. D., 1979.

7. Kozmetsky, G., 1980; Morris, P. W. G. and DeLapp, S. E., 1983.

8. Bignell, V. and Fortune J., 1984; Turner, B., 1976, 1979.

9. Pfeffer J., 1981; Pondy L. R. *et al.*, 1983.

10. Elton, J. R., 1985; Franks, J., 1984; Hayes, R. W., 1983; Hayes, R. W., Perry, J. G. and Thompson, P. A., 1983; Perry, J. G. and Hayes, R. W. 1985a, 1985 b; Perry, J. G., 1985; Thompson, P. A., 1981; Vicklund, C. A. and Craft, W. S., 1981.

11. Hodgkinson, C., 1983.

12. Alexander, A. J. and Nelson, J. R., 1972; Department of Energy, 1976; Harman, A. J., 1970; Henderson, P. D., 1977; Kharbanda, O. P. and Stallworthy, E. A., 1983; Large, J. P., 1974; Marshall, A. W. and Meckling, W. H., 1959; Merrow, E., Chapel, S. W. and Worthing, C. A., 1979; Myers, C. W. and Devey, M. R., 1984; Perry, R. L. *et al.*, 1969, 1971; Stinchcombe, A. L., 1979a; Summers, R., 1965.

13. Bryson, L., 1982; Merrow, E., Chapel, S. W. and Worthing, C. A., 1979; Murphy, D. C., Baker, B. N. and Fisher, D., 1974; Pugh, P. G., 1985.

14. Cochran, E. G., Patz, A. L. and Rowe, A. J., 1978; National Audit Office, 1986.

15. Cochran, E. G., Patz, A. L. and Rowe, A. J., 1978; General Accounting Office, 1985; Harvey, T. E., 1980; National Audit Office, 1986.

16. Hayfield, F., 1985.

17. National Economic Development Office, 1970, 1982; Ruskin, A. M. and Lerner, R., 1972.

18. Gott, H. H., 1969: National Audit Office, 1986.

19. Caro, R., 1974; Hall, P., 1980; Knight, G., 1976.

20. Baum, W. C. and Tolbert, S. M., 1985; Feldman, E. J., 1985a, 1985b.

21. Paul, S., 1982, 1983.

22. Hannah, L., 1982.

23. Williams, R., 1980.

24. Hall, P., 1980.

25. Edmonds, M., 1975; Hayward, K., 1983; Henderson, P. D., 1977; Williams, R., 1980.

26. Jenkin, M., 1981.

27. National Audit Office, 1986.

28. Bignell, V. and Fortune, J., 1984.

29. House of Commons, 1986.

30. Luffman, G. A. and Reed, R., 1984.

31. Cook, J., 1985; Geistants, G. and Hauck, V., 1979; Horwitch, M., 1979, 1982.

32. Feldman, E. J., 1985b; Persson, B., 1979; Wilson, A., 1973.
33. Feldman, E. J. and Milch, J., 1982; Hall, P., 1980.
34. Canaday, H. T., 1980; Feldman, E. J., 1985b; Feldman, E. J. and Milch, J., 1982; Frame, A. G., 1978; Horwitch, M., 1984; Komanoff, C., 1981; Summers, R., 1965; Viana de Andrade, R. *et al.*, 1979.
35. Paul, S., 1982; Frame, A. G., 1978.
36. Glaser, P., 1985; Little, Arthur D., 1985.
37. Cochran, E. G., Patz, A. L. and Rowe, A. J., 1978; Patz, A. L., 1984.
38. Acker, D. D., 1980; Harvey, T. E., 1980.
39. General Accounting Office, 1985.
40. Myers, C. W. and Devey, M. R., 1984.
41. Personal comment to the authors.
42. Morris, P. W. G., 1986.
43. Canaday, H. T., 1980; Department of Construction Management, University of Reading, 1979; Hayes, R. W., Perry, J. G. and Thompson, P. A., 1983; Ibbs, C. W. *et al.*, 1986; Nahapiet, H. and Nahapiet, J., 1985a, 1985 b; Ninos, G. E. and Wearne, S. H., 1974; Perry, J. G., Thompson, P. A., and Wright, M., 1982; Theodore Barry Associates, 1979.
44. Moolin, F. P. and McCoy, F., 1979.
45. Collier, K., 1979; Franks, J., 1984; Hayes, R. W., 1983.
46. Srinivasau, R. and Sassoon, D. M., 1982.
47. National Economic Development Office, 1970.
48. Ministry of Public Building and Works, 1964; National Economic Development Office, 1968.
49. Large, J. P., 1974.
50. Alexander, A. J., 1976; Belden, D. L., 1969; De Mong, R. F., 1978; Peck, M. J. and Scherer, F. M., 1962; Perry, J. G. and Thompson, P. A. and Wright, M., 1982.
51. Alexander, A., 1976.
52. Ibid.
53. Frame, A. G., 1985; Perry, J. G. and Thompson, P. A., 1982.
54. Hayes, R. W., 1983.
55. Collier, K., 1979; Srinivasau, R. and Sassoon, D. M., 1982.
56. Ibbs, C. W. *et al.*, 1986.
57. Baker, B. N., Murphy, D. C. and Fisher, D., 1982; Hayfield, F., 1985; Moolin, F. P. and McCoy, F., 1979.
58. Reis de Carvalho, E. and Morris, P. W. G., 1978.
59. Wearne, S. H., 1973.
60. Davis, S. M. and Lawrence, P. R., 1977; Whitmore, 1975.
61. Morris, P. W. G., 1973, 1974.
62. Youker, R., 1977.
63. Morris, P. W. G., 1982b.
64. Reis de Carvalho, E. and Morris, P. W. G., 1978.
65. Morris, P. W. G., 1973, 1974, 1982a, 1982 b.
66. DeWit, A., 1985; Warnock, G., 1979.
67. Asbury, A., 1982; Baker, B. N., Murphy, D. C. and Fisher, D., 1982; Bryson, L., 1982; Department of Construction Management, University of Reading, 1979; Frame, A. G., 1978; Herbert, E., 1983; Morris, P. W. G. and Hodgson, P. J., 1985; Myers, C. W. and Devey, M. R., 1984; Ninos,

G. E. and Wearne, S. H., 1974; Paul, S., 1982; Reeser, C., 1968; Reis de Carvalho, E. and Morris, P. W. G., 1978; Souder, W. E., 1978.
68. Reis de Carvalho, E. and Morris, P. W. G., 1978.
69. Gray, K. G., Jaafari, A. and Wheen, R. J., 1985; Seamans, R. and Ordway, F. I., 1977.
70. Myers, C. W. and Devey, M. R., 1984.
71. Gemmill, G. and Thamhain, H. J., 1972, 1974; Rubin, I. M. and Seelig, W., 1967.
72. Ruskin, A. M. and Lerner, R., 1972.
73. Baum, W. C. and Tolbert, S. M., 1985; Honadle, G. and Van Sant, J., 1985.
74. Caro, R., 1974; Horwitch, M., 1982; Morton, G. H. A., 1984; Sapolsky, H., 1972.
75. Murphy, D. C., Baker, B. N. and Fisher, D., 1974.
76. Allen, T. J., Lee, D. and Tushman, M., 1980; Allen, T. J., Tushman, M. and Lee, D. 1979; Archibald, R. D., 1976; Martin, M. and Cavendish, P. C., 1982; Sayles, L. R. and Chandler, M. K., 1971; Seamans, R. and Ordway, F. I., 1977.
77. Sykes, A., 1979, 1982.
78. Baker, A. C. and Boyd, K. J., 1982; Geistants, G. and Hauck, V., 1979; Reis, F. W., 1986; Seder, A. R., 1986.
79. Hayward, K., 1983.
80. Thamhain, H. J. and Wileman, D. I. 1986.

Chapter 12

The Strategic Management of Projects

Chapter 1 raised certain questions about the performance of projects, particularly major ones, and the effectiveness of project management. It noted that the success rate of projects is generally very poor and that the inability of project management to accomplish projects within specification is often due to factors which are not traditionally the concern of project management. If we wish to manage our projects better, it was said in Chapter 1, we must manage these factors more effectively. To do this we must first understand them better.

Chapter 10 explored what is meant by success and failure in more detail. Three different measures of success were identified: project functionality, project management and contractors' commercial performance. It was noted that on many occasions there might have to be a fourth measure: in the event that a project needed to be cancelled, was the cancellation made on a reasonable basis and was the project terminated efficiently? It was also noted that the evaluation of success will vary over time. Partly this is because a project's success criteria vary according to the stage of the project, and partly because conditions change over time.

In Chapters 2 to 9 detailed case studies of eight projects were presented and in Chapters 10 and 11 the anatomy of these projects was examined in detail to see what lessons could be learned as regards the effective management of such projects. The projects were examined from a number of perspectives: the question of objectives, technical management, political/community concerns, schedule matters, finance, legal and contractual affairs, and project implementation. These headings, though they can of course be subdivided and regrouped in a number of ways, essentially represent the strategic issues which management must address in order to improve the success rate of projects, particularly major ones.

What, in summary, do the case studies tell us about these issues?

THE CHANNEL TUNNEL, 1960–75

(1) Although the primary objective was abundantly clear, many of the the secondary objectives were not. For instance, the role of British Rail was not clear, neither was the nature of the future competition with the ferries. Secondary objectives, their conflicts and management, are important.

(2) The overall organization of the project was flawed, allowing, as it did, for the consortium to break up relatively easily if there was a delay in the ratification of the treaty. There was no organization with the goal, the charter or the ability to fight to make the project a success.

> —The absence of a clear owner and owner organization was particularly dangerous, not just in questions of policy (and even detail, such as some of the design issues) but in the question of commitment to the project's eventual success.
> —The absence of an overall 'supremo' – someone who was 'in charge' and would 'champion' the project – seriously diminished the project's chances of survival.
> —The financing of the project ought to bear some commitment to the project itself, not just to getting the best return currently available.

(3) Certain critical aspects of the project were not under the control of project management. The implementation of the project was neither comprehensive nor entirely systematic. The most obvious example of this was the high-speed rail link. The budget for this ultimately fatal aspect of the project was in the hands of British Rail, not the Channel Tunnel's project management. Management must manage all those factors which can threaten its success. (This leads to the so-called systems approach to managing projects.)

(4) In its key stages, when government ratification of the international treaty was required, the project failed to obtain the political support it needed. Managers must pay the greatest attention to the strategic aspects of a project's schedule. The experience of this Channel Tunnel and the later one in 1986–7 raises the fundamental concerns that projects which are strongly dependent on government support may face problems due to the asynchronization of major project life-cycle activities, such as meeting planning objections and raising finance, with the timing of the political consequences of elections.

(5) The treaty ratification period represented a particularly dangerous period for the project – such danger periods need identifying and

guarding; instead this one was used as an opportunity to disband. A proactive owner, managing all elements which could threaten his project, conscious of the strategic influences on his project schedule, might have avoided this problem.

CONCORDE

(1) The objectives of the programme were extremely broad. Recognize that broad objectives imply vague, probably unreliable initial estimates.
(2) Avoid if possible a commitment to project go-ahead if the technology and the design are only in a preliminary or untested state. Proceed on a phased basis, testing the project concept in the early stages and committing only when the project definition is known to be secure and achievable.
(3) Like the Channel Tunnel, Concorde suffered from a weak owner organization and management due largely to the requirements mandated by its international treaty. Beware, then, of management structures designed primarily to reflect political needs; they are unlikely to be to the project's benefit.
(4) The project organization should work in an unified way. There should be one person or group in overall charge.
(5) It is possible that the building of preproduction aircraft (01, 02) could have been rationalized. There should be careful planning of the overall programme, including design, development and production. For example, in Concorde the number of prototypes and design steps and a duplicated final assembly facility increased the costs significantly. Difficult political issues are only fudged at great expense.
(6) Concorde suffered from ineffective control procedures. Inadequate design and project management procedures will lead to confusion and inefficiency.
(7) The lack of attention to the broader aspects of the project, such as air certification, sonic boom and landing rights, brought serious problems to the project later. Again, therefore, management must manage all these factors which can threaten its success.
(8) In international projects, nationalistic aspirations should be constrained within the management requirements of the project. On Concorde, detailed objective planning should have been used to a greater extent. On Airbus and Giotto, planning and organiz-

ation are based on thoroughly objective analyses. Similarly, Giotto's success sprang from comprehensive planning fed into an efficient project management.

APT

(1) There must be full support within the initiating organization(s) for the objective of the project. Without top management commitment the odds against success are very long.
(2) It is inadvisable for the same organization to act as both owner and contractor, otherwise objectives are not clear, specifications may be changed too readily, schedules may slip, project costs may rise, role and personality conflicts increase and efficiency decline substantially.
(3) There are extreme dangers in switching the design authority for different phases of the development. Continuity is lost and technical management – a key strategic area – suffers.
(4) Inattention to design detail can prove disastrous. Human beings make mistakes so managers should provide accordingly. Build in stringent Quality Assurance; provide walk-throughs at strategic points; do not do prototype testing in public, least of all under the full glare of the media.
(5) The existing practices of a company or institution may inhibit the introduction of new management technologies and so seriously prejudice the chances of project success.

THAMES BARRIER

(1) The crucial problem of the Thames Barrier was the initial failure to recognize and gear up for the size of the task presented by the project, particularly at the time of tendering and in the early days on site. To this day, some senior managers on the project claim that it was not that out of the ordinary; others speak of the outstanding size of the challenge from labour management and financial risk, and indeed engineering, viewpoints. Contracts were, however, let in the traditional manner and the claims and bonus games begun just as they so often do on civil engineering jobs. Thus, a first lesson must be the need to raise the level of the

game – i.e. management – commensurate to the challenge being presented; not to carry on as per usual.

(2) As a corollary, high quality of management leadership, demonstrated later in CTH, for example, is critical.

(3) Traditional owner/contractor roles and forms of contracting may sometimes require modifying for major civil engineering projects[1] (e.g. more active owner project management, possibly with management support contracts, or management contracting; key contractors brought onto the project earlier; different forms of competitive bidding; greater use of target reimbursement type contracts; less readiness to create a hostile, claims-conscious environment).

(4) Institutional factors can constrain effective management. Under the legal arrangements governing local authorities, the GLC project manager was only able to have limited executive power delegated to him. Further, militant labour was supported by some members of the GLC. There should in fact be political and other support for such tough, disciplined management as may be required. Thus, the political/institutional context of work significantly constrains the way projects can be organized and the manner and terms in which contractors are engaged.

(5) For the first year or two on site, labour was allowed to 'get away' with a number of demands, though not all, which in retrospect it would have been better to resist. There is a need to exercise firm, effective management right from the outset of the project/contract, e.g. in regard to labour.

(6) With no site agreement there were frequent clashes between the payment regimes of different unions and different contractors. Labour practices need to be consistent amongst and between contractors and unions.

HEYSHAM 2 AND THE AGR PROGRAMME

From the first generation of AGRs the following lessons arise.

(1) Beware of making expensive project commitments for political

---

[1] Thompson considers that the traditional forms of contracting should only be used under the following preconditions [1]:

1. The Engineer must be free to act in a truly independent manner.
2. The work included in the contract must be well defined.
3. The probable extent of a change and variation should not exceed about 20 per cent.

reasons. By all means recognize and respond to political forces, but proceed cautiously, as per the recommendation for Concorde, above.

(2) Contractors' consortia must be sufficiently experienced to perform the work.
(3) The design should be adequately tested before committing to full scale production – avoid concurrency if possible.
(4) There is an obvious danger if the bid evaluation team has a vested interest in one of the bids.
(5) Fixed-price, turnkey contracting is inappropriate, or at least very risky, possibly to the owner as well as the contractor, for work having high technical uncertainty. The form of contract should reflect the reality of the contractor's financial ability to absorb his contractual risks.

Turning to Heysham 2, and in fact the conventional power stations of the late 1970s and early 1980s, the following points arise.

(1) Strong leadership and the willingness of all – leaders, managers, teams, unions, operatives – to work towards common goals, as they generally did on Heysham 2, are invaluable.
(2) Contractors' responsibilities should be clearly defined. Where possible, contractors should be financially responsible for their performance; cost reimbursable contracts should be used only where absolutely necessary.
(3) There is much merit in providing adequate lead-in time for contractors to work on the project, through design contracts for example, before requiring firm production bids.
(4) When employed effectively, design management and other project management practices are of great benefit in controlling changes and maintaining work to plan.
(5) Technological change poses risk, particularly in complex technologies such as nuclear reactor pressure vessels. Such changes must be as analysed as vigorously as possible prior to implementation.
(6) As with the Thames Barrier, a disciplined approach to industrial relations must be exercised from the outset, as indeed it was with Taylor Woodrow. Similarly there is great value in discipline amongst and between contractors and unions, as was proved with the 'nominated site' status arranged under NAECI.

FULMAR

(1) Problems were created by beginning fabrication while the design still contained significant technical uncertainty. Hence, as with the first generation of AGRs, though to a considerably less dramatic degree, beginning implementation before the design is relatively stable will in all likelihood necessitate considerable future changes.

(2) As a corollary, where contract changes are to be expected, consider using flexible forms of contract.

(3) There were some inconsistencies in contracting and awkwardness in contract administration. Contract policies should be clearly defined and effectively administered.

(4) There should be a thorough appraisal of the contractors' abilities before letting contracts, particularly if the work is novel and the contractor's record of such work is not well known. Otherwise, schedule slippage or cost overruns should not be considered surprising.

(5) The owner should assess carefully whether his managerial capabilities justify his interference with the execution of a contract, which on Fulmar they probably did – a point which haunts the Thames Barrier and has proved important time and again to the CEGB, on COP and on many defence projects.

(6) Fulmar was somewhat caught in the strains of moving from a functional to a project form of owner organization. The project organization should be appropriate to the size, urgency and complexity of the project.

(7) On Fulmar, there was great emphasis placed on not going offshore until work was fully completed. This paid off handsomely. Hence, have worked performed in as controlled an environment as possible.

(8) Fulmar's project manager was a leader of subtlety and vigour, with regard to both his team and the joint venture. The importance of leadership cannot be underestimated.

COP

(1) COP benefited considerably from the steering committee. Top management support is essential.

(2) COP had a strong, consistent, dedicated champion and leader in

Steve Matheson. Consistent and effective senior management leadership is similarly very valuable.

(3) There should be a clearly defined and extensively researched prefeasibility/feasibility study.

(4) After the award of the ICL contract, almost one year was spent in validating design capabilities, and writing coding procedures and 'middleware', before project implementation (coding) was begun. Hence, as with the AGRs and Fulmar, the design should be appropriately developed before beginning implementation. Avoid rush-to-code.

(5) State-of-the-art project planning and control systems were used effectively. As with Heysham 2, there should be rigorous design and project management practices.

(6) Although the development of the Estriel programme provided not inconsiderable risk, there were fall-back strategies had this programme not worked out. Hence, in practice there should be realistic back-up strategies for the high risk aspects of any project.

(7) Contractors were managed vigorously, although to clear project goals of mutual benefit. Rescoping and renegotiation of contract terms were occasionally necessary. As with Fulmar, there should be effective owner administration of contracts and support for contractors' efforts.

GIOTTO

(1) Giotto benefited from clearly defined and validated objectives. The presence of an immutable end date was both essential to and of great benefit to project success.

(2) Once the BAeD bid was accepted, both the ESA and BAeD project managers made explicit efforts for their teams to work together positively and openly towards their shared project objectives. Organizational confidence, strong leadership and effective communications make an enormous contribution towards success.

(3) Giotto's project management focused carefully on areas of technical uncertainty and reduced these as a matter of priority. Design replication was employed to the extent possible.

(4) In situations of technical uncertainty and complexity, as in the Giotto project, there is a particular need for careful design management and effective project control. Both these received outstanding attention on Giotto.

(5) Where there are significant subproject interdependencies, as there

ADVANCED PASSENGER TRAIN	Ensure full support for project objectives	Differing national technical practices have to be controlled	Government financing brings political control of a project	Avoid weak owner organization and management	Attend to design detail	It is inadvisable to have the same organization as both client and contractor
					Recognize dangers of switching design authority	Existing company practices may inhibit new approaches
					Minimize technical risk and fully review before implementing	Carefully assess formation of new teams
THAMES BARRIER	Recognize and gear up for level of endeavour		Obtain political support necessary		Traditional approaches to contracting may need reconsidering	Firm management required in early stages of implementation, particularly of labour
HEYSHAM 2 POWER STATION	Design should be tested before commitment to full implementation				Impartial bid evaluation is important	Early firm discipline on industrial relations is necessary
					Contractors must be sufficiently experienced	Strong leadership invaluable

Table 12.1 Continued

Project name	Objective	Technology and design	Finance	Government	Schedule	Contract	Organization
		Avoid concurrency where possible				Ensure clearly defined responsibilities for contractors	
		Firmly employed design and other project management practices				Provide adequate lead-in time for contractors prior to bidding	
						Fixed-price contracting inappropriate/risky for high technical risk work	
FULMAR		Avoid implementation until design is (relatively) stable				Make thorough appraisal of contractors' abilities	Project organization should be internally consistent and appropriate to project's size and complexity

	Perform work under as controlled an environment as possible Complete onshore work to greatest extent possible before going offshore		Assessment of owner's managerial capabilities and consequences of his interference on contract objectives important Ensure clearly defined and effectively administered contract policies	Leadership very important
COMPUTERIZATION OF PAYE	Clearly defined and extensively researched feasibility are invaluable Design should be developed in detail before implementation Rigorous design and other project management practices should be employed	Have back-up strategies to support high risk approaches	Effective owner administration of contracts and support for contractors	Obtain top management support Consistent and effective senior management leadership is very important

Table 12.1 Continued

Project name	Objective	Technology and design	Finance	Government	Schedule	Contract	Organization
GIOTTO	Clearly defined and validated objectives are very beneficial	Focus on areas of technical uncertainty and reduce quickly as matter of priority Exercise great care in interface and design management					International projects, well managed, are neither more difficult nor more complex than national ones Exercise strong organizational confidence, leadership and effective communications

Table 12.2   Factors for project success arising from the case studies

---

Project definition
   Define comprehensively
   Communicate clearly
   Phase as appropriate
   Identify, assess and develop sub-objectives clearly
   Relate objectives to participants
   Do not force clarity until appropriate
   Beware of progressive change
   Avoid too early a commitment

Planning, design and technology management
   Attend to broader, systems aspects of projects
   Relate to phasing, logistics, geophysical uncertainties, and the design and
      production relation
   Have back-up strategies for high risk areas
   Develop the accuracy of estimates to an extent consistent with the uncertainties
      present, e.g. technology, methods
   Avoid concurrency (see below)
   Test design adequately before final project commitment is made
   Recognize the extent to which R & D is completed will affect accuracy of estimate
   Use flexible design philosophies
   Recognize that good design management is essential, especially where there is
      technical uncertainty or complexity
   Recognize that interface management is important where there are significant
      interdependencies
   'Freeze' design once agreed
   Beware of switching design authority during different phases of project
   Pay attention to detail since mistakes can prove costly
   Encourage replication where appropriate

Politics/Social factors
   Ensure effective sponsorship
   Recognize fiscal, safety, employment, etc., constraints
   Ensure support for such management actions as may be necessary
   Constrain nationalistic aspirations on international projects
   Manage community factors effectively

Schedule duration
   Recognize the major impact that output, price, regulation, technical developments,
      government or corporate changes can have on definition of success
   Phase projects where/as possible to avoid unnecessary over-commitment

Schedule urgency
   Avoid rushing
   Note possible disruptive effect on work sequencing
   Beware of impact on full discussion by all parties
   Beware of when urgency and technical uncertainty go together (concurrency)

Finance
   Undertake full financial analysis of all project risks: budget validity, political
      support, owner's commitment, etc., including inflation, and possible currency
      variations
   Be cautious over availability of funds
   Be prepared to stop funding where necessary
   Seek sponsors interested in success of project *per se*, not just a good return
   Beware of exchange rate movements
   Check definition of project success if business base of project changes
                                                            (continued overleaf)

Table 12.2   Continued

Legal agreements
 Ensure break clauses are adequate
 (Beware of 50–50 partnerships)
 (Beware of mixed public–private funding)
 Seek commitment to making contract work

Contracting
 Consider whether more innovative contractual arrangements may not be required
 Consider incentive contracts valuable where it is difficult to get competition, though beware of too high a level of technical uncertainty
 Ensure contractors are sufficiently experienced to perform the work
 Consider extent to which competitive bidding is appropriate
 Beware of same organization acting as contractor and owner
 Provide adequate bid preparation time
 Beware of the cheapest bid
 (Beware of having to manage a large number of contracts)
 Define contractor's responsibilities clearly
 Make contractors financially responsible for their performance as far as possible
 Beware of contract forms which unfairly penalize contractor, particularly for factors outside his control
 (Beware of mixing firm price and reimbursable forms)
 Question the threat of liquidated damages
 Appraise carefully whether interference by the owner in the execution of a contract is justified

Project implementation
 Seek appropriate client, parent company and senior management attitudes and support
 Control all those aspects of project which can affect the chances of success
 Recognize the magnitude of task and organize appropriately
 Obtain clear client guidance
 Foster good client–contractor relations
 Integrate the project teams' perspectives with the project aims during start-up
 Assess risks adequately
 Develop good planning, clear schedules, adequate back-up strategies
 Exercise firm, effective management from the outset
 Recognize the importance of effective, schedule-conscious decision making
 Provide clear and comprehensible project organization appropriate to the size, urgency and complexity of the project
 There should be one person, or group, in overall charge having strong overall authority
 Ensure effective leadership
 Strive for a well motivated, experienced team
 Develop appropriate controls, highly visible, simple and 'friendly'
 Check definition of success, where changes are allowed
 Ensure resources are adequate, properly planned and flexibly employed
 (Consider use of site labour agreements)
 Ensure labour practices are consistent amongst and between contractors
 Give full recognition to quality assurance and auditing
 Recognize that good communications are vital

Human factors
 Ensure top management support
 Recognize and demonstrate the importance of effective leadership
 Seek competent personnel
 Ensure communications are effective
 Consider which power style is appropriate
 Recognize that people are human and less than perfect

In describing our purpose in writing this book we noted two current fundamental problems. One was that project management has not addressed itself to the factors which often really cause projects to fail. The other is that our ability to manage major projects seems particularly poor. Since major projects are so important to society, we should work to improve this success rate.

The lessons we have derived from the eight case studies and the long list presented in Table 12.2 go a long way, we hope,.to articulating the environment which must be managed if projects, whether major or otherwise, are to be managed more successfully. But can there not be more straightforward guidance than the description of an environment? Despite our cautions, is it not possible to construct a simpler model of the strategic management of projects that would serve all classes of projects?

Having noted the dangers of simplification, we feel compelled to agree that the need for such a model is real. We have thus pared our findings down to 22 items which we consider to be the preconditions to project success. These 22 items are relevant to all kinds of project, major or otherwise (although again different kinds of projects will emphasize different factors to different degrees). These 22 factors we have structured as shown in Figure 12.1. Our model is based on the following thesis.

First, all parties to the project must have an attitude which is truly desirous of project success.

Second, the project must be properly defined and should not be fully committed to until that definition is shown to be workable; it should then be 'frozen' to the extent possible.

Third, external forces influencing this project definition must be monitored and their impact on the project managed.

Fourth, the effect on the project definition of schedule matters, finance and the manner in which the project is to be implemented must be assessed. Each can significantly compromise the realization of the project definition.

Fifth, of the three factors – schedule, finance and method of implementation – the latter is particularly complex:

(a) organization and contracting matters are significantly interdependent and exert a fundamental influence on the way the project is to be run;
(b) the communications and controls put into the project reflect how it is being assessed, valued and managed;
(c) the people one uses and the way their qualities can be maximized to the project's benefit is ultimately where success or failure begins.

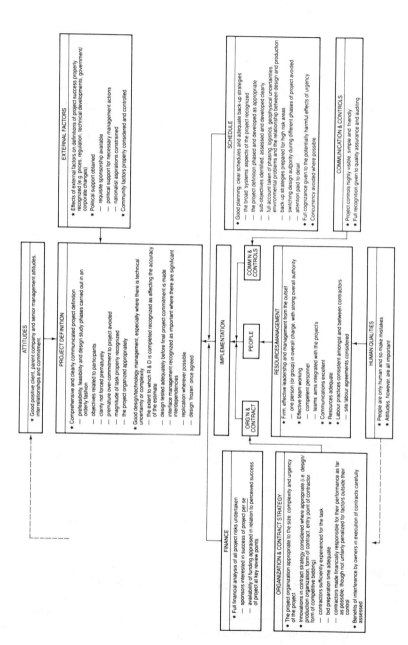

Figure 12.1 Research model: preconditions of project success

Sixth, projects are built by people. People are human and human beings are not perfect (and some are less perfect than others). The choice of the right person for the right job is of supreme importance. Expect errors. However, if attitudes are right. . . .

If all these preconditions are met, management deserves the fullest praise. More often, however, they will not be met, because of individual error or preference, or company circumstances or even institutional constraints. Even as we write we know of major projects being initiated or accomplished where these preconditions are not being met.

This book has illustrated the basic features of good management available to those working on projects today. As the book has demonstrated, considerable progress has been made over the last 20 or so years in the way projects are managed and in the tools and techniques used to control them. It is our hope that this work may stimulate the reader and those responsible for large organizations to reflect upon practices within their own companies. Perhaps then the success rate of projects of all kinds will begin to improve. Indeed we believe that there are already indications that this may be the case.

REFERENCES

1. Thompson, P. A., 1981
2. Morris, P. W. G. and Hough G. H., 1986

Appendix: Research Methodology

This book is based on a study conducted over an 18-month period by the Major Projects Association and Templeton College, Oxford. The objective of the study was the identification of those factors which may lead to the success or failure of a major project.

As with some of the major projects analysed in the book, this breadth of objective creates certain problems. As we saw in Chapter 10, since different project participants have different objectives and value systems, success may mean different things to different people. The researcher must consequently recognize the different conceptual frameworks that different project participants employ. There may be some commonality amongst these different frameworks, of course, for the good of the project if for no other reason, but it would be wrong to minimize these differences in perspective.

For this reason, the approach adopted in the research was purposely very broad. We were not interested in examining for their own sake limited theories or sets of factors which might influence the success or failure of a project. We wanted instead to capture the broad range of factors which affect the chances of success or failure. In consequence, our research was based on a broad review of the literature. Although the literature may seem heavier in some areas than others, e.g. more has been written about technology management than about finance, this does not reflect a difference of interest on our part.

We also recognized, as was noted in Chapter 10, that the factors affecting success and failure, as well as the perception of success and failure, vary through time. We therefore felt that a longitudinal study was essential in order to capture the temporal dimension of the projects. The bias towards a longitudinal analysis led us strongly to favour a case study approach to the research.

We felt that the case study approach was valid for several other reasons too. Case studies allow the organizational, managerial, political and other dynamics influencing the project to be understood better so that the reality of such large projects can be better appreciated. The difficulty of managing projects, particularly major ones, is not just that principles may or may not be understood properly. It is the reality of dealing with a variety of difficult management situations in a compressed time frame. If these pressures were to be ignored in the research the result would be a bland and superficial understanding of the projects' management challenges and our analysis of the reasons for their success or failure would be inadequate. Hence, the chapters in Part Two contain descriptions of the week-to-week pressures—the drama—of the case studies in order that the reader might appreciate better the reality of managing such projects. (Textbooks on project management, with few exceptions, not only miss many of the issues which are important to project success, they also often fail to get across the excitement which is so typical of the project world.) Further, having read the case studies, hopefully the reader should also have been in a better position when reading the analyses in Chapters 10 and 11 to recognize that, as in any effort of intellectual understanding, simplification is necessary. Those projects which in Chapters 10 and 11 would appear to have been really very successful, of course, had their problems; similarly those which appear to have been much less successful had their triumphs.

We hoped further that by adopting a broadly based comparative method of case study work, the insights on the management of major projects would be greatly increased. Previous work in the management of projects has generally been within a relatively narrow industry base. Although the topic of success and failure of major projects would appear to be of obvious importance, there are remarkably few studies of what influences success or failure in projects and there is little in the way of a case study tradition. (Table A.1 summarizes all the case studies we were able to locate relating to the success and failure of projects).[1] The selection of case studies was therefore designed to cover a broad range of major project types.

The distinguishing features of major project types were considered to be: (1) the industry/technology; (2) project purpose; (3) sources and pattern of sponsorship (public/private, nature of finance markets, loan/equity stake); (4) the degree of technological uncertainty, particularly the extent to which technology is 'advanced'; and (5) location.

---

[1] In addition to these studies, note should be made of Gilbreath's entertaining essay on success and failure tendencies in project management, in which he lists 130 failure factors and 13 success factors, and of the 1986 Project Management Institute Conference which had as its theme 'Measuring Success' and for which DeWit's paper, referred to in Chapter 10, was prepared [1].

Table A.1   Summary of studies of project success and failure

Study	Projects studied	Study findings	Comments
Murphy *et al.*, 1974	650 aerospace, construction and other projects	Coordination; relevant and agreed success criteria; project structure and control; project difficulty; funding pressure; project uniqueness; team build-up	Data primarily supplied by project managers; data dominated by US domestic (and possibly government) projects
Might and Fisher, 1985	103 system development projects	Organization design; authority of project manager; clarity of success variables	Research focused on project management
Myers and Devey, 1984	55 US and Canadian process plants	Extent of project definition (including regulatory requirements); focused on project responsibility drawn from all relevant corporation divisions; single project manager; concurrency dangerous; cost-plus contracts could experience slippage	60% of plants involve pioneering technology
Pugh, 1985	71 UK aerospace projects	Cost overruns are a function of poor project definition, concurrency and risk ((1) materials, (2) new scientific principles, (3) success required in other subsystems and (4) if new project)	
Baker, Green and Bean, 1986	211 R & D projects in steel, agriculture, chemicals, foods and industrial chemicals	110 projects successful technically or commercially. Success factors identified statistically were: experienced general management involvement, extent goals well defined	A carefully controlled analysis, ultimately not leading to any 'new' insights

Table A.1   Continued

Study	Projects studied	Study findings	Comments
Balachandra and Raelin, 1984	51 high-tech R & D projects	Important success/ failure factors are: top management support; rate of new product development; probability of technical success; technological route; project manager as project champion; technical/marketing relations; end use; effectiveness of project manager; commitment of project team; life-cycle of product; internal competition; cost schedules	Supporting evidence for such sensible comments very skimpy
Cooper, 1982	R & D projects in 103 firms	Success rate on average = 59%. Use of marketing resources more significant than amount of R & D	Success defined as commercial success
Gerstenfeld, 1976	11 successful projects, 11 unsuccessful ones and 10 innovations, all in West Germany 1974–5	Unsuccessful projects difficult to stop: need for more formal reviews. Successful project more likely to be demand pull in origin	Findings drawn largely from auto industry (also chemical and electrical)
Hopkins, 1980	148 companies	Half companies achieved success on 67% of new products. Failure caused by poor market research, timing and technical problems	Success defined as 'meeting management's objectives'
Mansfield and Wagner, 1975	R & D projects in 16 firms	Success rates vary considerably. Success is greater if economic evaluation is formally carried out early in the project and if marketing is integrated with R&D	R & D success defined in three ways: (1) technical completion, (2) commercialization and (3) economic success

Table A.1   Continued

Study	Projects studied	Study findings	Comments
Whipp and Clark, 1986	Study of the Rover 3500 (SDI) developed by British Leyland at the time Austin Morris and Rover merged	A longitudinal case study showing how different company cultures clashed, market definition was confused, design and production were poorly integrated, industrial relations were poorly handled and why major innovative leaps forward such as SD1 are so risky	An important, somewhat depressing work illustrating why major projects so typically go wrong even in general manufacturing
Kharbanda and Stallworthy, 1983	Glace Bay Canada; Concorde; UK refinery; Arzew; Trombay fertilizer complex; US nuclear plants; TAPS; Jubail and Yanbu; others	Careful preparation; control of changes	An enthusiastic and enjoyable but not overly detailed book on 'lessons' for project managers
Hall, 1980	London's third airport; London Motorway Box; Concorde; BART; Sydney Opera House; others	A more politically sensitive study of costs and benefits is required	Projects are approached primarily from a planner's perspective
Horwitch, 1982	US SST project	Many lessons to be inferred, though Horwitch gives few very explicitly. The power of people and politics in a major project is hugely evident	A factual account of what happened
Horwitch, 1984	US synfuels programme	Broader aspects of technology management, hostile political environment, absence of champions, changing corporate strategies not taken sufficiently into account. Need for broader top management 'project' training	Horwitch uses US public-sector experience as his paradigm of project management

Table A.1   Continued

Study	Projects studied	Study findings	Comments
Bignell and Fortune, 1984	Humber Bridge, RB211	Develops general descriptions of why things fail: problems of communication, control and the individual	Uses 'systems approach'; not very detailed
Edmonds, 1975	Rolls-Royce RB211 aero-engine	Inadequate project appraisal; fascination with technology; unhealthy regard given to government backing; unrealistic contract conditions and pricing; underestimation of technical challenges—all conspired to create a disaster which should have been foreseen	A useful if disjointed account leaving the reader anxious to learn more
Paul, 1982 and 1983	Dozen or so successful Third World development projects	Political commitment, capital, technology and leadership are key 'enabling conditions'; strategic management embraces management strategy, structure, process and environment in a congruent way; government plays a key role	While focusing on the individual characteristics of Third World projects, Paul makes several points of general relevance in a thoughtful, readable, if at times somewhat academic study
Rycroft and Szyliowicz, 1980	Aswan High Dam	The predominant factor affecting decisions on the dam was politics. Decision taking was primarily 'satisficing' (muddling through) rather than 'optimizing'	The case is written primarily as an administrative science case study rather than an investigation into project success and failure
Szyliowicz, 1982	Eregli iron and steel works (Turkey)	While the project was ostensibly analysed and managed very rationally, the underlying assumptions were often weak or false. Political considerations were dominant	A well documented account of a major project, analysed 'in the round'

Table A.1   Continued

Study	Projects studied	Study findings	Comments
Feldman, 1985b	Charles de Gaulle and third London airport; Concorde	Elitist approach to state support for high visibility projects similar in both United Kingdom and France; frequency of political change created uncertainty; political and industrial pressure kept Concorde going, despite objective evidence against doing so	Approaches projects from a public policy view point. A provocative, well researched book
Knight, 1976	Concorde	Like Horwitch's SST, a factual account of what happened without any overt analysis of success or failure; written by an enthusiastic supporter	A valuable account of the challenges encountered and overcome
Wilson, 1973	Concorde	A detailed rehearsal of what happened on the project	An anti-Concorde book, highly critical in tone
Sapolsky, 1972	Polaris	Memorable comments on Admiral Raborn's outstanding leadership and on the suspect value of PERT	A thoroughly informed, critical review of the management of the Polaris programme commissioned by the US Navy. A classic account of program management in its very earliest days
Seamans and Ordway, 1977	Apollo and the Energy Research Development Administration	Discusses management of state-of-the-art technology, funding, selling, support, manpower, planning, communications, visibility, decentralization, risk, control and flexibility	An authoritative attempt to extract high level nuggets of management know-how

Table A.1   Continued

Study	Projects studied	Study findings	Comments
Feldman and Milch, 1982	Dallas–Fort Worth, London, Milan, Montreal, New York, Paris, Toronto and Vancouver airports	Problems of technocratic business orientated decision making (on airports) in democratic, urban societies about a complex, uncertain business (air traffic) are explored. A bias towards phased development with greater recognition of due process is displayed	A very detailed discussion of a complex subject, based on a wide range of research
Marschak, Glennan and Summers, 1967	A dozen or so aero-engine, fighter, bomber and missile radar projects are described, together with several discussions of the defence development process	The case studies concentrate on problems of technical and environmental uncertainty; two opposite extremes of development strategies compared: the flexible (broad specifications until uncertainty is reduced) and the inflexible (assuming clear future requirements and hence having detailed specifications)	Much interesting material sandwiched between a mass of microeconomic formulae and prose
General Accounting Office, 1981, 1983 and 1985	2 coal liquefaction programmes, submarine construction, 6 weapon systems	The dangers are highlighted of premature commitment to contracting (coal liquefaction), poor QA and shipyard productivity (submarines), inadequate attention to production matters and programme uncertainty (weapon systems). Concurrency is discussed in detail	A most valuable set of 'snapshots' showing how the same problems keep appearing, even after years of study, experience and recommendation

Table A.1 Continued

Study	Projects studied	Study findings	Comments
National Audit Office, 1986	12 large, expensive UK defence projects	The Comptroller and Auditor General notes: the effect of technical uncertainty on underestimation; the significant likelihood of cost growth with concurrency; the danger of poor project definition and weak design control; difficulties of estimating the work associated with software; over-optimism of contractors; problems of cost control; and that cost growth follows from interrupted funding. Recent attempts to rectify these problems have had only limited success	NAO reports briefly on the current state of managing major UK defence projects and in so doing highlights many of the issues raised in this book
Canaday, 1980	US nuclear power industry	Huge cost increases due to a suspect cost reduction incentive system (regulation); underestimation of technical and organizational difficulties; inflation; increased safety requirements; weak contracting policies	An excellent, thoughtful, thorough study
Mason et al., 1977	US nuclear power industry	Identified as major areas of difficulty: design/construction interfacing, construction methods, coordination and communication, manpower and productivity	A construction management, somewhat overly academic report

Table A.1   Continued

Study	Projects studied	Study findings	Comments
Monopolies and Mergers Commission, 1981	The Central Electricity Generating Board (and thus the British nuclear power story)	Very comprehensive review recounting the principal problems faced by the CEGB. Advocates national site agreements; firm-price contracting; design contracts; broad-based manufacturing competition, with performance guarantees; unified overall control	A rich source of information
Wilson, 1969	The Central Electricity Generating Board's power stations (36 in total; 70 units)	Adverse site conditions, manufacturing difficulties, design faults, labour problems	
National Economic Development Office, 1976	3 ethylene units, 3 distillation units, 3 refineries, 3 methanol plants, 6 power stations	Construction projects took longer in the UK than abroad and absorbed more man-hours, mostly, it was suggested, because of better industrial relations	Comparative data are brief

(1) Each *industry* has its own way of managing projects, determined partly by its culture and partly by the technological requirement of the work. The aerospace and process industries have a longer history of project management, due partly to their relative youthfulness and also to the technical uncertainty typical of them. The civil building and information systems industries, on the other hand being a lot more differentiated, and in the construction case much older, have a much weaker tradition of integrated project management. Recently, information systems projects have been adopting the project management approach with vigour. The civil and building industries are making less certain attempts, partly because of their history and differentiation, but also perhaps because of their smaller degree of technical uncertainty.

(2) As we saw in Chapters 10 and 11, a project's *purpose* influences its definition of success or failure, and hence the way it is set up and managed.

(3) Different *funding* sources mandate different management practices

commercial sources may look primarily at the bottom line but tend to assess the various different risks in full. Government and multilateral lending agencies generally have objectives other than simply financial ones and will require that these 'success variables' be achieved too. Different patterns of funding—equity rather than loan, a number of investors or just a few—also affect the way the project is run, as we saw in the case studies.

(4) The influence of *technical uncertainty* on both overrun performance and management control was extensively noted in Chapters 10 and 11.

(5) *International* projects pose quite different challenges from *domestic* ones. The management challenge of cultural differences, staffing, communications, logistics and so on are evident; political risk is different; so too is financial risk, not only because of financial and managerial uncertainty but also for concurrency reasons. Domestic projects' managerial challenges are often quite different from, though just as distinct as, those of overseas ones: environmentalist opposition and the problems of labour relations, for example.

Table A.2 characterizes the eight case studies eventually selected in the light of these different factors: there is a range of industry types going from low to relatively high technical uncertainty; some projects are purely commercial, one is totally non-commercial (the Thames Barrier); most are domestic but three are multinational and Fulmar has significant international contracting.

Finally, the case study approach was selected since it was also hoped that the preparation of case material in this still relatively under-researched area of management would be of value in itself to the future teaching and study of major projects.

In selecting case studies, the question arises of whether one should study project successes or failures. Paul, for example, made much of this, arguing, along with Hirschman [2], that to study failures and thereby identify what went wrong on a project may not be helpful, for simply learning how to overcome the obstacles to success is not the same as learning what it is that brings success [3]. Indeed, the factors which achieve success may outweigh those which cause failure. One should therefore study successful projects, Paul says, not failures. By the same token, he argues, taking projects around the mean of a normal distribution, or at random, would be mistaken. Since one should be studying successes, one should be choosing projects from the right tail of the distribution, so to speak.

Such care in deciding whether to choose successful projects or unsuc-cessful ones assumes, of course, that such a distinction is at least rela-

Table A.2   Case studies used in the research

Project	Industry/ technology	Purpose	Sponsor	Degree of technological advance	Domestic/ inter- national
Channel Tunnel	Construction (tunnelling)	Public transport	90% government 10% private	Low	50:50
Concorde	Aircraft	Political/ commercial	100% UK and French governments	High	50:50
Advanced Passenger Train	Rail (mechanical engineering)	Improve rail service competitive- ness	50% government 50% BR (a nationalized industry)	Medium	Domestic
Thames Barrier	Construction (marine)	Public safety	100% government	Low	Domestic
Nuclear power	Power	Utility	100% government entity	Medium/high	Domestic
Fulmar: North Sea oil	Oil and gas	Commercial	100% private	Medium	Domestic/ interna- tional
PAYE computeri- zation	Computeri- zation	Improve efficiency	100% govern- ment	Low/medium	Domestic
European spacecraft Giotto	Space	Scientific measure- ment of physical properties of Halley's Comet	ESA—multi- government funded	High	Inter- national

tively clear; yet, as has been pointed out, there are several measures of success and failure in projects, some of which may be quite separate from each other. Also, of course, the perception of success and failure is temporal. The definition of whether a project is a success or a failure, then, is not always an easy one. Deciding *a priori*, before the investigation, to an extent begs the very question being asked. For this reason, the cases studied in this research did not follow Paul's strictures. Instead, projects were chosen on the basis of being major projects, posing substantial managerial challenges, bearing in mind the distinguishing criteria of industry/technology, purpose, funding, tech- nical uncertainty and domestic/international location.

The disadvantage of a project-specific case study method is that its 'findings' may only be relevant to the particular industry practices prevailing at the time, to the particular characteristics of a project sponsor, and indeed to the project itself. This may create problems of generalizability. Earl has argued that descriptive, classificatory research is valid in young fields, with models, theories and principles following later [4]. In fact, there is no way in broadly based, project related research such as this, which spans several industries and a couple of dozen years, that rigorous up-to-date data of undeniable generalizability can be obtained other than through a study which would be so large as to have almost certain difficulties in getting sponsors.

Having said this, the analysis of the case studies has been additionally strengthened very considerably by the testing of some 22 hypotheses, carefully formulated as a result of the literature review, which were applied to each of the projects on a systematic basis. The hypotheses were as follows.

Project Definition

(1) The limits of a project's viability should be *evaluated on an objective basis* in the light of the participants' own objectives, strategies and resources [5].
(2) *Unclear objectives* increase the likelihood of an unsatisfactory project [6].
(3) *Changes in commercial, technical, cost and schedule specifications* may lead to overruns and are often associated with problems of project management or performance [7].

Technical Factors

(4) *The amount of technical uncertainty* or innovation required increases the chances of difficulties and overruns [8].
(5) Problems in *coordinating project interfaces* can create technical difficulties [9]
(6) *Design management* difficulties can cause considerable problems later in a project [10].

Finance and Commercial Considerations

(7) The *amount of finance required* may cause difficulties in both initiating a project and keeping it on schedule, particularly if there is subsequent cost-growth [11].

(8) Projects financed with a mix of *public and private sources of funds* are liable to suffer from mixed financial objectives, which may cause problems [12].

(9) The *financial risk* posed *and the difficulty of forecasting* final costs, the business base, fiscal changes and exchange rate changes are clear indicators of potential future problems [13].

Environmental, Social and Political Pressures

(10) Severe *geophysical challenges* can increase the chances of over-runs significantly [14].

(11) *Political, social, community, environmental and other 'external' factors* can radically impact a project and alter its chances of success [15].

Schedule Makers

(12) Schedule *length* should be chosen so as to minimize risks of adverse political, financial and commercial changes; schedules should be phased to allow for *strategic review points* [16].

(13) *Urgent* schedules create increased management pressures and can lead to problems [17].

Managerial and Organizational Factors

(14) Inadequate *planning* will greatly increase the likelihood of project failure [18].

(15) *Legal agreements, contract strategy and terms and conditions* fundamentally influence project structure and the roles project participants can adopt [19].

(16) *Organization structure* should 'fit' the project and the participants

and should be dynamic, changing as the needs of the project change [20].

(17) The absence of effective *project controls* can seriously increase the chances of overruns and poor project performance [21].

(18) *Leadership* has a strong influence on the conduct of a project and hence on its chances of success [22].

(19) *Human relations factors and teamwork* are particularly important on projects and strongly influence project management success [23].

(20) *Labour relations* problems can seriously disrupt project implementation [24].

(21) If *internal and external communications* are poor, the chances of project success are reduced [25].

(22) *Human error or incompetence, incapacity of incapability* can jeopardize project success [26].

It was not the purpose of the research to test rigorously these 22 hypotheses. The hypotheses were intended to be used as analytical tools, their value being in the systematic application of the conceptual frameworks underlying them to each of the case studies. This process brought a degree of intellectual rigour to the case study analyses which, we feel, added substantially to the reliability of the research findings. (This process is presented clearly at the conclusion of each case study in the research report, MPA Technical Paper No. 3 [27].) Table A.3 summarizes the findings resulting from the hypotheses for each of the case studies. The rigour and validity of the case study analysis and the conclusions and observations made in Chapters 10, 11 and 12 were as a result, we feel, strengthened considerably.

We conducted the case studies first by undertaking background reading and then by interviewing senior executives associated with the projects. Notes were made of the interviews. Interviews tended to be wide ranging but concentrated on obtaining missing data and on exploring issues raised by the hypotheses. There are, of course, numerous parties to any project, and on major projects they tend to be particularly numerous; it would have been impossible to interview everyone we might have liked. Nevertheless, as far as possible all those persons who had a comprehensive view of the project's success or failure were interviewed in each case study. The descriptions of the case studies were then reviewed by senior persons who had worked on the projects and who had been interviewed prior to preparing the studies. In some instances material was omitted in consequence of comments made, but in none was new material added,

Table A.3 Summary of the findings resulting from the hypotheses for the eight case studies

Hypotheses	Channel Tunnel 1960–75	Concorde	APT	Thames Barrier	Heysham 2 and the AGR programme	Fulmar	COP	Giotto
(1) Evaluation of project viability should be objective and realistic from participants view	Very objective individual evaluations; but no 'project champion' to respond to these evaluations	Viability study was really a somewhat optimistic feasibility study	No viability study undertaken	Managerial aspects evaluated neither in detail nor objectively	Evaluations made in depth; objectivity increased by (a) previous record, (b) fixed-price bidding	Contractors appeared to have problems in assessing viability	Very objective evaluations by all parties, as project scope changed as well at outset	
(2) Unclear objectives can mean an unsatisfactory project	Primary objective clear but inconsistencies and conflicts amongst secondary objectives	Being broadly stated led to unsatisfactory project performance	Clear objectives but their point of origin led to difficulty (lack of top management commitment)	Conflicting objectives with Port of London led to delays	Very tight specification	Clear objectives although not all uncertainties could be resolved thereby creating future delays	Clearly stated, exhaustively researched but later compromised by the ICL and CODA decisions	Carefully examined and defined in detail

(3) Changes in specification can lead to management or performance problems	The introduction of a mandatory high-speed rail link (in 1973) triggered the project's collapse	No changes to the basic requirement though, of course, thousands of design changes		Heysham 2 had minimum changes; the first AGRs suffered badly from changes (concurrency)	Changes trickled down throughout project causing severe problems	Changes rigorously controlled	A few small changes, quickly dealt with
(4) Technical uncertainty/ innovation increases chances of difficulty	Innovation high; design evolution took more effort than planned	High innovation from BR view, perhaps rather unnecessarily and dangerously so	Technical problems caused setbacks but could have been overcome with greater experience	The first AGRs presented substantial technical uncertainties; sometimes with inexperienced consortia. Technical uncertainties in the second phase were minimised	Technical uncertainty created difficulty; innovation was low	Substantial uncertainties faced. Fall-back positions adopted to cover the risks posed	Uncertainty minimized by using established technology and resolving outstanding uncertainties on a priority basis

Table A.3 Continued

Hypotheses	Channel Tunnel 1960–75	Concorde	APT	Thames Barrier	Heysham 2 and the AGR programme	Fulmar	COP	Giotto
(5) Interface coordination can create difficulties		Difficult because of both technology and bi-national division of work			Significant during construction; very important	Coordination and communication of vendor information a little awkward	Very important and given much attention	A very large task: received considerable attention and very well done
(6) Design mangement difficulties can cause problems		The complex management structure caused design difficulties			Design managed as rigorously as possible	Design management difficulties *did* cause problems	Great effort made to create standardized design environment	Enormous effort put into creating absolute design control
(7) Amount of finance required may cause difficulties					Uncertainty over commitment affected pace of project in early stages		Assumed financing available for whole duration even though not literally true	

(8) Mixed public/private funding can create difficulties	Mixed funding created uncertainty contributing directly to final abandonment				
(9) Financial risk/difficulty of forecasting final costs, etc., indicative of problems	The perceived risks led to good cancellation terms being negotiated	Early forecasts were guestimates; the science of project cost estimating and control were barely appreciated and so risks went unchallenged	Senior 'owner' management was not interested in determining the financial risks; this cannot have been good for the project	Financial risk and out-turn cost estimated and controlled in detail	
(10) Geo-physical challenges increase chances of overruns	River working created delays	Site conditions created complex logistics; seismic matters important	Winter working in North Sea added around 3 months' delay	Networking between the 11 areas is a challenge	Space encounter and global communications added geophysical risk

Table A.3 Continued

Hypotheses	Channel Tunnel 1960–75	Concorde	APT	Thames Barrier	Heysham 2 and the AGR programme	Fulmar	COP	Giotto
(11) Political, social, community and other 'external' factors affect success chances	Change in government single biggest factor affecting abandonment. Community opposition	Initiated politically, affected dramatically by community reaction, maintained for political reasons—Concorde was intimately affected by all these factors	Support of minister was crucial to the project's initiation and central to its later problems (and cancellation)	Influences were many, complex and generally indirect, particularly political ones. Interaction with PLA and community affected design	Decisions re reactor type were very political. Heysham 2 has been relatively free of political interference. Community problems have been minimal	Politics affected Fulmar via PRT, the Varley assurances and the objection to exporting oil via Ekofisk	Politics directly influenced the choice of mainframe supplier and consequent system design	USA, USSR, Japanese collaboration provided data for corrections to the final intercept path
(12) Schedule phasing chosen so as to minimize risks of political, finacial, etc., changes	Schedule was at its most vulnerable when political changes occurred					Several early reviews. Perhaps more detailed reviews prior to letting fabrication contracts would have been beneficial	Schedule was designed to minimize risk of failure and to allow strategic review	

(13) Urgent schedules can create problems	Urgency was removed when US SST was cancelled		Urgency slowed progress (because of labour problems); urgency also eased the threat of contractual sanctions	PRT and other factors led to great urgency. This clashed with technical uncertainty (concurrency) and caused problems		The finite window (launch date) was of very great value to the mangers of the project
(14) Inadequate planning increases the likelihood of failure	Planning largely adequate, with exception of integrating British Rail		Technically excellent but possibly insufficient for construction work	Heysham 2 benefited greatly from previous AGRs. CEGB developed a systematic project philosophy and management plan	Detailed plans prepared but uncertainties continued and caused future disruptions	A great quantity of high quality planning entered into COP · Considerable planning work resulted in accurate project estimates
(15) Legal agreements and contract strategy and conditions influence structure and roles	The sponsor's legal agreement meant that when the project was threatened it was easier to abandon it than continue · Most manufacturers required cost-plus contracts because of substantial risks		CTH's experience demonstrates the limited threat onerous contract conditions can have in certain project situations	Firm price contracts assisted the CEGB and helped ensure realistic planning and budgeting	Owner took an active role. Contract conditions (and type) changed where and when necessary	COP able to exert considerable leverage over its suppliers to everyone's benefit

Table A.3 Continued

Hypotheses	Channel Tunnel 1960–75	Concorde	APT	Thames Barrier	Heysham 2 and the AGR programme	Fulmar	COP	Giotto
(16) Organization structure should fit project needs and be dynamic	British Rail not sufficiently integrated into project team	Organization structure was governed by the treaty and was bureaucratic and unwieldy	Railways Board was both client and contractor; this caused difficulties, particularly given the division of opinion within the Board about the project		Project orientation found to be useful	Mixture of project and functional arrangements was awkward and possibly led to management difficulties	Structure evolved to fit requirements	Organization structure based on ESA's long experience was tailored to project's various requirements
(17) Absence of effective project controls increases chances of overruns and poor performance		Considerable difficulties experienced in project control. Government had great difficulty in getting information on the project				Control difficulties experienced on several parts of the project	COP had a detailed, regular, extensive control system which contributed significantly to the project's success	Very effective systems with ESA having on-line access to BAeD data

Statement								
(18) Leadership has a strong influence on chances of success	Lack of a champion was a major problem	Technically brilliant, managerially lacking	Leadership changed at the prototype stage. No evident qualities of leadership of the requisite quality	Very important, at every step. More experienced management might have prevented the initial problems becoming so serious	Very important, particularly in teamwork, organizational development, industrial relations and contract negotiations	Personality and qualities of project manager very important, particularly in team building and the joint venture	Outstanding—top management commitment and a manager with vision and leadership	Without its strong leadership early difficulties might have wrecked this project
(19) Teamwork is important to success	Early cultural tensions between the British and French subsided; lack of teamwork by British Rail was disastrous		Had relations between the 'new' researchers and the 'old' engineers been better, the project might have been more successful	Important in keeping joint venture staff working effectively	Important	Important	Important and effective. Being based in a new town contributed significantly to the project's success	Teamwork throughout the project as a whole was important
(20) Labour relations can disrupt project implementation			Union blacking and later strike action contributed substantially to the abandonment of APT	Labour militancy had a direct and dramatic impact on the project. A site agreement and tougher early management might just have helped	NAECI and the Management Group have been of great benefit	Overall not major though difficulties experienced on the RSV and Ashlow contracts	Not a major issue	Union problems at BAeD could have jeopardized the project had industrial relations not been closely monitored

Table A.3 Continued

Hypotheses	Channel Tunnel 1960–75	Concorde	APT	Thames Barrier	Heysham 2 and the AGR programme	Fulmar	COP	Giotto
(21) Poor communications reduce the chances of success			Overemphasis on 'standard practice' created communication problems	Perversely, almost too good: operatives knew of GLC decisions sometimes before management did		Geography, contract arrangements and organizational conflicts impeded communications during engineering and procurement	The steering committee an important vehicle for communications. Team and union communications at Telford good	Maximum effective communications particularly between the client and the contractor. Contract terms reflected the desire for this
(22) Error, incompetence, incapacity or incapability can jeopardize the project success			'Trivial' design faults and reliability finally killed the project			Difficulties encountered through, for example, misunderstandings between owner, fabricators and suppliers		

except in a few instances where the proposed new material accorded with our own observations.

While some of the conclusions made in Chapter 12 are undoubtedly project or industry specific, where the conclusions from the case studies fit the list of factors derived from the literature, we might feel reasonable confidence in their general validity. The factors set down in Chapter 12 were carefully prepared to represent such a general list.

REFERENCES

1. Gilbreath, R. D. 1986; Project Management Institute, 1986
2. Hirschman, A. O., 1958.
3. Paul, S., 1982.
4. Earl, M. J., 1983
5. Baum, W. C. and Tolbert, S. M., 1985; Camillus, J. C., 1984; Hellings, J, 1985; Hodder, J. E. and Riggs, H. E., 1985; Pinches, G. E., 1982.
6. Baker, B. N., Murphy, D. C. and Fisher, D., 1982; Baum, W. C. and Tolbert, S. M., 1985; Feldman, E. J. and Milch, J., 1982; Hayfield, F., 1985; Herbert, E., 1983; National Economic Development Office, 1982; Ruskin, A. M., 1982; Vicklund, C. A. and Craft, W. S., 1981; Waterson, A., 1965.
7. Frame, A. G., 1978; Hall P., 1980; Horwitch, M., 1982, 1984; Horwitch, M., 1984; Kutner, S., 1979; Navarro, P., 1982; Turner, B., 1976.
8. Bryson, L., 1982; David, E. E., 1981; Department of Energy, 1976; Hall, P., 1980; Harman, A. J., 1970; Hayfield, F., 1985; Henderson, P. D., 1977; Hess, R. W., 1985; Kharbanda, O. P. and Stallworthy, E. A., 1983; Marshal, A. W. and Meckling, W. H., 1959; Merrow, E., Chapel, S. W. and Worthing, C. A., 1979; Murphy, D. C., Baker, B. N. and Fisher, D., 1974; Perry, R. L. *et al.*, 1971; Pugh, P. G., 1985; Summers, R., 1965.
9. Hayfield, F., 1985; Viana de Andrade, 1979.
10. Feldman, E., 1985a,b; Hayfield, F., 1985; Kharbanda, O. P. and Stallworthy, E. A., 1983; Knight, G., 1976; National Economic Development Office, 1970, 1982; Whipp, R. and Clark, P., 1986.
11. Baker, B. N., Murphy, D. C. and Fisher, D., 1982; Ferdinands, D. *et al.*, 1985.
12. Major Projects Association (confidential).
13. Antl, B., 1980; Frame, A. G., 1978; Haache, G. and Townend, J. C., 1981; Jaycobs, R., 1984; Kimball Brooker, T., 1979; Luetchford, M. A. C., 1978; Merrett, A. J. and Sykes, A., 1980; Stringer, J., Lobl, M. and Wheen, R., 1985.
14. David, E. E., 1981; Department of Energy, 1976; Frankhouser, H. S., 1981; Geistants, G. and Hauck, V., 1979; National Committee on Tunnelling Technology, 1974; Seamans, R. and Ordway, F. I., 1977; Stinchcombe, A. L., 1979b; Vicklund, C. A. and Craft, W. S., 1981.
15. Canaday, H. T., 1980; Caro, R., 1974; David, E. E., 1981; Feldman, E. J., 1985a, 1985b; Geistants, G. and Hauck, V., 1979; Greene, M. R. and

Cury, M. G., 1977; Grindle, M. S., 1980; Hall, P., 1980; Honadle, G. and Van Sant, J., 1985; Horwitch, M., 1979, 1982, 1984; Knight, G., 1976; Kutner, S., 1979; McEachron, B. and Teige, P. J., 1977; Navarro, P., 1982; Rycroft, R. W. and Szyliowicz, J. S., 1980; Sapolsky, H., 1972; Szyliowicz, J. S., 1982.

16. Little, Arthur D., 1985; Frame, A. G., 1978; Glaser, P., 1985; Kharbanda, O. P. and Stallworthy, E. A., 1983; Paul, S., 1982, 1983; Sykes, A., 1982.

17. Cochran, E. G., Patz, A. L. and Rowe, A. G., 1978; Department of Energy, 1976; Fox, J. R., 1984; Gemmill, G. and Thamhain, H. J., 1972, 1974; Hayfield, F., 1985; Honadle, G. and Van Sant, J., 1985; Kelley, A. J. and Morris, P. W. G., 1981; Morris, P. W. G., 1974; National Audit Office, 1986; National Economic Development Office, 1982; Rothwell, D. L. *et al.*, 1975; Rubin, I. M. and Seeling, W., 1967; Ruskin, A. M. and Lerner, R., 1972; Stinchcombe, A. L., 1979b.

18. Baum, W. C. and Tolbert, S. M., 1985; Coopers & Lybrand, 1973; Department of Energy, 1976; Frame, A. G., 1978; General Accounting Office, 1985; National Committee on Tunnelling Technology, 1974; National Economic Development Office, 1982; Seamans, R. and Ordway, F. L., 1977; Whipp, R, and Clark, P., 1986; Vicklund, C. A. and Craft, W. S., 1981.

19. Canaday, H. T., 1980; De Cotiis, T. A. and Dyer, L., 1979; Department of Construction Management, 1979; Jaafari, A., 1985; Nahapiet, H. and Nahapiet, J., 1985a, b; Ninos, G. E. and Wearne, S. H., 1974; Perry, J. G., Thompson, P. A. and Wright, M., 1982; Sharp, D., 1982; Thamhain, H. J. and Wilemon, D. I., 1986; Theodore Barry & Associates, 1979.

20. Asbury, A., 1982; DeCotiis, T. A. and Dyer, L., 1979; Might, R. J. and Fischer, W. A., 1985; Moolin, F. P. and McCoy, F., 1979; Morris, P. W. G., 1982a, b; Paulson, B. C. Fondahl, J. W. and Parker, H. W., 1977; Thamhain, H. J. and Wilemon, D. L., 1986.

21. Hayfield, F., 1985; Hayward, K., 1983; Might, R. J. and Fisher, W. A., 1985; Philips, S. C., 1967.

22. Baker, B. N. and Wilemon, D. L., 1974; Baker, B. N., Murphy, D. C. and Fisher, D., 1982; Baum, W. C. and Tolbert, S. M., 1985; Caro, R., 1974; Fox, J. R., 1984; Honadle, G. and Van Sant, J., 1985; Horwitch, M., 1982; Kolman, E. H., 1972; Morton, G. H. A., 1984; Murphy, D. C., Baker, B. N. and Fisher, D., 1974; Ninos, G. E. and Wearne, S. H., 1974; Seamans, R. and Ordway, F. I., 1977; Sykes, A., 1982.

23. Baker, B. N., Murphy, D. C., and Fisher D., 1982; Bocherding, J. D., 1976; Chapman, R. L., 1973; Sayles, L. R. and Chandler, M. K., 1971; Wilemon, D. L., 1971.

24. National Economic Development Office, 1970, 1976.

25. Allen, T. J., Lee, D. and Tushman, M., 1980; Allen, T. J., Tushman, M. and Lee, D., 1979; Andrews, D., 1984; Archibald, R. D., 1976; Baker, B. N., Murphy, D. C. and Fisher, D., 1982; Katz, R., 1982; Katz, R. and Allen, T. J., 1985; National Economic Development Office, 1982; Sayles, L. R. and Chandler, M. K., 1971; Seamans, R. and Orway, F. I., 1977; Vicklund, C. A. and Craft, W. S., 1981.

26. Dixon, N. R., 1976, 1982; Janis, I. L., 1972.

27. Morris, P. W. G. and Hough, G. H., 1986.

Bibliography

Acker, D. D., 'The maturing of the DOD acquisition process', *Defense Systems Management Review*, 3(3), 1980, pp.7–77.

Adams, J. R. and Bardnt, S. E., 'Organizational life cycle implications for major projects', *Project Management Quarterly* 9(4), 1978, pp.32–9.

Alexander, A. J., Appendix B in 'Alternative institutional arrangements for developing and commercializing breeder reactor technology', Johnson, L. L., Merrow, E. W., Baer, W. A. and Alexander, A., Rand Corporation, R-2069-NSF, Santa Monica, California, November, 1976.

Alexander, A. J., and Nelson, J. R., 'Measuring technological change: aircraft turbine engines', Rand Corporation, R-1017-ARPA/PR, Santa Monica, California, June 1972.

Allen, J. M. and Norris, K. P., 'Project estimates and outcomes in electricity generation research', *Journal of Management Studies*, October 1970, pp.271–287.

Allen, T. J., Lee, D. and Tushman, M., 'R & D Performance as a function of internal communication, project management, and the nature of work', *IEEE Transactions on Engineering Management*, 27, 1980, pp.2–12.

Allen, T. J. Tushman, M. and Lee, D., 'Technology transfer as a function of position on research, development, and technical service continuum', *Academy of Management Journal*, 22, 1979, pp.694–708.

Allison, G., *The Essence of Decision*, Little, Brown & Co., Boston, Massachusetts, 1971.

Andrews, D., *The IRG Solution: Hierarchical Incompetence and How to Overcome It*, Souvenir Press, London, 1984.

Angremond, K. d', and Kooman, D., 'Eastern Scheldt storm surge barrier', *International Journal of Project Management*, 4(3), August 1986, pp.149–157.

Antl, Boris (ed.), *Currency Risk and the Corporation*, Euromoney Publications, London, 1980.

Archibald, R. D., *Managing High Technology Programs and Projects*, John Wiley, New York, 1976.

Archibald, R. D., 'Project management in the USA', *International Journal of Project Management*, 3(4), November 1985, pp.195–7.

Arditi, D., Akan, G. T. and Gurdamar, S., 'Reasons for delays in public projects in Turkey', *Construction Management and Economics*, 3(2), 1985a, pp.171–81.

Arditi, D., Akan, G. T. and Gurdamar, S., 'Cost overruns in public projects'

International Journal of Project Management, 3(4), November 1985b, pp.218-24.

Asbury, A., 'Summary of the discussion at the forum on large-scale project management', *IEE Proceedings*, Part A, 129(8), November 1982, pp.629-33.

Baker, A. C. and Boyd, K. J., 'Fast tracking nuclear power plant construction—concepts to make fast tracking a viable concept', *Proceedings of the 7th World Congress on Project Management*, Copenhagen, Internet, Zurich, 1982.

Baker, N. R., Green, S. G. and Bean, A. S., 'Why R & D projects succeed or fail', *Research Management*, November–December, 1986, pp.29-34.

Baker, B. N., Murphy, D. C. and Fisher, D., 'Factors affecting project success' in *Handbook of Project Management*, Cleland, D. I. and King, W. R. (eds), Van Nostrand Reinhold, New York, 1982.

Baker, B. N. and Wilemon, D. L., 'A summary of major research findings regarding the human element in project management', *Project Management Quarterly*, 5(2), 1974, pp.27-30.

Balachandra, R. and Raelin, J. A., 'When to Kill that R & D project', *Research Management*, July-August, 1984, pp.30-33.

Bladridge, J. and Burnham, R. A., 'Organizational innovation: individual organizational and environmental impacts', *Administrative Science Quarterly*, 20(2), June 1975, pp.165-76.

Baum, W. C. and Tolbert, S. M., *Investing in Development*, Oxford University Press, Oxford, 1985.

Baumgartner, J. S., *Systems Management*, Bureau of National Affairs, Washington DC, 1979.

Beard, E., *Developing the ICBM*, Columbia University Press, New York, 1976.

Bedell, R. I., 'Terminating R & D projects Prematurely', *Research Management*, July-August, 1983, pp.32-35.

Belden D. L., 'Defense procurement outcomes in the incentive contract environment', Ph.D. dissertation, AD 668561, Stanford University, 1969.

Beteille, R., 'The coordination of European research', *Aeronautical Journal*, May 1969, pp.417-21.

Bignell, V. and Fortune, J., *Understanding Systems Failures*, Open University Press/Manchester University Press, Manchester, 1984.

Blake, C., Cox, D. and Fraize, W., *Analysis of Projected vs Actual Costs for Nuclear and Coal-Fired Plants*, Mitre Corporation, Fairfax, Virginia, 1976.

Bocherding, J. D., 'Applying behaviour research findings on construction projects', *Project Management Quarterly* 7(3), 1976, pp.9-14.

Bondi, H., 'London flood barrier', unpublished report to the Ministry of Housing and Local Government, London, 1967.

Boocock, D. and King, I., 'The development of the prototype Advanced Passenger Train', *Proceedings of the Institute of Mechanical Engineers*, 196(6), 1982.

Boocock, D. and Newman, M., 'The Advanced Passenger Train', *Proceedings of the Institute of Mechanical Engineers*, 190(62), 1976.

British Standards Office, *Glossary of the Terms Used in QA*, BS 4778, London, 1978.

Brooks, F. P., *The Mythical Man–Month*, Addison-Wesley, Reading, Massachusetts, 1982.

Bryson, L., 'Large scale project management', *IEE Proceedings*, Part A, 129(8), November 1982, pp.625-9.

Bryson, L., 'All at sea', *IEE Proceedings*, Part A, 133(1), January 1986.

Bunyard, J. M., 'Today's risks in software development—can they be significantly reduced?' *Concepts*, **5**(4), 1982, pp.73–94.

Camillus, J. C., 'Designing a capital budgeting system that works', *Long Range Planning*, **17**(2), April 1984, pp.111–16;

Canaday, H. T., 'Construction costs overruns in electric utilities; some trends and implications', Occasional Paper No.3, National Regulatory Research Institute, Ohio State University, November 1980.

Caro, R., *The Power Broker*, Vintage, New York, 1974.

Carter, E. E., 'What are the risks in risk analysis', *Harvard Business Review*, July/August 1972, pp.72–82.

Channel Tunnel, The, HMSO, Cmnd 5430, London, 1973.

Chapman, R. L., *Project Management in NASA*, National Aeronautics and Space Administration, Washington DC, 1973.

Checkland, P., *Systems Thinking, Systems Practice*, John Wiley, New York, 1981.

Cleland, D. I. and King, W. R., *Systems Analysis and Project Management*, McGraw-Hill, New York, 1983.

Cochran, E. G., Patz, A. L. and Rowe, A. J., 'Concurrency and disruption in new product innovation', *California Management Review*, Fall 1978.

Collier, K., *Construction Contracts*, Reston Publishing, Reston, Virginia, 1979.

Connell, J., *The New Maginot Line*, Secker & Warburg, London, 1986.

Cook, J., 'Nuclear follies', *Forbes*, 11 February 1985.

Cooper, R. G., 'New Product success in industrial firms', *Industrial Marketing Management*, **11**, 1982, pp.215–23.

Coopers & Lybrand, *The Channel Tunnel—A United Kingdom Transport Cost-Benefit Study*, HMSO, London, 1973.

David, E. E., 'Synfuels superprojects: new challenges for project management', Henderson Memorial Lecture, Massachusetts Institute of Technology, 30 April 1981.

Davidson, F. P., *Macro: A Clear Vision of How Science and Technology will Shape our Future*, Bond, London, 1986.

Davidson, F. P., Giacoletto, L. J. and Salkeld, R., *Macro-Engineering and the Infrastructure of Tomorrow*, Westview Press, Boulder, Colorado, 1978.

Davidson, F. P., and Meador, C. L. *Macro-Engineering and the Future—A Management Perspective*, Westview Press, Boulder, Colorado, 1982.

Davidson, F. P., Meador, C. L. and Salkeld, R., *How Big and Still Beautiful? Macro-Engineering Revisited*, Westview Press, Boulder, Colorado, 1980.

Davies, C., Demb, A. and Espejo, R., *Organization for Program Management*, John Wiley, New York, 1979.

Davis, S. M. and Lawrence, P. R., *Matrix*, Addison-Wesley, Reading, Massachusetts, 1977.

DeCotiis, T. A. and Dyer, L., 'Defining and measuring project performance', *Research Management*, January, 1979, pp.17–22.

Delp, P., Thesen, A., Motiwalla, J. and Seshadri, N., *Systems Tools for Project Planning*, International Development Institute, Indiana University, Bloomington, Indiana, 1977.

De Marco, T., *Controlling Software Projects: Management, Measurement and Estimation*, Yourden Press, New York, 1982.

De Mong, R. F., 'The effectiveness of incentive contracts: what research tells us', *National Contract Management Quarterly Journal*, **12**(4), December 1978.

Department of Construction Management, University of Reading, *UK and US*

Construction Industries: A Comparison of Design and Contract Procedures, Royal Institution of Chartered Surveyors, London, 1979.

Department of Energy, 'North Sea costs escalation study', Energy Paper No.7, HMSO, London, 1976.

DeWit, A., 'Cost-effective owner project management—the challenge for the future, *Proceedings of the 8th World Congress on Project Management*, Internet, Zurich, 1985.

Dickson, J. R., 'Project management: a new agenda', *Proceedings of the 8th World Congress on Project Management*, Internet, Zurich, 1985.

Digital System Development Methodology, Computer Sciences Corporation, London, 1985.

Dinsmore, P. C., *Human Factors in Project Management*, Amacom, New York, 1984.

Dixon, N. F., *The Psychology of Military Incompetence*, Jonathan Cape, London, 1976.

Dixon, N. F., 'Some thoughts on the nature and causes of industrial incompetence, *Personnel Management*, **14**(12), December 1982, pp.26–30.

Dunne, E., 'How six management techniques are used', *Research Management*, March-April 1983, pp.36–41.

Earl, M. J., *Persepectives on Management*, Oxford University Press, Oxford, 1983.

Economic Consultants Limited, *The Channel Tunnel—Its Economic and Social Impact on Kent*, April 1973.

Edmonds, M., 'Rolls-Royce' in *Policy and Private Interests: The Institutions of Compromise*, Hague, D. C., MacKenzie, W. J. M. and Barker, A. (eds.), Macmillan, London, 1975.

Elliot, J., 'Sir Keith tears up his own rule-book', *Financial Times*, 20 March 1981.

Ellis, W., 'Welcome to a new white elephant', *Financial Times*, 17 August 1985.

Elton, J. R., 'Management contracting' in *Management of International Construction Projects*, Institution of Civil Engineers, London, 1985, pp.73–83.

ESA, Arianspace, CNES, British Aerospace, *Giotto: ESA's Mission to Halley's Comet*, Paris, July 1985a.

ESA, *Status Document*, Paris, September 1985b.

Fangel, M., 'Twelve methods of project start-up, *Proceedings of the 8th World Congress on Project Management*, Rotterdam, Internet, Zurich, 1985.

Federal Aviation Authority, 'Civil aircraft sonic boom. Nature of proposed rule making', Docket 10261 Notice to 70–16 Federal Register, Washington DC, April 1970.

Feldman, E. J., 'Patterns of failure in governement megaprojects: economics, politics and participation in industrial democracies' in *Global Dilemmas*, Huntingdon, S. P. and Nye, J. S. (eds.), Center for International Affairs, Harvard, and University Press of America, Cambridge, Massachusetts, 1985a.

Feldman, E. J., *Concorde and Dissent: Explaining High Technology Failures in Great Britain and France*, Cambridge University Press, New York, 1985b.

Feldman, E. J. and Milch, J., *Technocracy Versus Democracy*, Auburn House, Boston, Massachusetts, 1982.

Ferdinands, D., Gibbons, C., West, J. and Conway, K., 'Arranging finance' in *Macroprojects: Strategy, Planning and Implementation*, Gray, K. G. *et al*, (eds.), Warren Centre, University of Sydney, Sydney, 1985.

Finch, U. C. and Postula, F. D., 'Risk evaluation of alternative energy sources', *AACE Transaction*, 1983, P:B.2.1–B.2.5(5).

Flippo, E. B. and Munsinger, G. M., *Management*, Allyn & Bacon, Boston, 1976.

Fox, J. R. 'Evaluating management of large, complex projects: a framework for analysis', *Technology in Society*, 6(2), 1984, pp.129–39.

Frame, A. G., 'Influence of the nature, size and location of projects on organizations', Institution of Civil Engineers' Conference: *Management of Large Capital Projects*, 17–18 May 1978; Institution of Civil Engineers, London, 1978, p.89.

Frame, A. G., Inaugural Address to the Project Management Forum, Institution of Electrical Engineers, London, November 1985.

Frankhouser, H. S., 'Project management (North Sea)—basic and variable factors', *Journal of Petroleum Technology*, 33(10), October 1981, pp.1821–7.

Franks, J., *Building Procurement Systems*, Chartered Institute of Building, Englemere, Ascot, 1984.

Fraser, D. C., *An Approach to Major Projects*, Major Projects Association, Templeton College, Oxford, 1984.

Fremgem, J. M., 'Capital budgeting practices: a survey', *Management Accounting*, May 1973, pp.20–1.

Geistants, G. and Hauck, V., *The Trans-Alaskan Pipeline*, East–West Center, East–West Resource Systems Institute, Honolulu, Hawaii, 1979.

Gemmill, G. and Thamhain, H. J., 'Project performance as a function of the leadership styles of project managers', Project Management Institute Conference, Philadelphia, 1972. Project Management Institute, Drexel Hill, Pennsylvania.

Gemmill, G. and Thamhain, H. J., 'Influence styles of project managers: some project performance correlates', *Academy of Management Journal*, 17(2), 1974, pp.216–24.

General Accounting Office, 'Financial status of major federal acquisitions, September 30, 1979', PSAD–80–25, Washington DC, 12 February 1980.

General Accounting Office, 'Controlling federal costs for coal liquefaction program hinges on management and contracting improvements', PSAD–81–19, Washington DC, 4 February 1981.

General Accounting Office, 'Cost growth and delivery delays in submarine construction and electric boat are likely to continue', MASAD–82–29, Washington DC, 19 April 1982.

General Accounting Office, 'Status of major acquisitions as of September 30 1982', GAO/NS IAD–83–32, Washington DC, 7 September 1983.

General Accounting Office, 'Status of Bonneville Power Administration's efforts to improve its oversight of three nuclear power projects', GAD/RCED–84–23, Washington, DC.

General Accounting Office, 'Why some weapon systems encounter production problems while others do not: six case studies, GAO/NSIAD–85–34, Washington DC, 24 May 1985.

Gerstenfeld, A., 'A study of successful projects, unsuccessful projects and projects in progress in West Germany', *IEEE Transactions on Engineering Management*, EM–23(3), August 1976, pp.116–23.

Gilbert, S. and Horner, R., *The Thames Barrier*, Thomas Telford, London, 1984.

Gilbreath, R. D., *Winning at Project Management*, Wiley, New York, 1986.

Gittinger, J. P., *Economic Analysis of Agricultural Projects*, Johns Hopkins University Press, Baltimore, Maryland, 1972.

Glaser, P., 'The solar power satellite—a goal for the economic development of space', *Solar Power Review*, **5**, 1985, pp.83–90.

Gott, H. H., 'The engineering of large projects', in *Comparative Project Management*, Institution of Mechanical Engineers, London, 1969.

Gray, K. G., Jaafari, A. and Wheen, R. J. (eds.) *Macroprojects: Strategy Planning and Implementation*, Warren Centre for Advanced Engineering, The University of Sydney, Sydney, 1985.

Greater London Council, *Thames Flood Prevention, First Report of Studies*, London 1969.

Greene, M. R. and Cury, M. G., *Management of Social and Economic Impacts Associated with the Construction of Large Scale Projects: Experiences from the Western Coal Development Communities*, Department of Energy, June 1977.

Grice, J. R. and Hepplewhite, E. A., 'Design and construction of the Thames Barrier cofferdams', *Proceedings of the Institution of Civil Engineers*, Part I, **174**, May 1983, pp.191–224.

Grindle, M. S. (ed.), *Politics and Policy Implementation in the Third World*, Princeton University Press, Princeton, New Jersey, 1980.

Hacche, G. and Townend, J. C., 'A broad look at exchange rate movements for eight currencies, 1972–80', *Bank of England Quarterly Bulletin*, December 1981, pp.489–501.

Hall, P., *Great Planning Disasters*, Weidenfeld & Nicolson, London, 1980.

Hammond, R. and Fox, D., 'Organizing the macroproject' in *Macroprojects: Strategy, Planning and Implementation*, Gray, K. G. *et al.* (eds.), Warren Centre, University of Sydney, Sydney, 1985.

Hannah, L., *Engineers, Managers and Politicians*, Macmillan, London, 1982.

Harman, A. J. assisted by Henrichsen, S., 'A methodology for cost factor comparison and prediction', Rand Corporation, R–6269–ARPA, Santa Monica, California, August 1970.

Harrison, F. L., *Advanced Project Management*, Gower, London, 1985.

Harvey, T. E., 'Concurrency today in acquisition management', *Defense Systems Management Review*, **3**(1), Winter 1980, pp.14–18.

Hayes, R. W., 'A study of management contracts', M. Sc. Thesis, University of Manchester Insitute of Science and Technology, Manchester, 1983.

Hayes, R. W., Perry, J. G. and Thompson, P. A., 'Management contracting', CIRIA Report No.100, London, 1983.

Hayfield, F., 'Project success and failures, *Proceedings of the 8th World Congress on Project Management. Internet*, Rotterdam, 1985.

Hayward, K., *Government and British Civil Aerospace*, Manchester University Press, Manchester, 1983.

Hazelrigg, G. A. and Roth, E. B., *Windows for Innovation: A Story of Two Large-Scale Technologies*, National Science Foundation, Washington DC, 1982.

Healey, J. M., 'Errors in project cost estimates', *Indiana Economic Journal*, July–September 1964, pp.44–57.

Hellings, J., 'The cost of capital in the real world', *Management Accounting*, **62**(5), May 1984, pp.18–20.

Hellings. J., 'Capital budgeting in the real world', *Management Accounting*, **63**(4), April 1985, pp.38–40.

Henderson, P. D., 'Two British errors: their probable size and some possible lessons', *Oxford Economic Papers*, **29**(2), July 1977, pp.159–204.

Herbert, E., 'Superproject management', *IEEE Spectrum*, **20**(9), 1983, pp.68–9.

Hertz, D. B. and Thomas, H., *Risk Analysis*, John Wiley, Chichester, 1983.

Hess, R. W., 'Review of cost improvement literature with emphasis on synthetic fuel facilities and the petroleum and chemical process industries', Rand Corporation, N–2273–SFC, Santa Monica, California, March 1985.

Hirschman, A. O., *The Strategy of Economic Development* Yale University Press, Hartford, Connecticut, 1958.

Hodder, J. E. and Riggs, H. E., 'Pitfalls in evaluating risk prospects', *Harvard Business Review*, **63**(1), January–February 1985, pp.128–35.

Hodgkinson, C., *The Philosophy of Leadership*, Basil Blackwell, Oxford, 1983.

Honadle, G. and Van Sant, J., *Implementation for Sustainability. Lessons from Integrated Rural Development*, Kumarian Press, West Hartford, Connecticut, 1985.

Hopkins, D. S., *New Products: Winners and Losers*, Conference Board, New York, 1980.

Horwitch, M., 'Designing and managing large-scale, public–private technological enterprises: a state of the art review', *Technology in Society*, **1**, 1979, pp.179–92.

Horwitch, M., *Clipped Wings: The American SST Conflict*, MIT Press, Cambridge, Massachusetts, 1982.

Horwitch, M. (ed.) *Strategies for Macro Projects: Challenges and Opportunities*, Ballinger, Cambridge, Massachusetts, 1987.

Horwich, M., 'The convergence factor for successful large-scale programs: The American Synfuels experience as a case in point' in *Matrix Management Systems Handbook*, Cleland, D.I. (ed.), Van Norstrand Reinhold, New York, 1984.

House of Commons, Select Committee on Science and Technology, *United Kingdom Nuclear Reactor Programme*, HMSO, 1967.

House of Commons, Thirty First Report from the Committee of Public Accounts 1985–86, 'Financial assistance to the Lear Fan Aircraft Project, Industrial Development Board for Northern Ireland', HMSO, 10 July 1986.

Hufschmidt, N. M. and Gerin, J., 'Systematic errors in cost estimates for public investment projects' in *The Analysis of Public Output*, Margolis, J. (ed.), Columbia University Press, New York, 1970.

Ibbs, C. W. Back, W. E., Kim, J. J., Wall, D. E., DeLaGarza, J. M., Hassamein, M. A., Schram, S. M. and Twardock, R. R., 'Determining the impact of various construction contract types and clauses on project performance', Department of Civil Engineering, University of Illinois at Urbana-Champaign, March 1986.

Innes, G., 'Early production versus staged development' in *North Sea Development, Experiences and Challenges*, proceedings of a conference sponsored by the Institute of Petroleum and the Norwegian Petroleum Society, Heyden, London, April 1979.

Institute of Industrial Economics, 'Delays and project administration in the North Sea' (unpublished), Bergen, Norway, 1979.

Jaafari, A., 'Contractual relationships, agreements and potential liabilities' in *Macroprojects: Strategy, Planning and Implementation*, Gray, K. G. *et al.* (eds.), Warren Centre, University of Sydney, Sydney, 1985.

Janis, I. L., *Victims of Group Think*, Houghton Mifflin, Boston, Massachusetts, 1972.

Jaycobs, R., 'Getting it right at the right time', *Euromoney* August 1984, pp.148–54.

Jenkin, M., *British industry and the North Sea*, Macmillan, London, 1981.

Jenkins, R. H. and Link, D. C. R., 'Giotto: Europe's exploratory mission to the Comet Halley', *Journal of British Interplanetary Society*, **37**, 1984, pp.17–27.

Johnston, K. F. A., *Electrical and Mechanical Engineering Contracts*, Gower Press, London, 1971.

Jones, S., 'Economic high-speed running of railways', *Electronics and Power*, February 1975.

Jones, S., 'The Advanced Passenger Train: an economic alternative to the construction of new track', *South African Institute of Electrical Engineers Technology in Ground Transport*, **68**, Part 6, June 1977.

Katz, R., 'The effects of group longevity on project communications and performance', *Administrative Science Quarterly*, **27**, 1982, pp.81–104.

Katz, R. and Allen, T. J., 'Project performance and the locus of influence in the R & D matrix' *Academy of Management Journal*, **28**(1), 1985, pp.67–87.

Kelley, A. J. and Morris, P. W. G., 'Strategies for managing very large projects', *Proceedings of the 1981 Joint Internet–PMI Symposium, Boston*, Project Management Institute, Drexel Hill, Pennsylvania, 1981.

Kerzner, H. D., *Project Management: A Systems Approach to Planning, Scheduling and Controlling*, Van Nostrand Reinhold, New York, 1979.

Kharbanda, O. P. and Stallworthy, E. A., *How to Learn from Project Disasters*, Gower, London, 1983.

Kimball Brooker, T., 'The successful financing of projects' in *The Successful Accomplishment of Giant Projects*, Willis Faber, London, 1979.

Kloman, E. H., *Unmanned Space Project Management—Surveyor and Lunar Orbiter*, National Academy of Public Administration, Washington DC, 1972.

Knight, G., *Concorde: The Inside Story*, Weidenfeld & Nicolson, London, 1976.

Komanoff, C., *Cost Escalation of Nuclear and Coal Power Plants*, Komanoff Energy Associates, New York, 1981.

Kozmetzky, G., 'Evaluation of macro-systems: models and case analysis' in *How Big and Still Beautiful? Macro-Engineering Revisited*, Davidson, F. P., Meader, C. L. and Salkeld, R. (eds.), Westview Press, Boulder, Colorado, 1980.

Kutner, S., 'The impact of regulatory agencies on superprojects' in *Planning, Engineering and Constructing the Superprojects*, American Society of Civil Engineers' Conference, Pacific Grove, 1978: ASCE, New York, 1979.

Large, J. P., 'Bias in initial cost estimates: how low estimates can increase the cost of acquiring weapon systems', Rand Corporation, R–1467–PA & E, Santa Monica, California, July 1974.

Lavers, B. A., *The Management of Large Projects*, Shell UK Exploration and Production, London, 1985.

Little, Arthur D., *Federal Policy and MacroEngineering for Energy*, report to the National Science Foundation, Washington DC, United States of America, April 1985.

Little, I. M. D. and Mirless, J. M., *Manual of Industrial Project Analysis in Developing Countries*, OECD, Paris, 1968.

Litwak, E. and Rothman, J., 'Towards the theory and practice of co-ordination between formal organizations' in *Organizations and Clients: Essays in the Sociology of Service*, Rosengren, W. R. and Lefton, M. (eds.), Merrill, Columbus, Ohio, 1970, pp.137–86.

Lock, D., *Project Management*, Gower, London, 1984.

Long Term Demand for Scientific Manpower, Cmnd 1490, London, 1961. HMSO, (the Gibb–Zuckerman Report).

Luetchford, M. A. C., Comment at the Institution of Civil Engineers' Conference: *Management of Large Capital Projects*, Institution of Civil Engineers, London, 1978.

Luffman, G. A. and Reed, R., *The Strategy and Performance of British Industry, 1970–80*, Macmillan, London, 1984.

Maciariello, J. A., *Program Management Control Systems*, John Wiley, New York, 1978.

Maieli, V., 'Sowing the seeds of project cost overruns', *Management Review*, August 1972, pp.7–14.

Mansfield, E. and Wagner, S., 'Organizational and strategic factors associated with probabilities of success and industrial R & D', *Journal of Business*, **48**(2), April 1975.

Mao, J. C. T., 'Survey of capital budgeting: theory and practice', *Journal of Finance*, May, 1970, pp.349–60.

Marquis, D. G. and Straight, D. M., 'Organizational factors in project performance', Working Paper 133–165, Sloan School of Management, Massachusetts Institute of Technology, Cambridge, Massachusetts, 1965.

Marsh, P. D. V., *Contracting for Engineering and Construction Projects*, Gower, London, 1969.

Marschak, T., Glennan, T. K. and Summers, R., *Strategy for R & D: Studies in the Microeconomics of Development*, Springer-Verlag, New York, 1967.

Marshall, A. W. and Meckling, W. H., 'Predictability of the costs, time and success of development', Rand Corporation, P–1821, Santa Monica, California, December 1959.

Martin, C. C., *Project Management: How to Make it Work*, Amacom, New York, 1976.

Martin, M. and Cavendish, P. C., 'Coping with cross-cultural differences in the international project environment', *Proceedings of the 7th World Congress on Project Management*, Copenhagen, Internet, Zurich, 1982.

Mason, G. E., Larew, P. E., Bocherding, J. D., Okes, S. R. and Rad, P. F., 'Delays in nuclear power plant construction', United States Research and Development Administration, E(11–1)–4121, Washington DC, December 1977.

McCaskey, M. B., *The Executive Challenge*, Pitman, London, 1982.

McEachron, B. and Teige, P. J., 'Constraints on large-scale technological projects', Research Report No.CSS–4676–14, Stanford Research Institute International, 1977.

Meredith, J. R. and Mantel, S. J., *Project Management: A Managerial Approach*, John Wiley, New York, 1985.

Merewitz, L., 'How do urban rapid transit projects compare in cost estimating experience?' *Proceedings of the International Conference on Transporation Research*, Bruges, Belgium, 1973.

Merrett, A. J. and Sykes, A., *The Finance and Analysis of Capital Projects*, Longman, London, 1980.

Merrow, E., Chapel, S. W. and Worthing, C. A., 'A review of cost estimation in new technologies: implications for energy process plants', Rand Corporation, R–2481–DOE, Santa Monica, California, July 1979.

Metzger, P. W., *Managing a Programming Project*, Prentice-Hall, Englewood Cliffs, 1981.

Might, R. J. and Fischer, W. A., 'Role of structural factors in determining project management success', *IEEE Transactions on Engineering Management*, **EM–32**(2), May 1985, pp.71–7.

Ministry of Programme Implementation, *Towards Effective and Speedy Implementation: Report 1985–86*, Govenement of India, New Delhi, 1986.

Ministry of Public Building and Works, *The Placing and Management of Contracts for Building and Civil Engineering Work* (the Banwell Report), HMSO, London, 1964.

Ministry of Technology, *Report of the Steering Group on Development Cost Estimating* (the Downey Report), HMSO, London, 1969.

Monopolies and Mergers Commission, *Central Electricity Generating Board. A Report on the Operation by the Board of its System for the Generation of Supply of Electricity in Bulk*, HMSO, London, 1981.

Moolin, F. P. and McCoy, F., 'The organization and management of large projects . . . realities vs theory' *Proceedings of the Project Management Institute Symposium*, Drexel Hill, Pennsylvania, 1979.

Morgan, H. and Soden, J., 'Understanding MIS failures', *Database*, **5**, Winter 1979, pp.157–171.

Morris, P. W. G., 'Organizational analysis of project management in the building industry', *Build International*, **6**(6), 1973, pp.595–616.

Morris, P. W. G., 'Systems study of project management', *Building* CCXXVI(6816–7), 1974, pp.75–80 and 83–8.

Morris, P. W. G., 'Project organizations: structures for managing change' in *New Dimensions of Project Management*, Kelley, A. J. (ed.), Lexington Books, Lexington, Massachusetts, 1982a.

Morris, P. W. G., 'Managing project interfaces—key points for project success' in *Project Management Handbook*, Cleland, D. I. and King, W. R. (eds.), Van Nostrand Reinhold, New York, 1982b.

Morris, P. W. G., 'Programme management in a developing nation telecommunications company', *International Journal of Project Management*, **1**(4), November 1983, pp.204–8.

Morris, P. W. G., 'Work at Templeton College with the Major Projects Association in the study of the initiation, assessment, securing and accomplishment of major projects', Large Scale Programs Institute, University of Texas at Austin, Texas, 1985a.

Morris, P. W. G., 'Issues raised in seminars of the Major Projects Association: December 1981–June 1984', Technical Paper No.1, Major Projects Association, Templeton College, Oxford, 1985b.

Morris, P. W. G. (ed.), 'The MPA on finance' Technical Paper No.2, Major Projects Association, Templeton College, Oxford, 1986.

Morris, P. W. G. and De Lapp, S. E., 'Managing change through project management', *Project Management Quarterly*, **XIV**(2), June 1983, pp.60–72.

Morris, P. W. G. and Hodgson, P. J., 'The Major Projects Association and other macro-engineering societies: their activities and potential contribution to the development of project management', paper presented at the 8th World Congress on Project Management. Internet, Rotterdam, 1985.

Morris, P. W. G. and Hough, G. H., 'The Preconditions of success and failure in major projects', Technical Paper No.3, Major Projects Association, Templeton College, Oxford, 1986.

Morton, G. H. A., 'Become a project champion', *International Journal of Project Management*, **1**(4), November 1984, pp.197–203.

Murphy, D. C., Baker, B. N. and Fisher, D., 'Determinants of project success', National Technical Information Services, Springfield, Virginia 22151, USA. Accession No.N–74–30392, 15 September 1974.

Myers, C. W. and Devey, M. R., 'How management can affect project outcomes: an exploration of the PPS database', Rand Corporation, N–2196–SFC, Santa Monica, California, August 1984.

Nahapiet, H. and Nahapiet, J., *The Management of Construction Projects: Case Studies from the USA and UK*, Chartered Institute of Building, Englemere, Berkshire, 1985a.

Nahapiet, H. and Nahapiet, J., 'A comparison of contractual arrangements for building projects', *Construction Management and Economics*, **3**(3), 1985b, pp.217–31.

National Audit Office, 'Ministry of Defence: control and management of the development of major equipment', report by the Comptroller and Auditor General, HMSO, London, 12 August 1986.

National Committee on Tunnelling Technology, National Research Council, *Better Contracting for Underground Construction*, National Academy of Sciences, Washington DC, 1974.

National Economic Development Office, *Contracting in Civil Engineering Since Banwell* (the Harris Report), HMSO, London, 1968.

National Economic Development Office, *Large Industrial Sites*, HMSO, London, 1970.

National Economic Development Office, *Report on Engineering Construction Performance*, HMSO, London, 1976.

National Economic Development Office, *Guidelines for the Management of Major Projects in the Process Industries*, HMSO, London, 1982.

National Nuclear Corporation, 'New advanced gas-cooled reactors incorporate design imporvements', *Nuclear Engineering International*, March 1981, pp.27–36.

Navarro, P., 'Our stake in the electric utility's dilemma', *Harvard Business Review*, May–June 1982, pp.87–97.

Newey, S. F., 'The reasons for change', *Nuclear Engineering International*, March 1981, pp.36–43.

Newey, S. F., 'Progress report on Heysham 2 Power Station', *Nuclear Energy*, October 1985, pp.287–93.

Ninos, G. E. and Wearne, S. H., 'Responsibilities for project control during construction', Report No.TMR 17, School of Technological Management, University of Bradford, November 1974.

Nuclear Regulatory Commission, *Improving Quality and Assurance of Quality in Design and Construction of Commercial Nuclear Power Plants*, NRC, Bethesda, Maryland, 1984.

Olsen, R. P., 'Can project management be defined?', *Project Management Quarterly*, **2**(1), 1971, pp.12–14.

Owen, K., 'ICL: A taxing problem for the government, *The Times*, 18 July 1980.

Patterson, D. R., Mull, H. M. and Sprouse, M. N., 'Lessons learned by TVA', *National Nuclear Engineering International*, March 1982, pp.33–9.

Patz, A. L., *Innovation Pitfalls and Management Solutions in High Technology Industries*, University of Southern California, Los Angeles, California, 1984.

Paul, S., *Managing Development Programs: The Lessons of Success*, Westview Press, Boulder, Colorado, 1982.

Paul, S., *Strategic Management of Development Programmes*, International Labour Office, Geneva, 1983.

Paulson, B. C., Fondahl, J. W. and Parker, H. W., 'Development of research in the construction of transportation facilities', Technical Report No.223, Construction Institute, Department of Civil Engineering, Stanford University, Stanford, California, 1977.

Peck, M. J. and Scherer, F. M., *The Weapons Acquisition Process*, Harvard University Press, Cambridge, Massachusetts, 1962.

Perry, J. G., 'The development of contract strategies for construction projects', Ph.D. thesis, University of Manchester, January 1985.

Perry, J. G. and Hayes, R. W., 'Construction projects—know the risks', *Chartered Mechanical Engineer*, February 1985a, pp.42–5.

Perry, J. G. and Hayes R. W., 'Risk and its management in construction', *Proceedings of the Institute of Civil Engineers*, Paper 8809, Part 1, February 1985b.

Perry, J. G., Thompson, P. A. and Wright, M., 'Target and cost-reimbursable construction contracts. Parts A, B and C', CIRIA Report No.85, London, 1982.

Perry, R. L., DiSalvo, D., Hall, G. R., Harman, A. L., Levenson, G. S., Smith, G. K. and Stucker, J. P., 'System acquisition experience', Rand Corporation, RM–6072–PR, Santa Monica, California, November 1969.

Perry, R. L., Smith, G. K., Harman, A. J. and Henrichsen, S., 'System acquisition strategies', Rand Corporation, R–733–PR/ARPA, Santa Monica, California, June 1971.

Persson, B. (ed.)., *Surviving Failures: Patterns and Cases of Project Management*, Almqvist & Wiksell International, Stockholm, Sweden, 1979.

Pfeffer, J. 'Management as symbolic action: the creation and maintenance of organizational paradigms' in *Research in Organizational Behaviour*, Stair, B. M. and Cummings, L. L. (eds.) JAI Press, Greenwich, Conn., 1981.

Philips, S. C., 'Management schemes for Apollo', in *Mangement of Aerospace Programs*, Burgess, E. (ed.) American Astronautical Society, Washington DC, 1967.

Pinches, G. E., 'Myopia, capital budgeting and division-making', Financial Management, Autumn 1983, pp.6–18.

Pondy, L. R., Morgan, G., Frost, P. J. and Dandridge, T. C. (eds.) *Organizational Symbolism*, JAI Press, Greenwich, Conn., 1983.

Project Management Institute, *Measuring Success—proceedings of 1986*

Montreal Seminar/Symposium, Project Management Institute, Drexel Hill, Pennsylvania, 1986.

Project Management Journal, special summer issue:'Education and training for project managers', Project Management Institute, Drexel Hill, Pennsylvania, August 1984.

Project Management Journal, special summer issue: 'Project management body of knowledge', Project Management Institute, Drexel Hill, Pennsylvania, August 1986.

Proposals for a Fixed Channel Link, HMSO, Cmnd 2137, London, 1963.

Pugh, P. G., 'Who can tell what might happen? Risks and contingency allowances', paper presented at the Royal Aeronautic Society Management Studies Group, Spring Convention, 1985.

Putnam, W. D., 'The evolution of Air Force system acquisition management', Rand Corporation, R–868–PR, Santa Monica, California, August 1972.

Reeser, C., 'Some potential human problems of the project form of organization', *Academy of Management Journal*, December 1968, pp.459–67.

Reis, F. W., 'A requirement for successful macro–projects: good management––labor relations', paper presented at conference *Macro-Engineering: The New Challenge*, The American Society for Macro-Engineering, March 1986; to be published in *Strategies for Macro projects: Challenges and Opportunites*, Horwitch, M. (ed.), Ballinger, Cambridge, Massachusetts, 1987.

Reis de Carvalho, E. and Morris, P. W. G., 'Project matrix organizations – or how to to the matrix swing', *Proceedings of the 1978 Project Management Institute, Los Angeles*, Project Management Institute, Drexel Hill, Pennsylvania, 1978.

Report of the Channel Tunnel Advisory Group (Chaired by Sir Alec Cairncross), HMSO, London, 1975.

Report of the Commission on Government Procurement, US Government Printing Office, Washington DC, 1972.

Report of the Committee of Inquiry into the Aircraft Industry (chaired by Sir Edmund Plowden) Cmnd 2853, HMSO, London, 1965.

Reshaping of British Railways, British Railways Board, (chaired by Lord Beeching) Ministry of Transport, HMSO, 1962.

Roman, D. D., *Managing Projects: A Systems Approach*, Elsevier, New York, 1986.

Rothwell, D. L., Thompson, P. A. and Wearne, S. H., 'Management of an urgent public works project', School of Technological Management, University of Bradford, 1975.

Rowley, C. S., 'Methods of capital project selection', *Management Planning*, March/April 1973, pp.22–34.

Rubin, I. M. and Seelig, W., 'Experience as a factor in the selection and performance of project managers'. *IEEE Transactions on Engineering Management*, E–131(35), September 1967, pp.131–5.

Ruskin, A. M., 'Twenty questions that could save your project', *IEEE Transactions on Engineering Management*, EM–29(3), August 1982, pp.101–3.

Ruskin, A. M. and Estes, W. E., *What Every Engineer Should Know About Project Management*, Marcel Dekker, New York, 1982.

Ruskin, A. M. and Lerner, R., 'Forecasting costs and completion dates for defense research and development contracts', *IEEE Transactions on Engineering Management*, EM-19(4), November 1972, pp.128–33.

Rycroft, R. W. and Szyliowicz, J. S., *Decision-Making in a Technological*

Environment: The Case of the Aswan High Dam, University of Denver, Colorado, 1980.

Salkeld, R., Davidson, F. P. and Meador, C. L., *Macro-Engineering: The Rich Potential*, Westview Press, Boulder, Colorado, 1981.

Sapolsky, H., *The Polaris System Development: Bureaucratic and Programmatic Success in Government*, Harvard University Press, Cambridge, Massachusets, 1972.

Sayles, L. R. and Chandler, M. K., *Managing Large Systems: Organizations for the Future*, Harper & Row, New York, 1971.

Scott, P., *The Commercial Management of Engineering Contracts*, Gower, London, 1974.

Seamans, R. and Ordway, F. I., 'The Apollo tradition: an object lesson for the management of large scale technological endeavours', *Interdisciplinary Science Reviews*, 1977, pp.270–304.

'Sector management', *Railways Gazette International*, April 1984.

Seder, A. R., 'Building the nation's first commercial coal-gasification plant', paper presented at conference *Macro-engineering: The New Challenge*, The American Society for Macro-Engineering, March 1986; to be published in *Strategies for Macro Projects: Challenges andOpportunites*, Horwitch, M. (ed.), Ballinger, Cambridge, Massachusetts, 1987.

Segelod, E., *Kalkylering och avvikelsor* (Capital Expenditure, Planning, Planning Deviations: Empirical Studies of Large Scale Local Government and Industrial Projects), LiberForlag, Malmo, Sweden, 1986.

Sharp, D., 'Design engineering and construction contracts in major resource projects', *Proceedings of 6th Annual Conference of the Australian Mining and Petroleum Law Association*, Melbourne, 1982.

Souder, W. E., 'Effectiveness of product development methods', *Industrial Marketing Management*, 7, 1978, pp.299–307.

Squire, L. and van der Tak, H. G., *Economic Analysis of Projects*, Johns Hopkins University Press, Baltimore, Maryland, 1975.

Srinivasau, R. and Sassoon, D. M., *International Contracting and Procurement for Development Projects*, International Law Institute, Georgetown University Law Center, 1982.

Stinchcombe, A. L., 'Controlling cost uncertainties in project administration', unpublished paper, University of Arizona, 1979a.

Stinchcombe, A. L., *Delays and Project Administration in the North Sea*, Rapport nr. 14, Institute of Industrial Economics, Bergen, Norway, 1979b.

Stringer, J., Lobl, M. and Wheen, R., 'Formulating the macroproject' in *Macroprojects Strategy, Planning and Implementation*, Gray, K. G. et al. (eds.), Warren Centre, University of Sydney, Sydney, 1985.

Summers, R., 'Cost estimates as predictors of actual weapon costs: a study of major hardware articles', Rand Corporation, RM–3061–PR, Santa Monica, California, March 1965.

Supersonic Transport Aircraft Committee, Report of the Royal Aircraft Establishment, Farnborough, 1959.

Sykes, A., 'The project overview—the key to successful accomplishment of giant projects' in *The Successful Accomplishment of Giant Projects*, Willis Faber, London, 1979.

Sykes, A., 'Reducing neglected risks on giant projects' in *New Dimensions of Project Management*, Kelley, A. J. (ed.), Lexington Books, Lexington, Massachusetts, 1982.

Sykes, A., 'Success and failure of major projects', *Civil Engineering*, January/ February 1986, pp.17–18.

Szyliowicz, J. S., *Planning, Managing and Implementing Technological Development Projects: The Case of the Eregli Iron and Steel Works*, University of Denver, Colorado, 1982.

Thamhain, H. J. and Wilemon, D. L., 'Criteria for controlling projects according to plan', *Project Management Journal*, XVII(2), June 1986, pp.75–81.

Theodore Barry & Associates, *A Survey of Organizational Trends in Power Plant Construction*, Theodore Barry & Associates, Los Angeles, 1979.

Thomas, W. A., 'North Sea field development: historic costs and future trends', paper presented at 1984 European Petroleum Conference, London, Society of Petroleum Engineers, Dallas, Texas, 1984.

Thompson, P. A., *Organization and Economics of Construction*, McGraw-Hill, London, 1981.

Treasury and Civil Service Committee, 'Supply estimates 1985–86', Minutes of Evidence, House of Commons, HMSO, London, 1 May 1985.

Turner, B., 'The organizational and interorganizational development of disasters', *Administrative Science Quarterly*, 21, Spring 1976, pp.378–97.

Turner, B., *Man-made Disasters*, Taylor & Francis, London, 1979.

Utility Data Institute, *Nuclear Plant Construction Cost Update—March 1985*, Washington DC. 1985.

Viana de Andrade, R., Bojanovich, F. L., Junqueira, Netto and Jose, Affonso, *Construction Planning and Interface Scheduling for Dams and Other Features of Itaipu*, International Congress on Large Dams, 13th Trans, New Delhi, India, 29 October–2 November 1979. International Commission on Large Dams, Paris, France, Vol.1, 1979, pp.749–78.

Vicklund, C. A. and Craft, W. S., 'Management of major offshore projects: an industry challenge', *Journal of Petroleum Technology*, 33, April 1981, pp.585–93.

Walker, A., *Project Management in Construction*, Granada, London, 1984.

Warnock, G., 'A giant project successfully accomplished—design risk and engineering management' in *The Successful Accomplishment of Giant Projects*, Willis Faber, London, 1979.

Waterson, A., *Development Planning: Lessons of Experience*, Johns Hopkins University Press, Baltimore, Maryland, 1965.

Wearne, S. H., *Principles of Engineering Organization*, Arnold, London, 1973.

Wearne, S. H., 'Contractual responsibilities for the design of engineering plants: a survey of practices and problems', *Proceedings of the Institution of Mechanical Engineers*, 198B(6), 1984, pp.97–108.

Webster, F. M., 'Ways to improve performance on projects', *Project Management Quarterly*, XII(3), September 1981, pp.21–6.

Whipp, R. and Clark, P., *Innovation and the Auto Industry*, Francis Pinter, London, 1986.

Whitehead, H., *An A–Z of Offshore Oil and Gas*, Kogan Page, London, 1983.

Whitmore, K. R. 'Matrix organizations in conventional manufacturing–marketing companies', M. S. Thesis, Sloan School of Management, MIT, Cambridge, Mass. 1975.

Wickens, A. H., 'Research and development on high-speed railways, achievements and prospects', *Transport Review*, 3(1), 1983, pp.77–112.

Wilemon, D. L., 'Project management conflict: a view from Apollo', *Proceedings of the Project Management Institute*, Drexel Hill, Pennsylvania, 1971.

Williams, G., Frank, G. and Simpson, J., *Crisis in Procurement: a Case Study of the TSR 2*, Royal United Services Institute, London, 1969.

Williams, H., *A Promise Unfulfilled*, Paul Ian Allen, London, 1985.

Williams, R., *The Nuclear Power Decisions. British Policies, 1953–78*, Croom Helm, London, 1980.

Wilson, A., *Committee of Inquiry into Delays in Commissioning CEGB Power Stations*, HMSO, 1969.

Wilson, A., *The Concorde Fiasco*, Penguin Books, Harmondsworth, 1973.

Wood, D., *Project Cancelled*, MacDonald & Jane's, London, 1975.

World Bank, *Tenth Annual Review of Project Performance Audit Results*, World Bank, Washington DC, 1985.

Youker, R., 'Organizational Alternatives for Project Management', *Project Management Quarterly*, **8**(1), 1977, pp.18–24.

Index